1. Hovis Mills—Westminster
2. St Katharine Dock
3. London Docks
4. Free Trade Wharf
5. Regent's Canal Dock
6. Lime Kiln Dock
7. South Dock (West India Docks)
8. West India Dock (Import)
9. East India Dock
10. Bromley gas works
11. Royal Albert Dock silos
12. King George V Dock
13. Royal Albert Dock Basin
14. Mark Brown's Wharves
15. Brewer's Wharf
16. Morocco Wharf
17. Aberdeen Wharf
18. Bellamy's Wharf
19. Surrey Dock
20. Odessa Wharf
21. Millwall Dock
22. Millwall Wharf
23. Charlton
24. Royal Victoria Dock silo
25. Ipswich
26. Colchester
27. Rowhedge
28. Fingringhoe
29. Maldon
30. Battlesbridge
31. Creeksea
32. Rochford
33. Hammersmith
34. Chelsea
35. Tilbury Dock
36. Aylesford
37. Rochester
38. Chatham
39. Rainham
40. Sittingbourne
41. Ridham Dock
42. Oare Creek
43. Faversham
44. Whitstable
45. Ramsgate
46. Dover
47. Calais
48. Boulogne
49. Dunkirk

KATHLEEN

Kathleen in her trading days as a staysail barge. *National Maritime Museum*

KATHLEEN

The biography of a sailing barge

by

RICHARD WALSH

TERENCE DALTON LIMITED
LAVENHAM . SUFFOLK
1986

Published by
TERENCE DALTON LIMITED
ISBN 0 86138 046 0

Text photoset in 10/12pt Garamond

Printed in Great Britain at
The Lavenham Press Limited, Lavenham, Suffolk

Contents

To *Kathleen*,
in the hope that she has not minded my
love for Mary.

Introduction

THERE can be few, if any, owners of traditional wooden craft who have not experienced the frustration of a deck leak which defies all attempts at cure. The position of the problem is identified; on the first available fine day deck seams are raked out, oakum rolled and laid with caulking iron and mallet, and each seam painstakingly payed with near boiling pitch to complete a totally professional repair. Then, with an inevitability akin to the ebb and flow of the tide, the next shower of rain manifests itself below as a clear lens-like formation on the deckhead, swelling by the minute until a fully formed drip is persuaded by gravity to make way for its identical brothers who will follow with ever-increasing rapidity.

It was such a leak, strategically placed over the skipper's berth aboard the Thames sailing barge *Kathleen*, that indirectly provided the inspiration for this book.

It was a wet Autumn night at Heybridge Basin in Essex. For the umpteenth time, despite many attempted repairs, the persistent drip which fell from a shake in the massive oak beam above had got the better of the absorbency of my kapok-filled sleeping bag. Turning on a torch, I climbed to my knees for yet another attempt at solving the mystery of the point of ingress. I was rewarded by a rather startling

Refitting a sailing barge is not all fun, to judge from the expression on Richard Walsh's face. *East Anglian Daily Times*

discovery. My massive oak beam sounded hollow when knocked, and closer examination the following morning revealed that it was indeed a fabricated imitation concealing a steel beam beneath. In the air space between the two lay a damp and tattered cargo book recording *Kathleen's* working life from 1923 to 1931.

In the fervour and activity of re-rigging *Kathleen* the cargo book was put in a drawer and forgotten until rediscovered a year or so ago. It formed the basis of a magazine article by Richard-Hugh Perks, which inspired me to research fully *Kathleen's* history and also to record the details of her restoration to sail.

This book is the result of those efforts. I believe it provides a unique record of a barge's years in trade and afterwards, a story which fortunately cannot be completed, for *Kathleen*, despite her eighty-odd years, is still afloat in Holland. I kept no notes during her restoration and therefore cannot be positive of some of the dates mentioned, nor for that matter are the events necessarily recalled in chronological order. I hope the Society for Spritsail Barge Research will forgive these inaccuracies, and also accept a certain amount of unintentional exaggeration in some of the Sailormen's stories.

I would like to thank all those who helped during the fitting out of the *Kathleen*, the late Fred Cooper, whose *Handbook of Sailing Barges* really is the bible for the amateur bargeman; Mona and Rene of the *Jolly Sailor* at Heybridge Basin who provided much-needed sustenance whenever we found time to stop, eat and drink; Bill Percy who helped with the rigging; and especially the late "Dilberry" Clark without whose encouragement, advice and sense of humour there would probably have been no story to tell.

Braughing

Acknowledgements

During the preparation of this work I have learnt that there is considerably more to a book than just an author! I am indebted to the many people who have assisted me; in particular the late Fred Cooper for reading and correcting the restoration portion of my manuscript, and providing a number of photographs; Captain Fred Wraight, who together with his late father traded with *Kathleen* for over thirty years, and Alf Kelsey, mate from 1918 to 1929, who between them furnished much valuable historical information. Thanks also to all those individuals, too numerous to name, who have provided such a wealth of other material, much of which has been included in the pages that follow. Finally a big "thank you" to Barbara Wisbey for her perseverance in converting my longhand scribblings into a comprehensible manuscript.

Kathleen among a fleet of square-rigged colliers in Whitstable harbour around 1910.
Douglas West collection

CHAPTER ONE

'A Spectacle Unique in Modern Times'

THE nineteenth century was drawing to a close. The Empire continued to flourish, and the unprecedented trade resulting from its creation converged on London, commercial capital of the world.

The waterfront at Gravesend saw much of this traffic go by. The pilots put off from there, and the tugs were based there, often scouring down Channel for their deep-sea customers, which were still using wind alone to carry them from far-off lands deep-laden to England.

An idle hour spent on the lawns of the Clarendon Royal Hotel would reward the onlooker with as colourful a maritime spectacle as could be witnessed anywhere. But it was not the bright funnels of tugs and ships, not the muddy green of the Thames, not the white upperworks, shiny black hulls and gold linework of the paddle steamers, that dominated the scene; it was the russet brown sails of the bustling spritsail barges, almost so common as to go unnoticed, so much were they a part of the Thamesside panorama. For this was the heyday of the Thames sailing barge, that workhorse of the coastal and river trade, a vessel so efficient that despite some seventy-five years' competition from the railways it still justified prolific building of new additions to the thousands already afloat.

So it was that in 1898 Lewis Glover came to Gravesend to establish a barge building yard. Strangely, in view of its maritime importance, the town had seen little shipbuilding activity for many years. It was in the late eighteenth and early nineteenth centuries that the yards of William Cleverly built sailing warships and merchant vessels of up to 2,000 tons. Spasmodic bursts of construction in other yards continued during the mid-eighteen-hundreds. This mainly comprised the building of small tiller-steered barges of around 35 registered tons. Of these, the *Amy Cecilia, Jessie,* and *Connaught*, of 1877, 1878, and 1879 respectively, were all for William Fletcher, a local coal and general merchant. He also had locally built the *Beatrice, Victoria* and *Mardy*, larger vessels of between 55 and 60 tons. The last barge built during this period was the *Wm. Paxton*, similar in size to Fletcher's smaller craft and owned by Robins (Northfleet) Cement Company. After her launching in 1881 there was no further Gravesend building until Mr Lewis A. Glover arrived on the scene.

In the Autumn of 1898 Lewis Glover entered into negotiations with the River Thames Conservators to obtain a "licence" to use their land to the West of the Royal

Dried out on Pin Mill hard, *Kathleen* shows off her underwater form.
C. Traill

Terrace Pier for the construction of sailing barges. It is not clear whether the yard, known as Terrace Pier Wharf, had previously been used for this purpose. The slipway at the western end of the site is covered by a large shed, thereby allowing construction to proceed unhindered by adverse weather conditions. Many of the barges built at this time were constructed on open sites, and this protection during building may well have contributed to the extraordinary longevity of the Glover barges. The shed, with its cast-iron girders and truss work, appears to date from this period, although it may have been somewhat earlier. Some of the decorative cast-iron in the roof is identical to that used in the construction of the Royal Terrace Pier, commenced in 1842, but not finally completed until many years later.

Three pieces of evidence seem to support the suggestion that both shed and slipway were built by Glover when his licence was granted. Firstly, the description of

Darnley Terrace, Gravesend, around the time that Lewis A. Glover lived at No 4.
Gravesend Library, Gould Collection

the property up to that time had always been Terrace Pier Wharf, which is inconsistent with that usually accorded to premises where vessels are built. Secondly, the period of time between acquisition of the site and the launch of the first barge was well over a year, but subsequent launchings came much more quickly, suggesting that the early period of tenancy may well have been taken up by building works. Thirdly, no known deeds or plans illustrate the shed and slipway until they appear on a document conveying the leasehold to Messrs Tuff, Miskin and West in 1903.

At the same time as Lewis Glover was concluding his licence for the bargeyard, he was also arranging to purchase a residential property, 4 Darnley Terrace, Gravesend, from a Mr Conrad Lockner. The terrace had been the first group of houses built on the road cut by the Turnpike Commissioners in 1801 and known as the Overcliffe. They were constructed in 1835 and could, in Glover's day, have been described as fashionable but by no means extravagant. They were demolished in the mid-1950s, the site now being occupied by a service station.

Construction of the first of Glover's barges commenced in the April of 1899 and caused great interest in the locality. In Royal Pier Road there were, in addition to

Terrace Pier Wharf, fourteen other properties. Thirteen of these were residences, five of which were occupied by river pilots, one by a marine surveyor and the remainder by others closely connected with the river. The other premises comprised the Clarendon Royal Hotel, standing on the site of a house built for James II, who had married Anne, daughter of the Earl of Clarendon, in the late seventeenth century, and therefore aptly named. Those who visited the Clarendon or had some other cause to travel to the waterfront watched keenly as the building progressed within the open-sided shed.

A frequent visitor to the yard was Mr Hamerton Hayne, of Rosherville, for whom the barge was being built. She was the largest sailing barge ever constructed in the town at that time, being 83 feet long, 19 feet 6 inches beam and of 6 feet side, designed to comply with Mr Hamerton Hayne's requirements of a 150-ton capacity.

By January, 1900, she was ready to be launched. The event was described by the local paper as a "unique spectacle in modern times" and crowds gathered from the town to witness the launching, arranged for high water on the afternoon of Thursday, 18th. Just before three o'clock amidst much enthusiasm Mrs Hayne, the owner's wife, stepped forward to christen the barge *Sir Richard.* A champagne bottle suspended on red, white and blue ribbon swung against the barge's stem which had been decorated with a bouquet of evergreen, and to rounds of applause the *Sir Richard* slid from the ways into the river. She was shortly secured alongside the

Terrace Pier Wharf, Gravesend, and the shed over the old slipway which housed *Kathleen* and other Glover barges while they were being built. *R. J. Walsh*

wharf area to the East of the slipway. The launching was attended by a number of local pilots and others connected with the river, as well as by the family of the owner and Lewis Glover's brothers and other relatives. A dinner at the Clarendon Royal Hotel followed in the evening, not only for the Hamerton Haynes but also for the shipwrights and apprentices who had helped with the construction.

The satisfactory performance of the yard on their first vessel led to a flurry of interest from other would-be purchasers, a firm order being received immediately from Samuel West (later to become proprietor of the business) and indications of interest from Mr C. S. Homewood, of Greenhithe, and from Lewis Glover's brother Edward, of Rochester.

To finance the construction of their barges both Homewood and Edward Glover decided to dispose of investment property they owned in Northfleet, Rosherville and surrounding areas. *The Gravesend and Dartford Reporter* carried an advertisement in April, 1900, under the heading of "property sales" describing various residences belonging to Messrs Glover and Homewood as being for sale by auction. The money raised enabled the order to be confirmed and so a second barge was commenced concurrently with that being built for Samuel West. It appears likely that this vessel was constructed almost in "kit form", her floors and frames being prepared ready for assembly once the slipway was vacant.

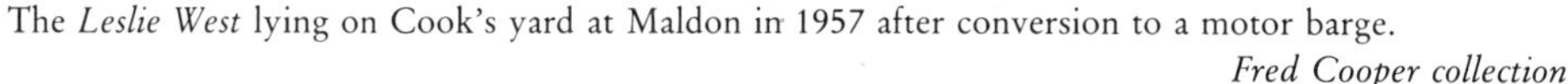

The *Leslie West* lying on Cook's yard at Maldon in 1957 after conversion to a motor barge.
Fred Cooper collection

The *Sir Richard* photographed in February, 1939, by Philip Kershaw. *F. Cooper collection*

On Wednesday, 12th September, 1900, Lewis Glover's second barge was launched by the wife of its new owner and named *Leslie West* after Samuel West's son. Approximately one foot longer and a foot wider than *Sir Richard*, she nevertheless was of only slightly larger capacity, with some 6 inches less side. No sooner was she clear of the slipway than the setting up of Edward Glover's barge from the timbers already selected and prepared was begun. Work proceeded at a considerable pace and the *Baden-Powell*, as she was to be christened, was launched only thirty days later by Mrs E. Glover at three o'clock on Thursday, 11th October. The ceremony was attended by a large crowd of spectators, the vessel's name being displayed on a flag unfurled at the bow as she slid into the water. The *Baden-Powell* was designed to carry 160 tons and was intended for "general trade on the river and around the coast".

Sir Robert Baden-Powell, after whom the barge was named, was the hero of the

The Brownie turning away from Strood buoy in February, 1950. *A. Cordell*

day as a result of his spirited defence of Mafeking during the South African War. The siege of that town had been lifted in May, while Glover was working on the *Leslie West*. Streets, terraces, villas and public halls throughout the country were named in Baden-Powell's honour. It is not surprising therefore that a few miles further down the coast at Faversham, Osborne Dan's bargeyard had built and launched another *Baden-Powell*, considerably smaller than the Glover-built barge. It seems strange how the careers of these two barges, both named the same and built the same year, had so many things in common. Both were at some time owned at Gravesend, and both eventually sank within a year or so of each other, Glover's *Baden-Powell* being wrecked on the Grain Spit in 1948 and Dan's barge sinking in the Lower Hope at Christmas, 1949. Some historians even go on to say that both hulks when raised were taken to Queensborough Creek as "constructive total losses". Certainly the Glover hulk lies there today, forlornly decayed now, but positively identified in 1961 from her official number which was still discernible at that time.

Mr C. S. Homewood's barge was next to be laid down at the yard, construction commencing straight away after the launch of the *Baden-Powell*. To be called *The Brownie*, she was to be the largest of Glover's barges, being of 170 tons burden, some 85 feet 6 inches overall, a beam of over 20 feet, and a depth of 6 feet 7 inches. Building took little over three months, and on Tuesday, 5th Febuary, 1901, the barge was launched during the afternoon by Kathleen Homewood, the owner's daughter. As was usual, a crowd witnessed the event, the families and friends of the builder and the owner being present.

The reader would be forgiven for imagining that there was a connection in the naming of the *Baden-Powell* and *The Brownie*. Baden-Powell was, of course, founder of the Scout and Guide movements, and the Brownies are an integral part of the Guide organisation. Such conjecture would, however, be unfounded, as Baden-Powell, then at 43 Britain's youngest ever major-general, had yet to inaugurate those youth movements. In fact Brownies did not come into being until some time after 1912, and then they were known as the Rosebuds for a time before receiving their more familiar name. The consecutive christening of these two craft by names which were later to become closely linked is therefore just a remarkable

The *Baden-Powell*, on the right, and another derelict barge at Queenborough in 1961. *A. Cordell*

coincidence. The Brownie was in fact a character not unlike the leprechaun which featured in a popular nursery story of the era; he was a helpful little fellow who tidied people's houses while they slept. He was only ever seen by children, and then only when they gazed into water. It was this nursery story that gave its name to Glover's fourth barge.

With *The Brownie* out of the way work started on what was to be Glover's final barge. This fifth barge was not as large as *The Brownie*, being of 155 tons deadweight capacity. In common with most of those he had previously built, she combined the large hatches of a Kentish river barge with the rig, size, and much of the build of a

William Henry Duttson, the original owner of a half share in *Kathleen*.
Lawrence Duttson Collection

coaster. Previously published material suggests that she was built on speculation by Lewis Glover, who traded with her when he disposed of his yard, but there seems to be insufficient evidence for this point of view, despite the Mercantile Navy Lists which indicate Lewis Glover's ownership until 1909, the year in which he moved from Darnley Terrace and apparently from Gravesend altogether. There is no doubt that Lewis Glover was manager of the barge during this time, but the original registration documents, filed subsequent to the launching on 16th November, state that another member of the Glover family, Arthur Glover, of Forest Hill, was owner of thirty-two shares, the other thirty-two belonging to a William Duttson from Sydenham.

William Henry Jones Duttson was born on 12th October, 1839. He became proprietor of William Duttson & Co, of Mincing Lane in the City of London, a company established in the brokerage of indigo and other colonial products. Indigo is a bright and durable blue dye obtained from the indigo plant in India, and was

A transcript of *Kathleen's* original registration.

Form No. 19. *Signal Letters (if any)*

Transcript of Register for Transmission to Registrar General of Shipping and Seamen

Official Number	Name of Ship	No., Year and Port of Registry
113708	KATHLEEN	24-1901-16 NOVEMBER ROCHESTER

No., Year and Port of previous Registry (if any)

Whether British or Foreign Built	Whether a Sailing, Steam or Motor Ship: if Steam or Motor how propelled	Where Built	When Built	Name and Address of Builders
BRITISH	SAILING	GRAVESEND	1901	LEWIS A GLOVER GRAVESEND

			Feet	Tenths
Number of Decks	ONE	Length from fore part of stem, under the bowsprit, to the aft side of the head of the stern post	82	8
Number of Masts	TWO	Length at quarter of depth from top of weather deck at side amidships to bottom of keel		
Rigged	SPRITSAIL	Main breadth to outside of plank	19	7
Stern	SQUARE	Depth in hold from tonnage deck to ceiling at midships	6	08
Build	CARVEL	Depth in hold from upper deck to ceiling at midships, in the case of three decks and upwards		
Galleries	✓	Depth from top of beam amidships to top of keel		
Head	✓	Depth from top of deck at side amidships to bottom of keel		
Framework and description of vessel	WOOD SAILING BARGE	Round of beam		7
Number of Bulkheads		Length of engine room, if any		
Number of water ballast tanks, and their capacity in tons	✓			

PARTICULARS OF DISPLACEMENT

Total to quarter the depth from weather deck at side amidships to bottom of keel .... Tons. Ditto per inch immersion at same depth .... Tons.

PARTICULARS OF PROPELLING ENGINES, &c. (if any)

No. of sets of Engines	Description of Engines	Whether British or Foreign made	When made	Name and address of makers	Reciprocating Engines: No. and Diameter of Cylinders in each set	Reciprocating Engines: Length of Stroke	Rotary Engines: No. of Cylinders in each set	N.H.P. B.H.P. I.H.P. Speed of Ship
		Engines	Engines	Engines				
No. of Shafts	Particulars of Boilers: Description ...... Number ...... Loaded Pressure	Boilers	Boilers	Boilers				

PARTICULARS OF TONNAGE

Gross Tonnage	No. of Tons		Deductions Allowed	No. of Tons
Under Tonnage Deck	71 · 13		On account of space required for propelling power	
Space or spaces between Decks CABIN. TOP	71		On account of spaces occupied by Seamen or Apprentices, and appropriated to their use, and kept free from Goods or Stores of every kind, not being the personal property of the Crew	
Turret or Trunk			These spaces are the following, viz.:— FORECASTLE & CABIN	11 07
Forecastle			(Number of seamen or apprentices for whom accommodation is certified ....)	
Bridge space			Deductions under Section 79 of the Merchant Shipping Act, 1894, and Section 54 of the Merchant Shipping Act, 1906, as follows:—	
Poop or Break				
Side Houses				
Deck Houses				
Chart House				
Spaces for Machinery, and light, and air, under Section 78(2) of the Merchant Shipping Act, 1894				
Excess of Hatchways	5 · 54	Cubic Meters	MASTER 4 · 85; BOSN'S STORE 1 · 90	6 75
Gross Tonnage	77 · 35	218 · 99		
Deductions, as per contra	17 · 82	50 · 43		
Register Tonnage	59 · 56	168 · 56	Total	17 · 82

Note.—1. The tonnage of the engine room spaces below the upper deck is .... tons, and the tonnage of the total spaces framed in above the upper deck for propelling machinery and for light and air is .... tons.

Note.—2. The undermentioned spaces above the upper deck are not included in the cubical contents forming the ship's register tonnage:

Name of Master — Certificate of Service No. / Competency — No.

Names, Residence, and Description of the Owners, and Number of Sixty-fourth Shares held by each, viz.,

ARTHUR GLOVER OF ELMSTEAD CLAYOW ROAD FOREST HILL IN THE COUNTY OF KENT } THIRTY TWO. 64THS

WILLIAM HENRY DUTTSON OF SOUTHWOOD SILVERDALE SYDENHAM IN THE COUNTY OF KENT } THIRTY TWO 64THS

Dated 16TH NOVEMBER 1901. SIGNED ILLEGIBLE. Registrar

Note.—Registrars in the Colonies are requested to distinguish the Managing Owner by placing the letters "M.O." against his name.

C. 345 N.B.—To be sent in an envelope addressed to the Registrar General of Shipping and Seamen, Llantrisant Road, Cardiff. (66165)

Instructions to Registrars of British Ships, para. 37.—Sec. F.66 (Sept. 1968)

widely used in mid-Victorian times for calico printing. Around 1885 alternative sources of blue dyes made a significant impact on Duttson's business and he became increasingly involved in the importation of invert sugars for the brewing industry. Most of the brewing sugar at this time came by ship to the lower reaches of the Thames, from where it was distributed by sailing barge to the riverside breweries in London and elsewhere. It is possible that it was this trade for which William Duttson's barge was intended. It would seem, however, that it was rather late in his career for him to be getting involved with a sailing barge; he was by then in his sixty-third year. Perhaps it was his sons that influenced him in the matter; Stanley Walter Duttson was in his early thirties and his brother Horace Leslie was just twenty-nine. Both had entered the family business and would probably have considered such an investment an appropriate move. In addition, their father had been recently widowed, and they may well have felt that visits to Glover's yard during the building would take his mind off the loss of his wife.

Why then, was Arthur Glover the chosen partner? It is certain that Arthur would have known that no further orders had been received by Lewis to follow on from *The Brownie*, and he might have volunteered to pay half towards the next barge if someone could be found to finance the remainder. It begins to appear, therefore, that the Duttsons were the invited party in the venture.

In delving into the background of these two families no connection whatsoever came to light until it was realised that the registration documents included an error in Arthur Glover's address. "Clayow Road, Forest Gate" should have read "Mayow Road"; Stanley and Horace Duttson were in fact close neighbours of Arthur Glover. All three lived virtually opposite one end of Bishopsthorpe Road, while William Duttson lived at the opposite end within the Sydenham postal area.

Having established the connection between Glover and Duttson it seems appropriate to explore the reasons for calling the barge *Kathleen*, a name she retained throughout a long life. Kathleen was a popular name at the time; two other barges with that name were registered at Rochester, one built at Sittingbourne in 1876 and the other constructed at Brentford in 1882, though no further barges shared the name after the launch of Glover's *Kathleen* in 1901.

It is obvious, under the circumstances of the partnership, that the prerogative of naming should have rested with William Duttson, and who better to christen the barge with her own name than his youngest child, and what better day to do it than her birthday?

Although the registration documents are dated 16th November, such records were frequently compiled a few days after the launching. It therefore appears likely that the launch took place on 6th November, 1901, Mabel Kathleen Duttson's 21st birthday. Why did the barge carry her second name instead of being christened Mabel? Almost certainly in memory of William Duttson's eldest son's wife Kathleen, who had died young of a tragic illness ten years previously.

Although William Duttson remained an active man until his death in 1920 at the age of eighty his partnership in the *Kathleen* lasted for only eight years, after which she was sold to the Whitstable Shipping Company. The Duttson name survives in the sugar business to this day in the guise of Duttson & Knight, part of the Manbré Sugars Group acquired some years ago by Tate & Lyle.

After completion of the *Kathleen*, Glover's yard undertook no new building under his proprietorship. Samuel West, for whom Glover had built the *Leslie West*, moved into the premises and commenced work on the *Saxon*, a large coasting barge of 82 registered tons. In association with a Mr Tuff, a broker from Rochester, and a Mr Miskin, a local man, he eventually purchased the leasehold of Terrace Pier Wharf in November, 1903, some time after the launch of the *Saxon*, and when construction of the *Lady Gwynfred*, a smaller barge of 66 registered tons, was well under way.

The firm of Tuff, Miskin and West was very shortlived and by 1904 Samuel West Ltd had come into being. However, Messrs Tuff and Miskin continued as barge owners until the mid-twenties. Samuel West's company thrived and was to survive for over half a century, for many of these years based in Lewis Glover's Gravesend yard. West went on to build the *Madge* in 1906 and the *Gwynhelen* in 1909. The latter was the last barge to be constructed in the yard, although the *Lady Gwynfred* was completely rebuilt there in 1935.

Spritsail barges are renowned for their longevity, in particular the fine craft from J. and H. Cann's yard near the old gasworks at Harwich, but surely no builder can match the performance of Lewis Glover. It is often said, even today, that Glover's barges were lightly built. We know, too, that they were often built very quickly.

Mabel Kathleen Duttson about the time of *Kathleen's* launching.
Lawrence Duttson Collection

Despite these factors only one of his barges, the *Baden-Powell*, is not intact today, and the loss of that barge in 1948 was certainly not attributable to any fault in design or construction.

The *Sir Richard* continued to be owned by Mr Hamerton Hayne until 1912, when she passed to the London and Rochester Barge Company. She was motorised in 1950 and her mast deck removed to create a large single hatch. By around 1960 she was laid up at Strood, subsequently being sold for conversion to a house barge. At the time of writing she is moored in the Medway Marina just downstream of the Motorway bridge near Rochester and looks as smartly kept as she ever was in trade.

The *Leslie West* traded for Samuel West for many years, being sold around the mid-twenties to John Sawyer of Brightlingsea and then joining the Francis and Gilders fleet based at Colchester. She was converted to auxiliary power by Priors of Burnham in 1949, having a 66h.p. Kelvin diesel installed. When eventually withdrawn from trade she was sold to Sadds of Maldon for timber lightering duties on the Blackwater. The circumstances of her conversion to a house barge are described in a later chapter; suffice to say she is still in use today at picturesque Pin Mill on the River Orwell in Suffolk.

Mr C. S. Homewood appears to have owned *The Brownie* for a very short time, the Mercantile Navy Lists showing Owen Parry of Colchester as her owner from the early years of the century. Around 1910 she was transferred to Jarvis of Brightlingsea and in 1932, like the *Sir Richard*, she was taken over by the London and Rochester Trading Company. Her half-century in 1951 proved a most eventful year. Bound for Southend from Silvertown with a freight of flour, she was run down by the *s.s. Pinto* and beached at North Woolwich. She was repaired, only to be run down a second time in the same year, again in the Thames. She was taken to Strood where she was

Left: *Leslie West* and *The Brownie* at Bell Wharf, Leigh, in July, 1952.
Fred Cooper collection

Opposite: *Kathleen* , on the right, in Whitstable harbour about 1910. The ketch barge lying alongside the same quay with the diving tender *Alert* outside of her is the *Lord Rosebery,* built at Upnor on the Medway in 1893.
Douglas West collection

surveyed; a credit to Glover's workmanship, she was considered worth repairing. Her sailing gear was removed, an engine installed and her two hatches made into one. She was eventually sold for conversion to a houseboat and is now moored on the Medway.

In common with her sisters, *Kathleen* has also enjoyed the benefits of the dedicated craftsmanship of Glover's shipwrights. On two separate occasions she has been considered worthy of the expense of major repairs, once in 1923, subsequent to the doubtful privilege of being sunk by a Cunarder, and again after being in collision with a shed in Whitstable some thirty years later! There can have been few if any among those present at *Kathleen's* launching who realised that she would outlive them all.

Powered flight was not then invented, but *Kathleen* was still to be sailing when man first set foot on the moon; changes surely beyond the imagination of the Glovers and the Duttsons as they witnessed her first contact with the busy waters of the Thames.

KATHLEEN

CHAPTER TWO

Construction

THE Thames sailing barge has a box-like hull with a vertical stem and a transom stern, as can be seen from the illustrations. This hull design evolved during the second half of the nineteenth century from the round bow of earlier years and from the "swim head" and "budget stern" types, similar in appearance to the dumb lighters still seen in use on the Thames today. Many present-day coasters have a hull form virtually unchanged from their sailing predecessors.

The corner formed between the side of the barge and its bottom is known as the chine, on the length of it depending the hull characteristics. Barges with short chines will undoubtedly have long, shapely runs towards bow and stern, limiting their carrying capacity but improving potential speed and handling. On the other hand, a barge like the *Kathleen*, built with long chines and bluff runs, provided maximum cargo space at the expense of her sailing performance.

All Glover's barges came into this latter category, a factor which was to ensure their viability, even through lean times between the two World Wars. It would be wrong, however, to presume that *Kathleen* and her sisters were disgraced when sailing in company with other barges. While rarely to the front of the fleet, *Kathleen* in particular did notch up some memorable passages, and she was noted for her consistent trading pattern under sail, averaging more than a freight a fortnight for much of her working life.

Unlike the wide beam shallow-sided stack barges designed to carry loads of baled straw piled high on deck from the remote Essex creeks, *Kathleen* was built with large hatches and narrow decks, making her easy to work in port. Her sides were deep enough to allow a six-foot man to stand upright under her decks anywhere in the hold.

Building was not an exact science, and there are recorded a number of barges with strange quirks of construction. *Kathleen* was no exception, with four inches more deck on one side of her hatches than the other. Much of a barge's strength comes from the use of long lengths of timber and though much of her deck planking will have been replaced over the years, there are still to be seen some pieces which run almost the full length of the hull.

When built, the majority of sailing barges embodied a main keelson sawn from a massive baulk of Oregon pine or pitchpine. This ran almost from stem to stern down

The *Leslie West* anchored in the Medway off Chatham in the late 1940s.
Fred Cooper collection

the centreline of the hull and was fixed on top of the floor timbers which stretch across from one chine to the other. Herein lies one of the main structural elements, combining enormous longitudinal strength with a resilience which allows the barge to sit on a bad berth with few if any after-effects.

Kathleen, however, was built with a steel keelson, a growing practice in latterday barge building which combined economy of construction with improved hold capacity. *Kathleen's* keelson was, in section, similar to a railway line, but in size comprised a six-inch wide base, an eleven-inch vertical height and a two-inch thick top edge. There were many sailormen who swore that a barge built in this manner, or one so modified later in life, seldom had the responsiveness and "feel" associated with those embodying a timber keelson.

Fixed approximately at right angles to each end of the floor timbers were the barge's frames or uprights, to which her outer skin was fastened. Like the bottom boards, which were married to the floor timbers with treenails, or wooden fastenings, the barge's sides comprised two layers of Oregon pine, each an inch and a half thick and bound together with cowhair and tar. The inside of the hold was lined in pitchpine, three-inch for the ceiling and two-inch for the sides. Where ceiling and side lining met, chine keelsons were bolted through both frames and floors. The deck was supported on heavy curved oak beams spanning the width of the hull, resting on the "inwale" and fastened to the tops of the frames. Where the hatches and cabin top aft prevented the use of full-width beams, smaller supports known as deck carlings extended inwards to the coamings. Where the beams and carlings met the frames, the "inwale", fashioned from 13 inch × 3¾ inch oak, ran the full length of the hold and

Kathleen's windlass and foc's'le scuttle. *R. J. Walsh*

beyond. This was matched by a corresponding sturdy "wale" fixed on the outside of the hull, where sides met deck, and running from stempost to transom.

There were two cargo hatches, the fore-hatch situated forward of the mainmast deck and the main hatch situated aft of that deck. To reinforce what would otherwise be a structural weakness, the large main hatch had a stout oak beam spanning the width of the opening midway. Known as the tie beam, it caused much inconvenience when loading bulky cargoes and was replaced by a removable iron substitute during the First World War.

To protect the hold were provided cambered hatch covers, some six for the fore hatch and seventeen for the main hatch. When in place they were covered with heavy tarpaulins known as hatch cloths which were retained behind battens wedged into a series of hooks all round the outside of the hatch coamings.

Immediately forward of the fore hatch was fitted the small foc's'le scuttle giving crew access to the accommodation and stores forward. A steep eight-runged ladder led down to a well-planned cabin, separated from the main hold by a strong bulkhead, to which was mounted the chain locker for the anchor cable. There were two bunks within the foc's'le, plus a coal-burning stove, numerous lockers and a vast cupboard forward in which was kept, apart from the third hand's belongings, the coiled up "stay-fall", a wire rope used for raising and lowering the mainmast. To left and right of this cupboard were fitted two large tapered pieces of oak, fixed at their lower end to the floor timbers and passing vertically upwards through the deck to support the most powerful winch aboard, the anchor windlass.

Aft of the fore hatch was the mast deck on which was mounted the mast case, made from riveted iron. Also positioned hereabouts were the forehorse to which the foresail was sheeted, the brail winch which was used to furl the mainsail, and the leeboard irons, on which the massive fan-shaped oak leeboards were attached, allowing them to pivot down into the water when the wind was abeam to prevent the barge blowing to leeward. Aft of the main hatch was fitted the mainhorse, a transverse round beam on which the mainsail was sheeted to an iron ring known as the traveller—appropriately named as it was free to traverse the full width of the barge.

Immediately behind the mainhorse was the wheel which turned the heavy oak rudder via a threaded centre spindle coupled by arms to the rudder post. This steering gear was mounted on the roof of the raised cabin top above the aft accommodation. Here too was fitted the mizzen mastcase, and on either side, within the rails which surrounded the deck, were the "crab" winches used for raising and lowering the leeboards.

A steep companionway, reached through a sliding hatch on the port forward edge of the cabin top, gave access to the main crew's cabin. This cabin was beautifully panelled in mahogany and provided two berths in cupboard-like bunks, the one to starboard traditionally that of the skipper, that to port being for the mate. Complete with coal-burning stove, on which meals were cooked and tea frequently brewed,

Mastcase, main brail winch and fore horse. The heel of the sprit, which has been lowered to a vertical position, can be seen. *R. J. Walsh*

this cabin provided a cosy environment and was home to all the crew, sometimes for weeks on end.

Kathleen's transom, fitted to the fore side of the sternpost on which the heavy rudder swung, curved gracefully from either quarter down to the waterline.

Almost 83 feet from stem to stern, 19 feet 9 inches wide and of 59.56 registered tons, *Kathleen* was in 1901 typical of the then current, albeit conservative, trends in barge building. She was neither extreme in size or shape nor in choice of construction; perhaps the ideal recipe for a successful career.

These brief, though of necessity somewhat complex, details of hull construction highlight the box section hull form which it can be seen formed such a capacity advantage over the round-bilge billy-boys and brigs of the nineteenth century. When viewed afloat, however, it was the distinctive sprits'l rig by which *Kathleen* and her type were identified. The spritsail barge is a unique craft which through the simplicity of its operation, despite the complexity of its gear, could be worked efficiently by a crew of two. The spritsail rig, and for that matter leeboards, were developed by the Dutch over five hundred years ago. They have been in use on the Thames for at least three hundred and fifty years and are commonly featured in many old engravings of the Tideway. The basic element of the spritsail is the long spar, known as the sprit or spreet, which supports the peak of the sail at its upper end, the other end being secured at the base of the mast. The typical Thames spritsail barge had two such sails, the mainsail, and a diminutive mizzen used to assist with steering, its boom being sheeted to the blade of the rudder. In addition to these sails, which were never lowered but merely brailed like a music hall curtain when not in use, *Kathleen* also set a topsail and foresail, plus from time to time a bowsprit jib and a staysail bent on to the long topmast stay as a flying jib. In all, over 2,500 square feet of sail, which together with her massive spars and rigging weighed upwards of five tons and were supported and worked by almost a mile of chain, wire and fibre rope.

Though functional in concept and build, few if any barges were devoid of traditional decoration, even steel and iron hulls often having carved wooden bow and stern badges bolted through their rails. These brightly coloured expressions of the shipwright's skills were often intricate in shape and detail, sometimes embodying the houseflag of the owner, or, as in the case of some of Howard's Maldon-built barges, displaying the flowers after which they were named.

A little less ornate, but still exhibiting much of the personal flair of her builder, *Kathleen's* bow badges were shaped like a breaking wave with incised yellow line work picked out on a mid-blue ground. A continuous yellow line gouged into the

Taken from the mainmast cap, this picture clearly shows *Kathleen's* unusual steering position, the result of her conversion to a motor barge. Most barges had the wheel and companionway hatch at the forward end of the cabin top. *Author's collection*

shiny black rails ran virtually to the stern badges, which in style and colour matched their forward counterparts. The quarterboards mounted above the rails aft and the covering board were painted white, contrasting attractively with the black-varnished hull. Her transom was painted green, and bore in addition to characteristic scroll work the name *Kathleen* and her port of registry, Rochester, skilfully carved and picked out in yellow. Incised into the saddle-chock, a transverse beam above the transom, was *Kathleen's* official number, 113708, and details of her ownership.

On her grey deck the mastcase, leeboard winches and other ironwork were painted green, with the cabin top, hatch coamings, the inside of the rails, windlass bitts and other timber work in "mast colour", a workaday mid-brown, rather restrained by comparison. All spars were clear varnished, except the topmast which was for much of its length given a few coats of raw linseed oil, a protection which unlike varnish allowed the topsail hoops to travel freely on the spar without binding.

Just one piece of ironwork appeared to escape the green paintwork. This was *Kathleen's* wheel. Perhaps out of envy for the fine wooden wheels of some of the larger coasting barges, *Kathleen's* cast-iron "chaff cutter" was carefully grained to imitate timber, despite its obvious foundry ancestry!

Kathleen lying in Whitstable about 1917 with a cargo which is stacked up well above hatch level.
National Maritime Museum, Nautical Photo Agency

CHAPTER THREE

Trade, Peacetime and War

IT IS unfortunate that many of the details of *Kathleen's* earliest years have been lost with the passage of time. The coastal trade was buoyant in the first decade of the century, and it is reasonable to assume that she plied in general trade, probably venturing to the near Continent from time to time.

It is also possible that some time was spent carrying invert brewing sugars to the river and creekside breweries of Kent from the merchant ships which unloaded into sailing barges in the lower reaches of the Thames. This was after all the business of her half-owner, but *Kathleen*, with her sizeable bowsprit and largely coasting build, was not ideally suited to the upriver trade. Perhaps it was this unsuitability for her owner's business that led to her disposal after only eight years with the Duttson-Glover partnership, for in 1909 she was sold to the Whitstable Shipping Company.

The port of Whitstable, *Kathleen's* home for half a century, is situated on the North Kent shore, just east of the Isle of Sheppey. Its major claim to fame stems from the fact that it was the world's first rail-linked port, Robert Stevenson's steam locomotive *Invicta* inaugurating a regular train service from the harbour to Canterbury as early as 1830. At a time when the carriage of goods by road was a laborious, expensive, and, during the winter, frequently impossible task, the convenience of a rail link from an important cathedral town to a port providing regular sailings to London and the Continent ensured the success of the harbour. Built by the Canterbury and Whitstable Railway Company for around £10,000, it was formally opened on 19th March, 1832. Within twenty years the harbour's value had increased tenfold, the South Eastern Railway taking it over for just under £100,000. This success gave rise to an increasingly prosperous maritime community, with no fewer than eighteen small shipyards operating during the second half of the nineteenth century.

James Robert Daniels, known to his skippers and friends as "Jim Bob", came from a long-established Whitstable family. With David and George Daniels, who had previously run the brewery in Oxford Street, Whitstable, and a certain Captain J. Dadd, he established a shipowning partnership which endured for twenty years. Subsequently, he was appointed Lloyd's agent and also became manager of the Whitstable Shipping Company. One of Jim Bob's sons, Alfred, went to sea at an early age, soon became a steamship captain, came ashore at thirty, and joined the firm as manager on his father's death. The company's main business was operating more than a score of schooners and barquentines of up to almost 300 tons. Much of their trade was in coal, but cereal and other dry cargoes were also a significant element.

H. K. Daniels

Captain J. R. Daniels

Captain A. W. Daniels

All R. K. Anderson collection

Alfred's brother, Harry Kingsford Daniels, was manager of the barge department which operated around a dozen vessels, one, the *Pearl*, being built for the firm as early as 1866. Much of their work centred on the grain trade from the London docks to the company's own store, erected in 1879 on the old west quay, but at times this work took the barges to Ramsgate, Dover, and beyond. General cargo was, however, carried whenever there was demand or capacity, and cross-channel passages were by no means rare.

Kathleen, in 1909 one of the Whitstable Shipping Company's larger barges, was one of those trading outside the estuary. It was on a Continental trip prior to the First World War that her first moment of notoriety occurred. Under the command of Whitstable skipper Frank "Dolly" Nicholls, *Kathleen* was returning home from Ostend with a freight of empty butts for the famous Whitstable oyster fishery. The Whitstable barges were accustomed to leaving the harbour light and arriving laden, as was the case on this occasion. Empty barrels, however, fill a barge with little more than air, so *Kathleen* with a mere 25 tons of freight was riding high in the water.

It was almost certainly this factor that led Captain Nicholls to misjudge his entry to the harbour, the extra windage on the barge's side sweeping her past the entrance. She drove ashore on the Horsebridge, an ancient landing place established on the beach long before the harbour was constructed. As luck would have it, this part of the foreshore was immediately adjacent to the stores of the oyster company, a very convenient coincidence. *Kathleen* suffered little if any damage and was soon refloated and back at work.

It was about this time, while *Kathleen* was under the command of "Dolly"

Nicholls, that a young man named Fred Wraight, also from Whitstable, had his first taste of the coasting trade. From a family background devoid of a seafaring connection, young Freddie shipped aboard *Kathleen* to earn his living afloat. He could not possibly have foreseen at the time that he would return to *Kathleen* as skipper some twenty years later, or that he would be joined by his son, also Fred; between them they gave fifty years' service aboard.

Shortly after the oyster barrel incident, around the time of the outbreak of the Great War, "Dolly" Nicholls left *Kathleen* to take a command of the *Eucrete*, a new Whitstable-built barge of 55 tons. She was, however, totally unsatisfactory in operation due, it is said, to persistent hull leakage and was quickly disposed of. "Dolly" Nicholls dearly wished to return to *Kathleen,* but her new master, Bill "Sluggs" Peyton, was equally keen to stay on, so "Dolly" took the *Lord Churchill,* which together with *Kathleen* and *Duluth* was put into the Channel trade. *Kathleen,* however, soon returned to river work until venturing abroad again early in 1918. The *Duluth,* Whitstable built in 1895, and the *Lord Churchill,* built at Littlehampton as a ketch in 1888 and converted to spritsail rig when purchased by the Whitstable Shipping Company in 1901, worked mainly to Calais, supplying the needs of our forces battling against the Kaiser.

After the start of the war, the Government requisitioned most of the firm's larger vessels, with the result that the scale of operation was much reduced, leading in 1916 to the winding up of the company. Harry Kingsford Daniels then started the firm of Daniels Brothers (Whitstable) Ltd. "H. K.", as he was universally known, partnered by his brother Alfred, took over the barge fleet from the then defunct Whitstable Shipping Company, becoming essentially concerned in the coasting trade, as well as carrying on business as shipbrokers and maintaining the agency for Lloyds.

From his office in London "H. K." would give orders to his skippers, frequently cotchel work (many small "parcels" of freight from various merchants) for the older and smaller craft, and sometimes for the larger craft as well. When these split cargoes involved grain, sacks would be hired, generally from Starkey's, filled at the P. L. A. hopper and stowed below. When a small "parcel" was loaded, the barge would often sail to another dock to load more part cargo, and so on until she was full, loading and unloading frequently consuming more time than the actual passage.

Daniels' crews were acknowledged as being among the hardest working in the business, and their system of remuneration, unique in the barging world, seemed to give a fair deal to all. "H. K.'s" generous nature led him to give a five-pound Christmas bonus to the crews, a considerable sum in those days; it is clear that a berth aboard a Daniels' barge provided a secure and rewarding occupation.

In the summer of the same year that Daniels' business was established the barge *Livonia* carried her last cargo. Ipswich-built in 1871, this 50-ton barge had by 1916 worked hard for a number of owners, having been bought by the Wright family in the late 1800s, owned firstly by Henry William Wright at Gravesend and around 1910 by Charles E. Wright at Maidstone. On 22nd July the *Livonia* sailed from

London with a freight of wheat and flour, bound for the River Medway. Anchoring at the mouth of the river for the night, Captain Jim "Sonny" Kelsey and his mate turned in for a few hours' sleep. By morning it was apparent that all was not well, the barge having taken a lot of water in the increasingly strong south-westerly.

With two pumps going, it was just about possible to keep pace with the leak, but that left no-one to sail the barge to safety. A little later Daniels' *Azima*, built in 1898 at Whitstable and by coincidence of the same tonnage, came alongside the *Livonia*. Her crew took turns with "Sonny" Kelsey and his mate at the pumps so that the wheat and flour, still dry, could be transferred into the *Azima's* empty hold. With luck the worst of the leak might be in *Livonia's* side planking, possibly above her waterline when unloaded. It was not to be.

Just before high water, with all the freight worth saving safely aboard the *Azima*, it became apparent that the leak was getting considerably worse. The pumps were no longer stemming the rising water. "Sonny" Kelsey decided to attempt to beach the barge, but with no feasible lee shore to run to he had to sail the half-submerged vessel to windward with the result that the *Livonia* soon foundered.

"Sonny" Kelsey thus found himself without a job, but was fortunate to find work with Daniels, apparently as a relief skipper; he did freights in a number of barges including the *Azima*.

There could hardly have been a better Christmas present for the Kelsey family than to learn from "H. K." Daniels that "Sluggs" Peyton was leaving the *Kathleen* to join the *George and Eliza*, a somewhat smaller but newer barge owned by the London and Rochester Barge Company, and that his berth on *Kathleen* was offered to "Sonny". On Thursday, 14th December, 1916, "Sonny" shipped aboard with his son Horace. The war effort still demanded a lot of work to France, but the Kelseys were to spend a year working *Kathleen* mainly within the limits of the Thames before venturing down Channel.

Their first trip was a London to Whitstable freight. Arriving at the Victoria Dock on 16th December, the 1s. 3d. bridge dues being paid on entry, *Kathleen* hired sacks for 111 quarters of wheat and 63 quarters of maize from Bradley Brothers. Christmas had come and gone before sufficient small parcels of cargo had been loaded, *Kathleen* calling at St Katharine's, Millwall and Tilbury Docks before taking the ebb to Whitstable on the 28th.

There was a total of 141 tons aboard for which 3s. 6d. per ton was paid, the gross income being £24 13s. 6d. From this sum was subtracted 5s., being Daniels' "commission" as brokers for finding the work. This left £24 8s. 6d. from which expenses were first deducted. On this occasion harbour dues at Whitstable were £1 1s. 5d. and at London 4s. 11d . A sum of 4s. was allowed for ale; presumably cotchel work created thirsty crews! Port Authority clearance cost 2s. 6d. and "help", probably a tow through the dock complex, came to 6s. A "guy boy" was hired to help with loading, his job being to assist with working the burton tackle rigged on the barge's sprit; he received 6s. for his efforts. The remaining basic expenses were 2s.

for coal to keep the lockers full and the cabin stoves burning and 1s. 8d. for paraffin oil for the navigation lamps. These items totalled £2 8s. 6d., half of which was met by the owners and the balance by the skipper. Daniels' always received half the freight money, in this instance £12 4s. 3d., after first taking their commission. Additional costs borne by the firm were postage stamps 1s., slinging 11s. 9d. and gratuities of 10s. Captain Kelsey therefore drew £14 11s. 3d. on his arrival at Whitstable, £1 4s. 3d. being the company's contribution to the basic expenses, £1 2s. 9d. for the stamps, slinging and gratuities, and the balance of £12 4s. 3d. his share of the freight. The mate was given approximately one-third of the freight and basic expenses, this proportion frequently varying, sometimes on account of the master's lack of mathematical prowess and at other times when the mate suffered deductions to take account of "advances" received during the voyage.

This first passage was typical of many which were to follow in 1917. *Kathleen* took 151 tons from London to Whitstable on 2nd January; 147 tons from the Surrey Dock on 15th February; 100 quarters of wheat and 600 quarters of maize from the Millwall and Surrey Docks on 2nd March; 151 tons on the 16th; 700 quarters of wheat loaded from the Ellerman steamer *City of Oran* in the Albert Dock and delivered to the Whitstable silo on the 23rd; yet another trip by the 30th, the fourth in March, certainly some remarkable passages. April was not so good, 147 tons of wheat loaded from a ship in the Victoria Docks not reaching Whitstable until the twelfth. Back to London's Millwall Dock on the 18th for 150 tons of cotton cake,

Horace Kelsey, who was mate under his father from 1916 to 1918. *Horace Kelsey collection*

making port on the 27th. Another two freights in May and one on 11th June were followed by a cotchel load totalling only 106 tons on 26th June. This particular trip was not quite so bad for the crew's wages as it might appear; 69 tons of the cargo were at 4s. 2d. per ton, largely offsetting the effect of working the barge one-third empty. The London to Whitstable work seemed to dry up for a while, so while without orders the Kelseys spent four days painting and maintaining the barge.

Kathleen's sail plan from the old sail book of Goldfinch's, sailmakers, Harbour Street, Whitstable. The likelihood is that this records her first new suit of sails after her arrival at Whitstable about 1909. Each new sail was superimposed on the original drawing if there was any change in dimensions; the last such addition was a triangular "leg o' mutton" sail set when *Kathleen* was trading under motor.

Ray Goldfinch

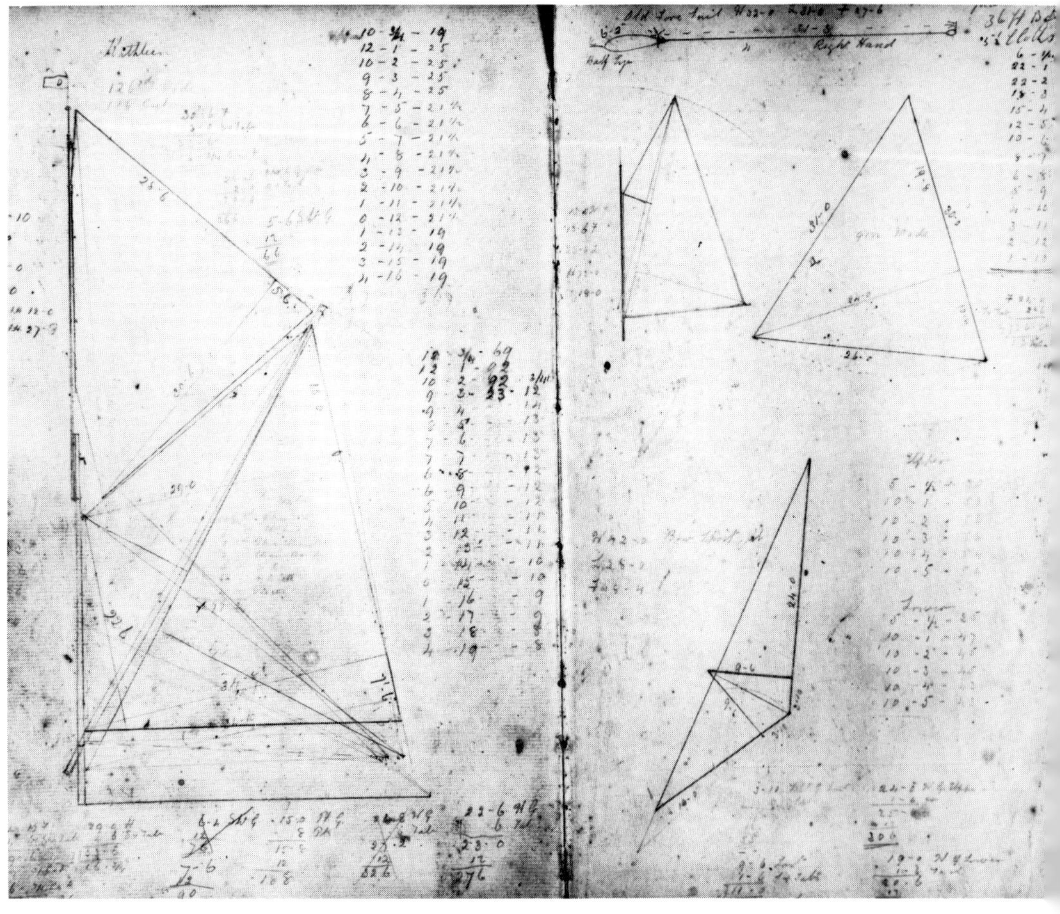

Kathleen's sails were unbent and Goldfinch, the local sailmaker, sent his cart, hauled by horses borrowed from the local undertaker, to bring them to his loft in Harbour Street. They were then repaired where necessary, the boltropes preserved with a liberal application of Stockholm tar, and the flax canvas dressed with an oil, ochre, and water mixture brushed on and allowed to dry in the sunshine. Spars were scraped and the hull cleaned of weed and barnacles. The main and mizzen masts and spreet, plus the bowsprit, were clear varnished and the topmast oiled. The hull down to the chines was given a coat of black varnish.

Kathleen's shiny sides mirrored the surface of the water as she took her tide to London in early July. A freight for Ipswich had been found, 660 quarters of wheat at a fixed price of 1s. per quarter. As was usual when she loaded a large cargo of bagged grain, she carried a small "stack" above her coamings. *Kathleen's* box-like hull made her a very good carrier, her biggest ever freight reputed to have been 167 tons of wheat to Whitstable. On this trip to Ipswich, one of *Kathleen's* very few trips northward from the estuary, the good freight money of around 4s. 4d. per ton more than compensated for a round trip lasting almost three weeks.

On the last day of the month, *Kathleen* was fixed with 118 tons of maize, London to Whitstable. By no means a full cargo, such a freight was not too bad when things were a bit slack, if all in one parcel.

A mixed load of wheat and oats from the Royal Albert Dock was carried on 14th August, followed on the 25th by 79 tons of bark for use by the Whitstable tannery, loaded in Tilbury Dock and earning 4s. 2d. per ton.

Early morning on 6th September found *Kathleen* leaving the South West India Dock with 135 tons of grain on the morning ebb, arriving at Whitstable the same day. Eight shillings had been enough to buy new bass mooring warps, and "Sonny" Kelsey settled his account with Frank Nicholls, the ship's chandler and ironmonger (not to be confused with Captain Frank Nicholls). At the same time he also paid the account relating to the *Thomas and Frances*, *Duluth* and *Globe*, a total of £9 4s. 0d. and was reimbursed at the office by Alfred Daniels. Then 131 tons of grain from the Victoria Dock silos were carried to Whitstable on the 15th, and another 151 tons ex Bellamy's Wharf on the 26th.

It was not until 18th October that *Kathleen* next found work, two parcels of wheat from the Victoria Dock silos and the Royal Albert Dock totalling 143 tons in all. Another split freight, this time 122 tons of barley and wheat from the Victoria and East India Docks, commenced loading on 2nd November. During the ensuing passage, when coming into Long Reach from Erith Rands, the Kelseys' gaze alighted on a barge high and dry on the south foreshore, just east of the River Darent. To all appearances the vessel was a derelict, with just her mizzen standing and her deck piled high with broken spars and other wreckage. There was, however, something familiar about the barge, and also the figure by then to be seen waving towards *Kathleen* from the vessel's taffrail. As the *Kathleen* stood in towards the shore, the barge soon revealed herself as the *Why Not*, another of the Daniels fleet, of some 40 registered tons, and built in 1866. The figure aboard her was none other than Horace's elder brother, Alf.

Kathleen anchored close in, and "Sonny" and Horace went ashore. "What are you waving for?" asked "Sonny" of Alf. "Do you need help?" "Just waving to say hello", replied Alf with a grin, but the state of *Why Not* warranted further explanation. Not only was the deck littered with torn sails and broken timber, but the remains of a military aircraft lay nose down in the barge's main hold. Young Alf explained. They were bound for London from Whitstable, empty. *Why Not* was carrying the last of the flood up Long Reach and Alf was down below tucking into his favourite dinner, streaky pork, when Jack "Farmer" Packman, the skipper, called down to him, "Come and look at this aeroplane, Alf, I've never seen one coming as low as this."

"Don't worry," Alf replied, "the government has commandeered land by the Joyce Green Isolation Hospital as an aerodrome for training new pilots; they'll be up to all kinds of antics near here." Before "Farmer" had a chance to reply, there was a rending crash, the *Why Not* stopping in her tracks. Alf rushed up on deck to find the skipper standing mesmerised at the wheel, his face a mixture of horror and disbelief. Forward of the mainhorse, everything was laid bare; rigging and spars had been demolished as the aircraft swept in over the bow, even wrenching the windlass and bollards from the deck.

"Farmer" rushed forward to see if there was anything he could do for the pilot, but he was beyond help, killed instantly at the moment of the crash. The barge was out of control and athwart the busy channel with no means of anchoring.

The Long Reach Tavern about 1936. *Evelyn Salmon*

"At that moment one of Cory's tugs came up and lashed alongside of us, though what he took a turn to, I can't imagine," Alf told his father and brother. "Anyway, he gives her full speed ahead, then slips us. We were going so fast *Why Not* slid right up on the mud by the Long Reach Tavern."

As the barge grounded there was a movement from the smoking tangle of fabric and metal, and a moment later a flyer emerged virtually uninjured to sit on top of the wreckage. He turned out to be the 'plane's observer.

Jack told his young mate he must leave for Daniels' London office and that he was to stay aboard until he returned. He left shortly after, walking to the station at Dartford, leaving Alf in the company of the dead airman. This macabre situation lasted through the first night, despite the arrival of officers from the nearby aerodrome who merely insisted that nothing at all should be touched until their investigators came to survey the scene. During that night, Alf, whose fitful sleep had endured only until shortly after midnight, was startled by a sound of movement coming from the other side of the main hold bulkhead.

Equally scared by the thought of investigating or doing nothing, he waited a moment, then grabbing a lamp climbed gingerly up the companionway. The flickering glow cast an eerie light into the hold. An overpowering smell of castor oil, the aeroplane's lubricant, came welling up from the wreckage. The sound came again, this time much louder than before. Then two beadlike eyes were caught in the soft beam from the lamp, and the rat to whom they belonged scuttled up and over the barge's side. The noise explained, Alf returned below with his heart still pounding.

Next morning, he went on to explain to his father and brother, the officers came back on board, though there was still no sign of the chaps who were going to investigate the crash. Having heard his story, they took pity on Alf, gave him a pass for the aerodrome, and offered him a bed in their billet.

"That was best part of a week ago and nothing much has happened since," Alf said. "I've stayed around the barge most of the days, walking to Dartford and back to get supplies when I needed them. They took the pilot's body away for the inquest which was held last Monday. No word from the skipper, and I'm still not allowed to touch anything on the barge."

"You come home for the weekend with us," suggested "Sonny". "Nobody will know, and the barge will be quite safe where she is. The tides have been taking off all this week, I don't suppose she's even got her rudder wet these last few days."

So "Sonny" and Horace returned to *Kathleen* with Alf, who was delighted to get a day or so respite from guarding the *Why Not*.

That night a storm sprang up, and by next morning the tide, much higher than expected, crept around the barge. The wind had managed to break out the mizzen, which was by then banging back and forth in the blustery gale. *Why Not's* stern began to lift to the rising waters. Down Joyce Green Lane from Dartford station came Jack Packman, climbing the sea wall just in time to see his barge inching her way from the mud back into the river. Hurling curses to the wind as he speculated on the whereabouts of his mate, "Farmer" ultimately succeeded in making the *Why Not* secure.

The *Dartford Chronicle and District Times*, reporting on the inquest, revealed that the dead airman was Captain Henry Griffith of the Royal Flying Corps. A witness, 2nd Lieutenant Stanley Fred Colver, said he had seen the two-seater aircraft from No. 63 Training Squadron at Joyce Green, looping among clouds at around 800 feet. Shortly after, it appeared in a spinning nose dive which continued until the aircraft crashed on to the *Why Not*.

Eventually the remains of the aircraft were removed, and the barge was repaired to work another day. Even Alf was forgiven by his skipper when all had been explained.

A cargo of 138 tons from Millwall Dock on November 15th, a large cargo of 162 tons from the West India Dock on the 25th and 146 tons from the London Docks on 13th December completed the Kelseys' first year with *Kathleen*.

Approximately 3,350 tons had been carried without mishap, and although war-time restrictions had from time to time affected the operations of the barge, hostilities had had little if any real impact on her trading pattern. "Sonny" Kelsey had earned for himself some £235 during the year, his son Horace getting about half that figure.

Hard but rewarding work when one considers that a typical wage at that time amounted to less than £100 per year.

On the Western Front the Battle of Cambrai had just seen the introduction of "Landships", code-named "Tanks" to avoid arousing the suspicions of enemy agents. Despite the potential of this new development, 1917 had been the blackest year of the war for the allies. Losses had been heavy in terms of men and equipment, and land regained from the German army minimal. At sea, the terrible toll wreaked by the German submarine fleet had averaged almost 200 ships each month. In the air, German bombing raids, primarily on highly populated areas of London, were sapping the spirit of the country.

The stubborn defence of the allied armies had, however, kept open the strategic French Channel ports of Dunkirk, Calais and Boulogne, all three well within earshot of the persistent gunfire. In addition to those deep-sea steamers which had evaded the U-boat menace, these hard-pressed ports were host to a multitude of sailing barges and other craft busily plying across the Channel to sustain the allied war effort.

For the first three months of 1918 *Kathleen* continued her regular London–Whitstable work, doing six round trips mainly with grain but including on one occasion a small parcel of bark for the Whitstable tannery. It was in early April that the Kelseys agreed to take a freight to Calais. They were to load Kentish coal, arranged through Alfred Gann, the Whitstable broker. This was lucrative work, rates being higher than those for the normal river trade.

Leaving Whitstable loaded and under tow was certainly a strange experience for "Sonny" and Horace. To help work the barge they had shipped a mate from another spritty as third hand for the trip.

The parade ground of Joyce Green aerodrome, with the Long Reach Tavern and sailing barges visible in the river beyond. *Major D. G. Nairn, via J. A. Tyler*

The enemy, unsuccessful in their land-based attempts to capture the Channel ports, were determined to deny their effective use to the Allies, and frequent German minelaying sorties kept the Royal Navy minesweepers constantly occupied in maintaining a swept channel. Even so, losses were quite considerable, a number of barges falling victim to mines.

To aid those navigating these treacherous waters, the swept channel was buoyed and the minesweepers and patrol vessels operated a simple warning system. The international code flag "N" indicated safe passage to the north of the sweepers; code flag "S" safe passage to the south; and so on. In addition "A" instructed the approaching vessel to anchor "at once" and "B" meant "stop instantly", a request as impossible for a sailing barge as it was for any other vessel.

A frequent practice for such passages was to assemble a small convoy of sailing barges at Dover, there to await a fair wind for their destination. Inevitably, times of arrival varied enormously despite the intentions of the naval authorities, who insisted that such a trip, starting at dawn, should always be completed by dusk the same day. Having left Whitstable on 2nd April, *Kathleen* spent a long time waiting for an unloading berth in the crowded harbour at Calais, but eventually returned to Whitstable unscathed some seven weeks after leaving. Although the freight rates were high, they in no way compensated for such delays in unloading as had been experienced. "Sonny" Kelsey visited the office, and the following day £50 demurrage was paid in new £10 notes to offset the crew's losses.

Orders were received on 3rd June to load a second cargo of coal for Calais. With consular fees, harbour dues, towage, etc, to be met abroad, a £15 float was provided as "ship's working money". The third hand carried during the first trip returned to

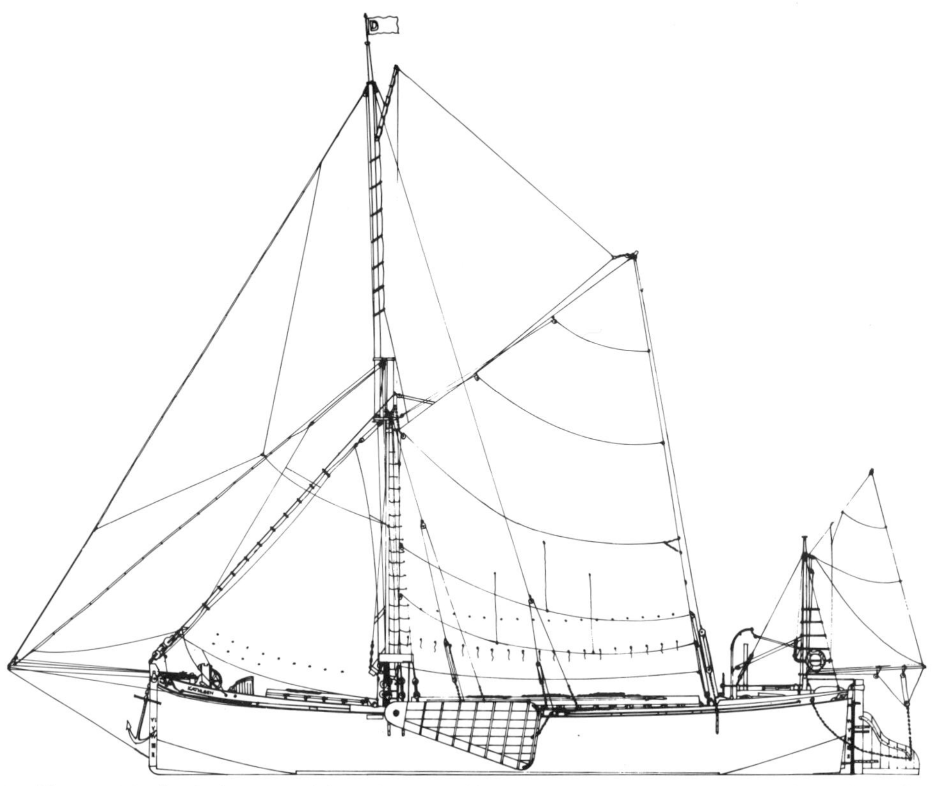

Kathleen's original sail plan, carried from the time of her building until 1926. Drawn by the author, after Edgar March.

his own barge and on 6th June a young man named Blackman came aboard as regular third hand and cook for a fixed wage of 15s. per week.

Leaving Whitstable on the 7th, *Kathleen* sailed to Calais via Dover, unloaded and returned light to Whitstable in under three weeks, a vast improvement on the first passage. A quicker turnround in Calais was probably a relief to skipper and crew alike, as the German army had started a violent assault on the allied lines, successfully advancing miles to the west. As it turned out, however, little progress was made near the coast and the stubbornly defended allied lines held firm.

The uncertainty in France probably influenced Daniels into putting *Kathleen* back in river work until the situation became more stable. The third hand was kept on during this period, pending further work cross-Channel. On 1st July 140 tons of grain was carried from Bellamy's wharf to Whitstable; 151 tons of wheat and maize on the 11th, and 146 tons on the 26th.

By the beginning of August, news that the German advance had been checked was being greeted with relief by the British people. Although few realised it, the tide had begun to turn.

More coal, this time destined for Boulogne, made up the Kelseys' third cross-Channel freight. Orders to load were given on 6th August, but departure for Dover was not until the 10th. The round trip was completed by the 22nd, the quickest cross-Channel passage by *Kathleen* so far.

The complicated system of charging half expenses and freight, as described earlier, was somewhat revised for the cross-Channel work, payment from receipts being divided between skipper and Daniels, though expenses were still debited in a similar but more complicated manner. On return from Boulogne, "Sonny" Kelsey computed his allowable expenses at £19 13s. "H. K.", however, made them come to £13 5s. 6d. The bone of contention appeared to be the halving of demurrage between owner and skipper. This amounted to £3 per day, a considerable sum. "Sonny" Kelsey revised his sums and eventually came to £13 6s. 2d., near enough to enable the two men to agree.

There followed one London to Whitstable cargo, 650 quarters of wheat, before *Kathleen* again loaded coal for Boulogne. This was to be an eventful trip, but it was the weather and not the war that was to take its toll. Loading started on 4th September and within a few days *Kathleen* was off round the Foreland, bound for Dover and Boulogne. The French port was crowded on arrival and it was 29th September before the return journey began. A fine southerly breeze had *Kathleen* romping home and by ten o'clock that evening she was about the Varne. The wind was freshening and by then south-easterly. On coming through the Folkestone Gateway *Kathleen* shortened sail and when in the Downs off Deal let go her anchor. She pitched awkwardly in the lumpy sea and lost her sprit. With plenty of chain she was in no immediate danger, and after doing as much as possible to tidy things up the Kelseys decided to wait until morning before assessing whether the barge could be sailed to port. At 7.30 next morning the lifeboat came alongside three times, offering to take off the crew. Each time "Sonny" Kelsey refused, having no wish to leave the barge to the mercy of the still worsening sea. Shortly after the lifeboat left, a Deal lugger came and offered assistance, which "Sonny" decided to accept. These luggers were operated by men who made a living from salvage and from assisting vessels in distress. Their crews, known as "Deal sharks" and often despised for their way of trade, were nevertheless much admired for their spectacular seamanship. The lugger sailed for Ramsgate and arranged for the tug *Aid* to tow the barge to the safety of the harbour.

Kathleen lay in Ramsgate for over a month, Daniels finding it virtually impossible to obtain a replacement spar. Blackman, the third hand, got a month's wages on 15th October, but not so lucky were the Kelseys, who got nothing when the barge was not working. Horace, fed up with doing little and earning less, took charge of the *Thomas and Frances*, a 37-tonner built some forty years previously in Sittingbourne. Shortly after he had left, Daniels found *Kathleen* a new sprit, a poor specimen, somewhat bent at one end, but it did the job. Alfred joined his father, taking over his brother's old job.

CHAPTER FOUR

After the First War

MID-NOVEMBER found *Kathleen* back in commission with 149 tons of wheat, London to Whitstable. Three more similar freights filled the remaining weeks of 1918, *Kathleen* returning to Whitstable on Christmas Eve with wheat and maize from the Victoria Dock silo, where Walter, the silo foreman, had received from "Sonny" a £1 Christmas box for his help during the year. The country was now at peace; 1919 was to be a year of rebuilding, of healing the wounds of the "war to end wars".

The first freight of 1919 was the last for the third hand, Blackman. He left on 18th January, some three days after *Kathleen* had delivered 700 quarters of wheat to Whitstable from the Surrey Dock. He was replaced by Edward Gambrill, a youngster of fifteen.

Eddie, as he was soon christened by the Kelseys, joined just in time for their first peacetime cross-Channel work. On Tuesday, 21st January, *Kathleen* slipped away from Whitstable for London, arriving at the East India Docks next day, fixed with a freight for Dunkirk. The busy docks were crammed with vessels of all descriptions. It was a whole week before they had fully loaded the hold and battened down on 131 tons of drainpipes, obviously intended for use in rebuilding the devasted battle areas of northern France.

Leaving London on the 29th, *Kathleen* carried the ebb down to the estuary, aided by a smart breeze, and brought-up overnight. The morning of Thursday, 30th January, greeted skipper and crew with the same south-westerly, but now blowing more strongly. Sailing east-south-east across the Cant, *Kathleen* headed for the Gore Channel, Whitstable soon being seen to the south. The wind had now risen to a full gale, and to have continued past the North Foreland would have been futile, so "Sonny" Kelsey decided to anchor in the Gore and wait for the gale to blow itself out. The main anchor would not hold her, so the second anchor was let go as well. After an uncomfortable night, the wind had if anything increased further and the skipper decided that they must get the barge to a more sheltered spot, as there was no sign of the gale abating. Turning with the flood, long and short tacks, *Kathleen* sped westward under foresail and half main. By nightfall she was safely anchored at Hollowshore, where Oare and Faversham Creeks combine before joining the Swale just east of Harty Ferry. There were already about thirty barges lying there, nearly all

Alf Kelsey aboard *Kathleen*, a photograph taken on 24th August, 1921.
Alf Kelsey collection

with freights for France. The weather did not improve for eleven days, but on the morning of the twelfth day, with the wind moderate from the north-west, the early morning air rang to the sound of the windlass palls clanking as the barges hove up their anchors and sailed for the Channel. At Dover by dusk, the fleet anchored for the night. The war might have finished, but the minefields still existed and passage was therefore only allowed in daylight.

There were five barges bound for Dunkirk, Daniels' ketch barge *Lord Churchill*, White's *Beatrice Maud*, a large coaster boasting a second place in the Medway Race of 1914, *Kathleen* and two others. At dawn, the patrol boat came alongside each barge in turn and announced that they were free to go, as long as they would be safely across by nightfall. As darkness approached, all but *Kathleen*, the last to leave, were safely in Calais roads; she was still about mid-Channel as the wind fell away to nothing and a thick fog enveloped everything, shrouding the swept channel markers completely from view. Concerned at the effect that the barge's chain might have on an isolated mine, "Sonny" Kelsey lowered the second anchor on a thirty-fathom rope; it was not long enough to reach the seabed. By the time it was retrieved the Kelseys, who understood much more of their predicament than the newly recruited third hand, realised that the tide had carried them out of the mile-wide swept channel into the heart of the minefields. For four days and five nights they drifted back and forth with the tide, enjoying the comparative safety of the swept channel for an hour or so twice in every twenty-four. This nervewracking experience was made all the worse by the persistent fog and by the terrifying sound of the tide rushing over mines which must surely, sooner or later, make *Kathleen* their victim. Lady Luck had different ideas: in the early hours of the fifth day a light breeze sprang up and above the fog there came into view some tall chimneys on the French coastline. Shortly afterwards the rest of the fog blanket disappeared as quickly as it had come. Unsure of their whereabouts, "Sonny" decided to sail towards the now clearly visible French coast. By mid-afternoon the sails of another barge could be seen, and to the Kelseys they had the familiar set of another Whitstable barge. *Kathleen* stood towards her and just before nightfall the two barges steered between the long piers of Dunkirk and into the inner harbour.

They waited almost a week for an unloading berth, but were then emptied in a day and spent the evening making ready for the passage home on the morning of Thursday, 27th February. Just before the barge crews turned in for the night a man sauntered along the dockside and, seeing *Kathleen* high in the water, paused to inquire when she was leaving. "In the morning if it's fine," replied "Sonny" Kelsey, to which the visitor responded with the offer of a tow to England. "How much?" asked "Sonny". "Nothing," replied the man, explaining that he was skipper of a London-bound tug. The crew of the *Kathleen* were very grateful, "Sonny" being only too ready to admit his lack of experience of the Channel. After the perilous happenings of the outward journey, a free hitch back was a great relief.

In the middle of the night they were awakened by the sound of voices, followed by what sounded like the noise of falling masonry. By the time "Sonny's" head peered from the companion hatch there was an astonishing sight ashore. The Dunkirk dockers were methodically smashing up the drainpipes just unloaded on to the quay. Next morning "Sonny" and his crew learnt that the happenings of the night were the result of a labour dispute between the dockers and their employer. Perhaps they might not have been so quick to destroy *Kathleen's* cargo had they been aware of the dramatic circumstances of its delivery.

They were towed that day all the way to the south east Margate buoy, where their line was slipped. *Kathleen* sailed on to Whitstable Bay, arriving in time for lunch on Friday. Entering the harbour on Saturday morning, she tied up alongside to await fresh orders. The third hand was paid up to the Sunday six weeks' money, amounting to £4 10s. The Kelseys shared the freight money with the owners, after taking account of expenses.

On Thursday, 6th March, *Kathleen* received orders for another cargo of drainpipes, this time destined for Calais. She arrived at the East India Docks on Friday, but it was the following Tuesday before loading commenced. By Thursday morning the loading was completed, *Kathleen* locked out from the dock and carried the ebb eastwards. On reaching the Swale, "Sonny" decided to bring up to await a fair wind for France. Dropping anchor just above the Nest Houses in the east channel, skipper and crew turned in for the night. In the morning the contrary wind was still blowing, so "Sonny" decided to go home to Whitstable. Alf sculled the barge's boat to the hard at Seasalter, from where his father could walk to his home town, a mile or so to the east.

Returning aboard, Alf and Eddie tidied the barge and chatted about the chances of a change in the weather and a fair slant to Calais. A couple of nights passed, and each morning showed no improvement in the wind direction. Both money and food were beginning to run out, so the mate and third hand decided that their daily jaunts sailing the barge's boat up and down the Swale to pass the time should be turned into hunting expeditions. Alf, armed with *Kathleen's* wartime issue rifle, managed to bag a few ducks which were cleaned and dropped into a stewpot on the cabin stove. A few vegetables, plus some undefined items, completed the concoction which simmered on and off for the next ten days! Topped up after each successful foray in the boat, the stew, accompanied by bread from a shop ashore, was the staple diet aboard till the skipper returned on Wednesday, 26th March.

Kathleen's stay at Shell Ness at an end with the coming of a fair wind at last, she slipped across the oyster beds of Whitstable Flats in the early hours of that Thursday morning. Entering her home port on the high water for a few much-needed stores, she bid the harbour goodbye on the same tide and sailed for Calais. In light airs *Kathleen* ghosted with the ebb to the Gore Channel and anchored for the night.

Eddie Gambrill was called upon to provide breakfast for "Sonny" and Alf. When, unknowingly late, he ventured down the companionway aft the following morning he found skipper and mate dressed and waiting. "What do you want for your breakfast?" inquired Eddie. "Too soon to say as yet," said "Sonny". A bemused third hand inquired as to the reason for this unusual reply. The skipper winked at his son and replied, "Well, we washed up this morning's twenty minutes ago, and it's a bit early to decide about tomorrow's!" Poor Eddie was not allowed to forget that little incident in a hurry; oversleeping has no part in the working of a sailing barge.

A good and trouble-free passage had *Kathleen* moored in Calais by next day. Unloading started on Monday, 31st, and was completed by the following Thursday, but it was Sunday before a fair wind let *Kathleen* sail for home. Coming straight

Eddie Gambrill
E. Gambrill collection

across the Channel, she headed boldly over the Goodwin Sands, leeboards raised to prevent them touching bottom.

Eddie was still not out of trouble. Bringing up for the night in a busy spot off the North Kent shore, "Sonny" asked the third hand to do a watch. Both the skipper and Alf had been about long hours and were keen for some sleep. For some reason "Sonny" was restless and later decided to go on deck. There was young Eddie fast asleep with a coat over his head! It could well be that the rebuke received over this incident made Eddie Gambrill realise, even at the age of fifteen, the significance of responsibility. He left *Kathleen* a few days later, joining Goldfinch's ketch *Mocking Bird*, of Rochester, as fourth hand. This was not demotion, as his pay was up from fifteen to thirty shillings a week, a spectacular increase by any standards. Eddie pursued a career closely associated with the sea, eventually becoming Harbour Master at Whitstable, a responsible and respected position in the community.

It was just over a week before fresh orders were received, this time a cargo of potatoes from Whitstable for Dunkirk. A new third hand, J. Sandy, came aboard on 24th April, the day *Kathleen* sailed for France. She lay overnight off Dover, and the morning of the 25th found Alf doing a bit of fishing and his father keeping a weather eye out for the patrol boat which would give them permission to leave. Unusually, *Kathleen* was the only barge waiting for clearance. "Look over there, here she comes," called out "Sonny". "That's funny, she's zig-zagging all over the place. They must be canned, that's what's the matter with them." It soon became apparent that this was not the patrol boat but a trawler weaving its way towards them. When she was nearly alongside, a hail from the trawler's wheelhouse was heard across the water. "Barge ahoy!" "Aye, aye," replied Sonny, "Where are you bound?" came the question. "Dunkirk". "So are we. Want a tow?" "That seems a bit strange," said "Sonny" to Alf, "I wonder if it's all right?" "Well, let's risk it," suggested Alf. They accepted the offer.

"Get your anchor," called the trawler skipper, so Alf and the third hand hove short the cable. The trawler steamed alongside and put a heaving line aboard, followed by a heavy towrope which was made fast to the bitt heads. *Kathleen's* anchor was catted to the rail and the trawler went slow ahead, then half, then full. It took both "Sonny" and Alf at the wheel to steer her, *Kathleen* foaming at the bow, and travelling her fastest ever. A mile south-west of Dunkirk the trawler blew four on its whistle, the signal to cast off the tow. Bringing the trawler round in a circle until she came alongside the barge, her captain called "Can't tow you no more skipper, the authorities will kick up a row if they know about this". As luck would have it, a nice little breeze sprang up and carried *Kathleen* smartly into harbour. The third hand had a four-shilling sub and went ashore to see the town. While the barge was discharging her cargo, the trawler skipper turned up on the quay. "This is when we'll have to pay up for the tow," muttered "Sonny" to Alf. "Skipper; mate; I want you to come and have a drink with me," said the trawler skipper. So the three of them found their way to a small cafe on the other side of the quay, leaving the third hand, by then returned and penniless, in charge of the barge.

Hot coffee and rum with chips was the order of the day. "How much do we owe you for that tow?" asked Sonny. "How much do I owe you?" the trawlerman replied. "You joking?" "No," he said, "we couldn't steer her. She was muddle headed because the hold was crammed full of coal. With you on our stern we could keep her straight!"

Back in Whitstable on 4th May, "Sonny" was greeted with the news of another Dunkirk trip, this time with more drainpipes from London. Mr Sandy was obviously having difficulty coping financially with the problems of being paid in arrears, borrowing 3s. in Whitstable and another 4s. in London on the 7th and 2s. on the 8th, the day *Kathleen* finished loading and locked out of the docks. After lying windbound at Whitstable, the third hand having a further 6s. in subs, *Kathleen* arrived at Dunkirk on Saturday, 24th May. Another 2s. on the day of arrival, an advance of five francs on Sunday and yet another five on Tuesday continued to keep the third hand in funds. A final sub of 2s. on return to Whitstable on the 30th left only £2 11s. 2d. to come from a wage of £4 10s. for the two trips. Perhaps he had learnt his lesson, for no more advances were necessary from then on, J. Sandy drawing his complete wage about every three weeks.

For *Kathleen*, the Dunkirk trip was to be her last passage to the Continent for fifty-six years. On her return she resumed her regular dry cargo work, mainly

London to Whitstable, occasionally to Ramsgate, Dover or Faversham. It was during a Faversham freight in early November that the rather poor specimen of a spreet, obtained with difficulty during the war years, decided to break. This time a replacement was found much more readily; a sound and straight spar of Oregon pine.

The year 1920 saw regular work in grain and animal feedstuffs. Rates had generally improved to around 4s. per ton, occasionally going as high as 5s. 3d.

On 12th May that year *Kathleen* was leaving Millwall Dock around 9 a.m. when her stern was hit by an Elephant! Neither Indian or African, this particular *Elephant* was a lighter so called by the Erith and Dartford Lighterage Company on account of its large capacity. The damage was confined to the taffrail.

Another Millwall freight followed on 25th May, after which *Kathleen* ran a series of trips from the Surrey Docks with bagged wheat. Towards the end of August, "Sonny" received orders for a cargo from Tilbury. While waiting to load in the dock he found time to yarn with some of the other skippers. Bargemen are generally a fit bunch of men, but poor "Sonny" was suffering from rheumatism, probably brought about by spending many hours in wet clothes during some of *Kathleen's* rougher passages. Someone suggested a remedy worth trying and "Sonny" wrote it down. It supposedly also provided relief from gout and probably other ailments too. Half an ounce each of "Powdered Turkish Rhubarb, Gum Guaiacum, Nitre in Powder, and Milk of Sulphur" were to be ground with a dram of aromatic powder and clove. The recipe called for "storage in a dry place", the dose was "one teaspoonful in half a cup of water, well stirred". Whether or not this concoction was of any benefit remains a mystery.

Regular work continued to be available for *Kathleen* throughout 1920, nearly all of it within the confines of the river and estuary. To start with, the services of the third hand were retained, despite the lack of Channel work, for freight rates were up as high as 8s. per ton and the extra help could be easily afforded. Towards the end of 1921 a far more competitive situation arose; *Kathleen* still found consistent work, but at prices which had fallen back to as low as 3s. 9d. The luxury of a third hand was no longer feasible, and for the remainder of *Kathleen's* trading life she was worked by skipper and mate alone. A look at her log book reveals a humdrum routine of similar cargoes and sailings. But in reality even passages of the most timetable regularity had variety, in wind, weather and tide. Occasionally, too, the routine would be broken for maintenance and repairs. The latter was usually on account of "fair wear and tear" but occasionally to remedy accident damage such as happened on 13th August, 1921, when the s.s. *Golfer* collided with *Kathleen* off Hope Point. All barges were built with the rigours of dock work in mind and their strong construction made them very resistant to knocks from tugs, lighters and other craft, but steamships were another matter entirely; although *Kathleen* survived this particular incident with negligible damage, she was not to be so lucky some eighteen months later.

CHAPTER FIVE

A Night off Greenwich

THE EVENING of Monday, 6th March 1923, was perhaps somewhat more pleasant than many that had preceded it. For *Kathleen* and the Kelseys were sharing work with two other Whitstable barges, both flying Daniels' house flag. The worst of the winter was by that time behind them, and the crews were looking forward to the warmer months ahead.

The three barges, *W. H. Randall,* of 35 tons and dating from 1876, the ten years older *Why Not,* and the *Kathleen* were lying alongside the Donaldson Line cargo ship *Tritonia.* A wartime standard steamer of 5,224 gross registered tons, she had been built by Caird & Co. Ltd. of Greenock in 1918 as the *War Emu.* She had recently arrived with a cargo of pitch in barrels from the asphalt lake of Trinidad. All four vessels were pointing upriver; the *Tritonia* moored fore and aft on the Folly House buoys at Greenwich, the barges moored to her starboard side with *Kathleen* amidships, *W. H. Randall* and *Why Not* ahead and astern.

Upriver from Greenwich in the Pool of London that same evening the *Virgilia* in Cunard Line service was making ready to leave for New York. Being another wartime standard ship, she shared a number of features with the *Tritonia.* Both were powered by triple expansion steam engines of identical dimensions, driving a single screw. The *Virgilia,* built by Russell & Co. of Port Glasgow, also in 1918, was the larger of the two at 5,697 tons.

Around mid-evening, as the last of the ebb chuckled its way round the piers and jetties of Greenwich, the skipper of the *Why Not* clambered aboard *Kathleen* for a yarn with the Kelseys. He descended the companion way aft, joining "Sonny" and Alf in the warmth of the cabin. The kettle was regularly boiled, and steaming hot mugs of tea interrupted the otherwise continuous chat. As was usual on such occasions, wide-ranging subjects were bandied about, but more often than not the conversation returned to life on the barges, the good passages and the bad, the narrow escapes, the freight rates, the weather, the memories of yesteryear. Around eleven o'clock their visitor bade farewell, the Kelseys checked their lines, and with the prospect of a hard day's work ahead to finish loading, they decided to turn in for the night.

"I don't like laying here," said Alf uneasily as he closed the companion hatch. "I'm not going to sleep in my bunk tonight; the locker top will do for me." Inexplicable though his comment was, it was sufficient to convince "Sonny" that he should do likewise. Had they not decided to forgo the comfort of their cupboard berths, it is almost certain that neither of them would have survived the night.

Around two in the morning three bow waves cleaved the early morning flood as the Cunarder *Virgilia*, in tow of the river tugs *Sun VII* and the *Sun IX*, headed seaward down Limehouse Reach. The tugs' speed eased as they swung to port round the southern end of the Isle of Dogs. The two seven-inch hauling lines fell momentarily slack as the *Virgilia's* way carried her forward. The incoming tide on her port bow caused her to sheer towards the Greenwich shore, the hauling line attached to the tug on the inside of the bend suddenly became taut and broke, and a few moments later as the remaining tug attempted to control the cargo liner's continuing wayward swing, the other line parted. It was immediately obvious to the tug skippers as the *Virgilia* slewed across the river, making four or five knots through the water, that the vessels lying to the buoys near the south shore were in terrible danger; though the tide was slowing the forward movement of the *Virgilia*, it was at the same time accelerating her swing towards *Tritonia* and the three barges.

Awakened by the urgent warning blasts from the tugs' whistles, "Sonny" and Alf leapt up from the lockers, climbed the companionway at the double, and arrived on deck just in time to see the towering stem of the *Virgilia* give a glancing blow to the stern of the *Why Not* before crashing headlong into *Kathleen's* starboard bow. Her destructive appetite unsatisfied, she slid down *Kathleen's* side, felling her gear as she went, then slammed into the *W. H. Randall* before carrying away the *Tritonia's* stern line. On she drove into Talbot's barge roads, damaging several lighters and breaking some adrift before running herself ashore by Woods Wharf.

At the moment of impact Alf recognised the consequences of the damage to *Kathleen's* bow and dashed below for his father's coat, wallet, and watch. Within seconds of his arrival back on deck the mast, sprit, sails and rigging came crashing down on them. Dismissing without a thought a blow on his head from a falling block, he struggled to the aid of his father who was being dragged by some heavy gear through the smashed hatches into the hold. From below came the sound of

The Donaldson liner *Tritonia*, alongside which the *Kathleen* was lying off Gravesend on the evening of 6th March, 1923. *The York Collection, Bristol*

The tug *Sun IX*, one of the tugs in charge of the Cunarder *Virgilia*. *Barry Collis collection*

inrushing water, explaining the forward cant of the barge as *Kathleen* settled by the head. Alf heaved his father back to the deck. As luck would have it, the barge's boat was moored to the stern and appeared undamaged. Alf managed to get to the cleat and free the boat, pulling it round alongside; the barge's deck was awash, so he was able to roll his injured and semi-conscious father into it. Letting go the painter, he allowed the tide to take charge of the boat just as *Kathleen* slid beneath the surface.

As the flood carried them upriver and away from the scene of the collision Alf considered his situation. He felt lucky to be alive. If they had slept in the bunks, "Sonny" and he would not have reached the deck before the falling spars trapped them below. But they were not yet safe, for the boat had lost its oars and was drifting with the tide. Looking around, he could see that the river was full of traffic; steamers, lighters, tugs and everything else posed a threat to their safety on such a dark night. Just then he noticed that there was a lot of water in the boat, which had not after all escaped damage and was obviously filling quite quickly. By good fortune, the flood set the waterlogged boat alongside a deep-laden lighter, and summoning his last reserves of energy Alf lifted his father aboard, then clambered on himself. The lighter turned out to be drifting; another victim of the *Virgilia's* rampage.

It was not long before a police launch spotted them and closed alongside. "Sonny", who couldn't move for his injuries, and Alf, still on his feet, were helped aboard and taken to a causeway near the Dreadnought Seamen's Hospital at Greenwich. To Alf's surprise the skipper of the *Why Not* was standing there. Suddenly the shock of the whole incident took hold; "I'm going aboard now," said Alf in a semi-delirious state as he and his father were whisked by ambulance to the hospital.

As dawn approached it was possible to assess the full extent of the incident. The *Kathleen* was sunk with no spars standing to mark her position, the *Why Not* was extensively damaged, and the *W. H. Randall* had been towed ashore in a sinking condition. In addition, the *Tritonia's* stern, broken from her mooring buoy, had swung inshore and grounded off Dreadnought Yard. She was towed off and re-moored by the tugs *Betty* and *Sun VII*. The *Virgilia* was also refloated and proceeded outwards under tow, anchoring at Gravesend to assess damage. At daybreak shipwrights were soon at work repairing her buckled plating above the waterline on the starboard bow. By evening the task was complete and the *Virgilia* resumed her passage during the early hours of the 8th.

The Port of London Authority, alerted to the accident during the early hours of the 7th, had a salvage vessel stationed over the *Kathleen* by mid-morning. Divers fixed lifting tackle to the barge, and at 12.40 p.m. she was raised to the surface and placed on the foreshore at Watergates, Deptford.

Daniels and the families of the barge crews involved were oblivious of the happenings of the night. "H. K." journeyed as usual to the firm's London office, only learning of his vessel's fate by telephone during the morning. Travelling immediately to Greenwich, he inspected the damage to the *Why Not*, *W. H. Randall* and *Kathleen*, commenting on the latter barge that she exhibited a hole in her bow big enough to drive a horse and cart through!

Meanwhile, back at Whitstable, Alf's sister had been visited by the police and informed that her brother and father had been drowned as a result of a collision on the river. She rushed to the shop where Alf's fiancee Frances lived and worked. Entering the store, tears streaming down her cheeks, she blurted out her story to Frances, who listened aghast. Mrs Spray, the proprietor, typing upstairs, came down to share the disastrous news. No details were known, but "H. K." would be on the train arriving at Whitstable at four that afternoon, and they were to meet him at the station.

As the train drew to a halt Alf's sister, Frances, and his mother looked eagerly for Mr Daniels. Grim-faced, he passed through the barrier to meet them, unaware of the tragic news which they had heard earlier in the day. As the group wended its way towards the harbour, "H. K." told them what he knew of the incident. Only when they arrived at the pavement outside the firm's office did he tell them the tidings they were least expecting.

"Well, my dears", he began, "Alf's all right, but Mr Kelsey, well, you won't be able to see him before Saturday."

The four days passed slowly, but each message from the hospital gave encouraging news of the casualties. On Saturday morning the anxious group set off for Greenwich. Horace, who had visited the hospital a day or so previously, did his best to prepare the others for the occasion. "I'm going to warn you," he said before they went in, "you won't recognise Alf, but don't upset yourselves." They entered the ward to find Alf sitting up in an old dressing gown, all done up with safety pins, and being fed with a baby's bottle. His head was completely bandaged and the rest of his body black and blue with bruises.

They were told that he had suffered a serious head wound; the hospital staff were amazed he had stayed conscious after the accident. His injuries were in fact far more serious than those of his father, who was up and about quite quickly. Dr Rowntree, a Harley Street specialist, pronounced his opinion that Alf might never walk, let alone work, again, but Alf's determination, spurred on by Frances, ensured that he was fit again by the time the barge was recommissioned.

Kathleen had been taken from the Deptford foreshore to Norton's yard at Bugsby's Hole, where more substantial repairs were carried out prior to towing the barge to Anderson, Rigden and Perkins' yard at Whitstable. "H. K." decided that the opportunity should be taken to sheath the barge, so she was "doubled" with an additional inch-and-a-half pitchpine skin all round, as well as making good the damage to her starboard bow. The cost of repairs was £1,144 16s. 6d.

An inquiry into the incident was obviously appropriate, but this was not held under the auspices of any independent body such as the Port of London Authority or the Board of Trade. With no loss of life involved, the investigation was left to Cunard, who appointed Sir William Corry from their own board of directors to interview witnesses, sift the available evidence and report back.

It was soon apparent that the direct cause of the collision was the parting of the tow, brought about by the imposition of a sudden and excessive load at a crucial

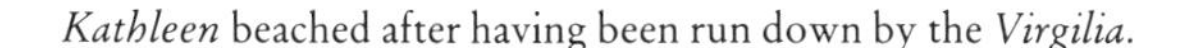

Kathleen beached after having been run down by the *Virgilia*. *Alf Kelsey collection*

moment on account of the geography of the river and the effect of wind and tide. The Cunard Executive Committee meeting on 25th April, 1923, noted Sir William's findings and endorsed his recommendation to the London Maritime Superintendent that towrope should be supplied for use in London instead of the seven-inch hauling line whose failure had been the major cause of the accident. In short, Cunard accepted the blame and Daniels' repair bill was met without argument.

After five months' intensive work, *Kathleen* was refitted and ready to resume trade. Also ready were "Sonny" and Alf, who while convalescing after their discharge from hospital had spent many days at the yard watching the skilled shipwrights at their work.

Looking like a new barge, with her smooth, unscarred black-varnished sides reflected in the dappled surface of the sea, she sailed for London on Monday, 6th August, freshly dressed sails once again spreading proudly from her lofty spars.

As a change from her usual grain cargoes, *Kathleen* carried a freight of timber to Faversham in September, 1934.

CHAPTER SIX

Cargoes and Running Costs

ALF and Frances set a date, Saturday, 10th November, 1923, for their wedding. The sixth of that month found *Kathleen* leaving Dover light, bound for the Surrey Docks, where she arrived on Thursday the 8th. She loaded 219 quarters of wheat on the Friday before skipper and mate caught the train to Whitstable for the wedding. There was to be no immediate honeymoon, for Alf and "Sonny" were back aboard on Monday waiting to load the remainder of their cargo, which was finally stowed on the 16th.

Frances had been fortunate in finding a couple of rooms not far from the harbour where she and Alf set up home on his return to Whitstable on the 17th. Only five days later *Kathleen* sailed to King George V Dock to load wheat and oats for Whitstable. Alf tried to persuade Frances to come for the trip, but she, never having had any love for the water, could not be tempted. During the ensuing weeks Frances prepared for the approaching festivities, making cakes and puddings and getting in other Christmas fare in the hope that she and Alf would be able to spend the holiday together in their new home.

Kathleen sailed for the Surrey Commercial Docks on 15th December, arriving to find that the freights fixed for her were not yet ready; the chances of being home for Christmas were looking slim indeed. After a few days' wait "Sonny" journeyed home by train, leaving Alf aboard. "Sonny" and his wife went to find Frances, who was helping her sister move house. Answering the door to her in-laws, she was greeted by a forceful "What are you doing here?" from "Sonny". "Come and get your bags packed," he continued, "Alf's waiting to meet you tomorrow morning at London Bridge." "He's got some hopes," retorted Frances, "I can't go." "Oh yes you can, you're going to spend your honeymoon up there," insisted "Sonny". So the next day she went to London to meet Alf, abandoning most of the Christmas things she had prepared for the flat, before going to the Surrey Docks and *Kathleen*. Frances was probably thankful that their floating "hotel" did not complete loading before 28th December, for this allowed the newlyweds almost a fortnight together. Then, deeply laden with wheat, with "Sonny" back aboard and Frances on the train home to Whitstable, *Kathleen* locked out from the dock bound for Dover.

London to Dover with wheat was a regular feature of 1924, no fewer than thirteen such freights being carried out of a total for the year of twenty-seven. Whitstable was the destination for another thirteen passages, and Ramsgate was visited once with a part cargo, *Kathleen* having first discharged at Whitstable en route. Once during the year she had the good fortune to secure a return freight from Dover, loading 172 bales of metal on 5th September for London.

The following year was to be almost a carbon copy of 1924. Again twenty-seven freights were carried, thirteen for Dover and the rest for Whitstable. Nearly three-quarters were wheat, the remainder all cereals or cereal by-products of one kind or another. This work was not always as simple as these bald statistics might indicate; it was frequently necessary to move from dock to dock and from ship to ship to obtain a full cargo. In April, for example, a freight of wheat and oats was loaded from three ships, the steamers *Perism*, *Otria* and *Valisia*; fortunately on that occasion all three were in the Royal Albert Dock together.

In November, a day or so at Whitstable between passages enabled "Sonny" and Alf to get a few things done to the barge. Top of the list of buys was a new nine-inch iron-bound double mainsheet block, complete with patent sheaves and costing the princely sum of £1 19s. 6d.; a new manilla mainsheet cost 9d. per pound and coir warps 6½d. per pound. Black varnish for the hull was 2s. 6d. per gallon and a Red Ensign six feet long cost 7s. 6d.

Daniels' barges were well and regularly maintained, but on occasions the sea still displayed the upper hand. Maybe superstition overlooked *Kathleen's* thirteen freights to Dover in 1924, but the thirteenth and last in 1925 was not to be so lucky.

Loaded with 648 quarters of wheat from the Victoria Docks silos, *Kathleen* sailed on 29th December for Dover. She carried a small stack aft which kept her about a foot by the stern, a trim which suited her well. With nine-tenths of her passage complete *Kathleen* began to make heavy weather of it off Walmer. The wind had freshened from the south and had made too much sea for the deep-laden barge. "Sonny" turned north and ran before wind and tide the short distance back to the Downs. *Kathleen* anchored to wait for the blustery conditions to abate and for a fair breeze and tide for Dover harbour.

The weather deteriorated further, and with the wind by then against the tide the barge pitched and rolled through the night. The "Deal Sharks" were watching *Kathleen's* riding light describing wild arcs in the wintry sky. At daybreak "Sonny" and Alf decided to run back to Margate Roads for more shelter. Such was the weight on her cable, however, that the anchor defied all their efforts at retrieval. The "Deal Sharks" came off to them and offered assistance. "Do you want help?" they yelled over the noise of the turbulent sea. "No. We're all right," replied "Sonny", anxious to avoid a salvage claim on the firm. So the boatmen returned to Deal, probably with more than an inkling that their services might yet be required. *Kathleen* lay fairly comfortably for the next few hours until the tide turned again. It was a particularly big spring tide and therefore very strong; things were not too bad while the barge lay head to it, but from time to time she would take a sheer athwart the breaking wave crests and be buried in a wall of water right across her hatches. Suddenly a particularly violent sea came crashing aboard and shattered the main hatch cover where it butted to the small stack aft. The hold was now open to the sea.

The "Deal Sharks" were watching. Off they came again. "Are you going to take help, or lay there and lose her?" Their question starkly summed up the Kelseys' predicament. There was really no choice. Four of them came aboard but they could not weigh the anchor, so the cable was buoyed and slipped in the hope that it could be recovered when the weather moderated. *Kathleen* was assisted into Ramsgate where it was discovered that 30 quarters of wheat had been damaged by water. The insurance assessors came and made a few notes, the hatch covers were repaired locally, and the local boatmen, having come to terms with Daniels, retrieved the barge's anchor. Some ten days after the gale, "Sonny" and Alf continued their interrupted voyage, arriving at Dover without further mishap.

Despite a marked decline in the proportion of work to Dover, 1926 saw a small drop in the number of freights carried. Much more cotchel work certainly accounted for the reduction in the number of passages. On one occasion *Kathleen* sailed from Whitstable on Monday, 8th March, arriving in London on the 9th; but it was to be the 23rd before she sailed for Whitstable, after visiting both Aberdeen and Odessa Wharves, plus the Millwall Docks. A few days later, the loading of another cotchel cargo of two different parcels of maize, pollards and sugar from the St Katharine Docks involved long periods of idleness. Such long-round trips resulted in a serious decline in the earnings of both crew and owners.

The process of maintaining the barge in good order was a continuous one, with various work being undertaken during unloading at Whitstable. In June two new leeboard pennants, forty-two feet long in quarter-inch galvanised chain, were made

Jim "Sonny" Kelsey and his son Alf aboard *Kathleen* at Whitstable about 1928. *Alf Kelsey collection*

up. These were complete with a long link at each end to enable a shackle to be passed through to attach them to the trailing edge of the leeboards, the other end being fastened to iron blocks through which new wire pennant falls were rove.

"Sonny" Kelsey, in discussion with "H. K." during July, was told that there was little likelihood of much work to Dover, so *Kathleen's* bowsprit was removed, making her much easier to work in the docks and river. As a staysail barge she needed a new topmast stay made up of 18lb of flexible steel wire at 10d. per pound, plus labour for splicing and serving, 2s. 6d., the whole job being done for just 17s. 6d. A new main brail leg was bought at the same time, for 7s. 1d. The major expenditure in 1926 was incurred during October when new side cloths (tarpaulins used to supplement the main hatch cloths when a stack was carried) were made up from 105 yards of 20oz natural wax dressed flax canvas at a cost of £18 7s. 6d. Also bought in October was 30 fathoms of six-inch coir rope for mooring warps, 109lb at 6½d. per pound, a total of £2 19s. A new "bob" for 2s. 10d. in December brought the total purchases for *Kathleen* in 1926 to £62 2s. 8d. including paint, sail dressing and black varnish for the hull. In December "Sonny" Kelsey "celebrated" his ten years in *Kathleen* with a rare occurrence, a laden departure from Whitstable, the freight being Kentish coal for Bromley Gas Works on Bow Creek.

Following the death in 1927 of his brother and partner Alfred, H. K. Daniels concentrated his efforts in Whitstable, only travelling to the firm's London office two or three times each week. Harry Blaxland, "H. K.'s" nephew, joined the company and took over the London end of the business. These changes in the organisation of the owners had little impact on the workings of the firm's craft and *Kathleen's* pattern of London–Whitstable work continued throughout 1927, a total of thirty round trips including one freight for Dover. Cargoes were still mainly cereals, with branded animal feeds and one consignment of tar making up the balance.

In the middle of the year *Kathleen* went on the gridiron at Anderson, Rigden and Perkins for a refit. Costs were moderate; £4 16s. bought 32 gallons of sail dressing, six gallons of black varnish for the hull cost 15s., a new stern light was purchased for £1 7s. 6d., and the mizzen rigging was replaced with galvanised iron wire for 17s. 4d. The two lifebuoys were re-covered and painted for 10s. each, then hung on the new mizzen shrouds, each displaying "*Kathleen*, Rochester" in block letters signwritten on to the canvas.

On the high water, 13th August, 1927, *Kathleen* floated from the blocks back into the estuary. Next day she sailed for the Surrey Docks where 696 quarters of wheat were loaded from the Cunarder *Ausonia*. This was delivered to Whitstable on the 18th, discharge into the silo being completed the following day. Against one entry in the cargo book that year "Sonny" had added the words "Stack, too much", a reference to the bulky cargo of branded wheat offal the size of which had perhaps gone a bit beyond the safe limits for the barge.

Maintenance costs for that year amounted to £107 10s. 8d., Goldfinch's

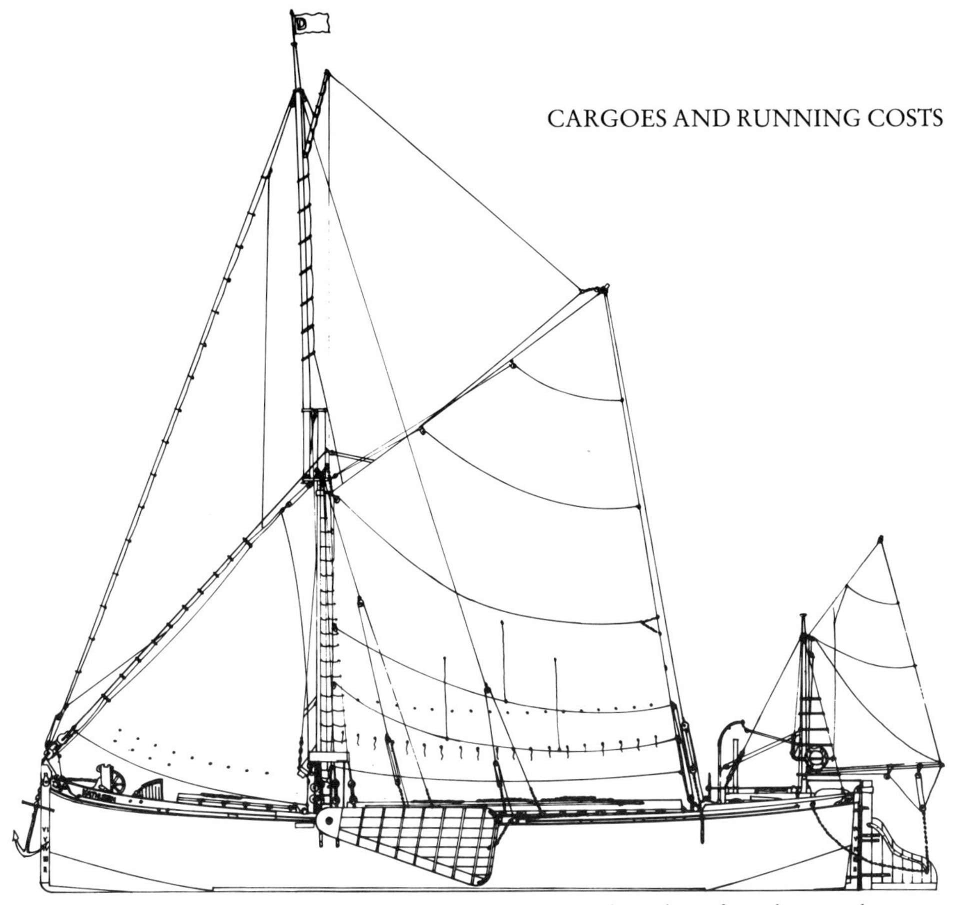

Kathleen's sail plan from 1926 until September, 1945. Drawn by the author, after Edgar March.

accounts totalling £54 14s. 7d., the balance comprising the Anderson, Rigden & Perkins invoices of 19s. 8d. for March, £22 12s. 5d. for June, £20 9s. 5d. for September, and £8 14s. 4d. for December.

In 1928 twenty-nine passages were achieved, twenty-seven to Whitstable, one to Dover and one to Ramsgate. Two unusual cargoes were carried during the year. One loaded from the s.s. *Southern Coast* in the London Docks in March was a mixed freight comprising 350 barrels of "Extract" and 809 bags of manure. The other was a cargo of string from Tilbury Docks for Whitstable on 7th November; just in time for wrapping the Christmas parcels, perhaps!

Principal items purchased during the year were 80 fathoms of flexible wire for the dolly winch costing £3 7s. 8d. and a new jib topsail (staysail) in 12oz cotton duck for £8 14s. 2d. Goldfinch's bills came to £67 13s. 5d. for the year, most of which was attributable to *Kathleen's* refit between 1st and 10th June. The shipyard charges were somewhat lower than average at £39 11s. 1d., resulting in a total maintenance cost of £107 4s. 6d., only 6s. 2d. different from the previous year.

CHAPTER SEVEN

A Change of Crew

SMALL "parcels" were a predominant feature of *Kathleen's* freights during the early part of 1929, and later in the year a number of passages were made with the barge far from full.

It is interesting to note that during this period cargoes became much more varied, and a few of what could be described as "less desirable" products were carried. The most significant feature of 1929 was, however, the departure of the Kelseys and Fred Wraight's return to *Kathleen* as her new skipper. Not that the Kelsey family's connection with the "firm" was finished, for Horace was later to take command of Daniels' auxiliary *Vicunia*, with his brother Alf going as mate. Nor for that matter was the association of the Kelseys with *Kathleen* at an end, for Alf's son Bill, nicknamed "Cod" for his fishing prowess, was to serve as an apprentice shipwright at Anderson, Rigden and Perkins, and both during his apprenticeship and after coming out of his time he worked on the maintenance and repair of *Kathleen*.

Nine freights in the four months January to April, 1929, was typical of *Kathleen's* trading pattern; less typical was the fact that no fewer than twenty-one separate parcels made up the cargoes. In addition to the more usual combination of cereals and cereal by-products, these cotchel freights also included manure for the Whitstable farmers, bark for the Whitstable tannery, and oyster shells for the famous Whitstable Native Oyster Company.

After discharging oats, cattle cake and oyster shells on 4th May, *Kathleen* lay windbound in Whitstable Harbour, waiting to leave light for London. "Sonny" was being pestered by the office to sail but at first refused, preferring to wait until the gale had abated. On 6th May, after a row with the owners, he reluctantly agreed to go, though conditions in the estuary were still very bad. Timing their departure so as to carry the flood upriver, the Kelseys turned *Kathleen* to windward with long boards across to the Essex shore and back. With the gale still blowing it was hard and wet work, *Kathleen's* bluff bow jarring against each vicious crest, sending curtains of spray across the deck. For Alf, who was tending the bowline, there was little escape from this regular drenching; at the wheel "Sonny" avoided the worst of the spray, but the spindrift-laden air still soaked him to the skin.

As they fought their way westward, the river became narrower, the boards became shorter, and the work therefore harder. As high water approached the wind

Deep laden with wheat in sacks from London, *Kathleen* enters Whitstable harbour under Captain Fred Wraight Snr. *F. Wraight collection* came in blustery squalls, straight across the low-lying marshes that bound the lower reaches. The confused chop became somewhat easier, and the tell-tale downriver swirl from the Yantlet buoy was confirmation if any was needed that the ebb had started. The head of the tops'l was dropped to ease the strain on the topmast, for the wind had increased again, and the tide had become its ally. "Sonny" hoped to reach Hole Haven where some shelter could be expected, though not much. The mizzen had long since been stowed, and a few cloths were taken off the mainsail as *Kathleen* came up to the East Blyth buoy.

The dark and menacing clouds that scudded low overhead seemed to contain and magnify the cacophony of sound as the barge thrashed to windward. The thump of the seas against the hull, the slatting of the sails and blocks as the barge surged through the eye of the wind at the end of each tack, the clanking of the heavy steering gear as it battled to control the massive rudder, the banging of the leeboards as they slammed against the side of the barge, the howl of the wind through the rigging, and the protesting creaks of the timbers as they strained and flexed to the movement of the boisterous swell.

"Sonny" and Alf glanced anxiously aloft to where the "rucked" tops'l writhed violently as if trying to be free of its spars and rigging. In the space of a few minutes it was in ribbons, the remnants streaming out to leeward from the topmast hoops and tops'l sheet. Moments later, with a crack like a rifle shot, *Kathleen's* mainsail split from sheet to throat. "Sonny" swung the barge's head into the wind and Alf wound like a demon on the main brail winch, gathering the damaged mainsail to the mast.

With no hope of reaching Hole Haven under foresail and mizzen, "Sonny" bore away to leeward before turning east to run before wind and tide back out of the river. The barge's motion was much easier as she sped before the gale, covering in minutes the miles so hard won in hours earlier in the day.

It took three weeks to get *Kathleen* back in commission. In addition to the necessary repairs, the opportunity was taken to overhaul and replace some of her running and standing rigging. New standing backstays and runners in flexible two-inch wire, two rolling vangs in two-inch galvanised iron wire, main brail legs and pennants from inch-and-a-half flexible wire, plus a new stayfall, 30 fathoms long, in two-and-a-quarter-inch wire, were made up and rigged. Four eight-inch iron-bound blocks for the main brails were bought for £1 10s. each, and despite the economic climate of that time the trucks of topmast and mizzen were gilded by Mr Cruttenden, of Cromwell Road, Whitstable, at a cost of 7s. 6d. A topsail of suitable size was located at Goldfinch's sail loft; it was a spare from the *H. K. D.*, a fine 65-ton coasting barge originally christened *Jewish* when built at Barking in 1899. She was given Harry Kingsford Daniels' initials on 1st November, 1928, after her purchase by the company in September of the same year. The old mainsail was repaired, needing 30 yards of number 1 flax canvas, plus 10lb of boltrope, to make it serviceable.

While *Kathleen* was refitting, "Sonny" and Alf had time to consider their futures. Their disagreement with the firm, which had in some measure contributed to their enforced inactivity, had left an atmosphere which was unlikely to be quickly forgotten.

At Tankerton, just east of Whitstable, "Sonny's" son-in-law had established a successful business with a pair of small motor boats carrying holidaymakers for short trips "around the bay". It was mid-May and the season would soon be in full swing. "Sonny" decided to go skipper of one of the boats and Alf, who did not wish to stay with Daniels' without his father, signed up for a job "navvying" on the roads for the water company. Before leaving the firm, the Kelseys did one last freight in *Kathleen*, leaving Whitstable on 1st June and returning with 200 quarters of oats and 550 quarters of wheat on the 13th, discharging next day.

Alf was not long away from earning his living from the sea. His brother-in-law with the boat trip business was driving through Whitstable one day and saw Alf labouring on the roads; a day or so later he called at Alf's house with a proposition. He proposed the building of a third trip boat which Alf would skipper during the summer months. At first the thought of a seasonal job, with earnings largely dependent on the weather, had little appeal when compared with the regular employment offered by the waterworks company, but Alf had the sea in his blood and the thought of a new boat, plus the success his father was enjoying, were sufficient to persuade him to accept the offer. So the boat was laid down, built, and

Captain Fred Wraight Snr. at the wheel, with an unknown passenger. *F. Wraight collection*

launched. Named *Seagull III*, she was designed to carry twenty people, but Board of Trade regulations limited her to twelve paying passengers. Nevertheless, like her sisters *Seagull I* and *II*, she was to earn her keep and provide a comfortable living for Alf and Frances over many years until the Second World War put paid to the local boating business.

During the years that had elapsed since before the First World War when Fred Wraight had shipped aboard *Kathleen* as third hand, Fred had married and raised a family. His son Fred Jnr was thirteen when his father took over as skipper from "Sonny" Kelsey. If he had been a little older he might well have gone as mate at the same time. As it was Alf Fryer, a Whitstable man in his mid thirties and a member of an established local seafaring family, took the job. Despite having skippered barges for nearly twenty years, Fred could not help but feel pleased at a new command, especially having served in her as a lad many years before. He could hardly have known at the time that *Kathleen* was to be his last barge; he was to serve in her for thirty years until he retired.

Fred Wraight and Alf Fryer sailed from the harbour on 15th June, 1929, bound as was usual for London, where *Kathleen* loaded a mixed cereal freight; they were soon back at Whitstable, the round trip taking only a week. It was to be nine months before the London—Whitstable pattern was broken with a freight to Dover, and during this time a remarkable thirty freights were carried with almost timetable regularity despite a programme of renovation and maintenance which was continued

A stack of timber for Faversham formed *Kathleen's* cargo in September, 1934. *F. Wraight collection*

almost every time *Kathleen* lay in Whitstable Harbour. At the end of June a new mainsail was purchased from Goldfinch's loft for £61 4s. It comprised 272 yards of No 1 "Extra Coker", a top quality flax canvas made in Devon by Richard Hayward, a firm still in the sailcloth business today. Unusually, the sail was bent on already dressed; it was normal practice to stretch a new sail for a month or so before the oil-and-water-based ochre dressing was applied. Also new at the same time was a topsail, from 126 yards of No 2 "Extra Coker" at a cost of £28 7s. The borrowed *H. K. D.* sail was unbent and returned. The old mainsail was put into store, and in the spring of 1931 was altered to fit the *Globe*, a 57-ton barge built at Frindsbury, Kent, in 1884 and bought by the Whitstable Shipping Company in 1902.

In July new running backstays were purchased, as well as an inch-and-three-quarter track line and a two-and-three-quarter-inch horse line, both in cotton rope. July was significant for another of *Kathleen's* rare laden departures from Whitstable, carrying 130 tons of slates for a London merchant.

By August, with the fitting of new backstay tackles, Fred Wraight was satisfied that *Kathleen's* gear was up to scratch. The year had proven expensive in repairs and maintenance. Goldfinch's charges covering rigging, sails, paint and "boatswain's stores" amounted to £182 9s. 6d., Anderson, Rigden and Perkins' account added up to £54 14s. 5d., giving a total of £237 3s. 11d. In present-day terms such a sum does not appear large, but to put this figure into perspective it should be noted that *Kathleen's* insurance in 1929 valued her at £800 , less than four times the year's expenditure on maintenance. It is also relevant to note that a year or two later a barge ready for work could be purchased second hand from Peters of Southend for less than £100 . Not until January, 1930, was further work on the barge's gear undertaken, a new yard tackle, mainsheet, topsail clewline, and a 60 fathom wire for the dolly winch replacing their worn predecessors.

The impressive performance of almost one round trip a week obviously reflected Fred Wraight's enthusiasm for his new charge, this rate being maintained in the face of a continuing high proportion of mixed cargoes. Three consecutive trips around Christmas, 1929, were achieved in eight days each, despite involving separate parcels of 212 quarters of wheat, 500 bales of cake, 39 tons of middlings and some flour on the first trip; 420 bales of cake, 50 quarters of maize, 140 quarters of oats, 375 bags of meal and a further 50 tons of cake on the second trip; and 338 quarters of wheat, 350 bales of cake and 50 tons of meal on the third trip. At least these dry cereal parcels were happy bedfellows. Not so a few months later when *Kathleen's* hold was shared by cattle cake, barley, oats and manure. This particular passage was shortly followed by a spell "cleaning and repairing", the former inside as well as out, presumably!

Alf Fryer stayed mate with Fred Wraight for just over six years before leaving on 9th August, 1935. This was the busiest period in *Kathleen's* history, with 208 round trips accomplished, carrying 444 different parcels comprising twenty-five different products. It would be wrong, however, to deduce that many trips comprised two parcels; for on most occasions complete cargoes of one commodity or cotchel freights of three, four or five parcels were the order of the day. Wheat was almost as common a cargo as Whitstable was a destination, and cereals and their by-products continued to form the basic constituent of *Kathleen's* trade. Exceptions during this period were the cargo of slates mentioned earlier plus others of shell grit, nuts, potatoes, bones and timber. In addition to the 176 freights to Whitstable, fourteen were carried to Dover, ten to Faversham, seven to Ramsgate, and just one north of the estuary, wheat to Ipswich in March, 1934.

It is remarkable that *Kathleen's* work load was maintained at such a high level at a time when the economy of the country was in such a depressed state. After a peak of thirty-seven freights in 1931 followed by thirty-six the following year, even 1933, when twenty-three out of every hundred of the working population were unemployed, provided Fred and Alf with an average of a round trip every twelve days. This was a time when barges lay for months on end on the famous "Starvation Buoys" at Woolwich while waiting for a freight. *Kathleen's* success during this period is probably attributable to a variety of circumstances. "Survival of the fittest" could well have been a factor, as there is no doubt that she was well maintained, efficiently operated (perhaps the threat of joining her less fortunate sisters at Woolwich constituted an incentive in this direction) and of a capacity ideally suited to her trade. Add to this the fact that many of the other barges which found themselves out of work had been engaged in trades such as the carriage of ballast and

building materials, items far less essential to a nation with its back to the wall than food and feedstuffs.

Leaving school at the age of fourteen shortly after his father took over the *Kathleen*, young Fred Wraight found regular work as an apprentice at George Fitts' garage in Tankerton. For five years he learnt about vehicles and their engines, picking up a mechanical knowledge which was in later years to influence his career in the coasting trade. Following the completion of his apprenticeship he went as an improver to a small garage in Canterbury for some six months, before leaving the land and joining his father as mate on 11th August, 1935, just short of his twentieth birthday.

Unlike his father, who on joining *Kathleen* had waited nine months for a break in the London—Whitstable trade, Fred Jnr followed his first freight from London to Whitstable, with maize and wheat, with visits to Faversham, Ramsgate, Dover and Ipswich, all within six months. Although various cargoes were carried, all four Ramsgate freights were in bulk wheat. On the first of these, towards the end of September, 1935, it appears that some mishap befell *Kathleen* either en route or in Ramsgate itself. Her cargo book tersely records "Repairs" on return to Whitstable, where *Kathleen* lay for a full week. It could be that this work was little more than routine maintenance, but the October account from Anderson, Rigden and Perkins was for £47 8s. 8d., the highest monthly bill for almost five years.

Opposite: Captain Fred Wraight Snr. on board *Kathleen* in the Millwall Dock in the early thirties. *F. Wraight collection*

Right: Alf Fryer, who was mate with Captain Fred Wraight Snr. from 1929 to 1935. *F. Wraight collection*

KATHLEEN

CHAPTER EIGHT

The Second World War

AS THE storm clouds were gathering in Europe, *Kathleen*, by then some thirty-five years old, continued to serve her owners and her crew with a minimum of fuss, and 1936 passed uneventfully. That year twenty-eight passages were accomplished, all to previously visited ports with *Kathleen's* familiar cargoes.

In April, 1937, orders were received for a London to Ipswich freight with wheat. Leaving the Thames on the 7th, *Kathleen* arrived next day after a good passage. It was often the case that visiting barges would be chartered by Cranfield's the millers or Paul's the maltsters, both Ipswich companies, to assist their own craft in unloading the large grain ships that would lie in Buttermans Bay or at Cliff Quay on the Orwell. This ferrying from the ship to the granaries in Ipswich Wet Dock went on apace to keep to a minimum the costly stay of the deep-sea vessel being unloaded. The company's barges and lighters would take priority at the granary, with the other barges, the "outsiders" as they were known, lying loaded as warehouses until the final day of their time charter, when they would be emptied to avoid payment of demurrage. It is interesting to observe that the River Orwell was one of the very few places where square-rigged ships were still to be seen from time to time. The last grain carried by sail from Australia arrived at Ipswich aboard the Swedish four-masted barque *Abraham Rydberg* in 1939.

Kathleen sailed from the Suffolk estuary on 22nd April, making London river on the 23rd and anchoring off the *World's End* public house when the last of the flood expired. This aptly named pub stands alone in a remote part of Tilbury Marshes, just west of the ancient fort and downriver from the Tilbury Landing Stage.

Brought up ahead of *Kathleen* was the London and Rochester Trading Company's 44 tonner *Rand*, built at Crown Quay, Sittingbourne, in 1898 by Wills & Packham, builders of many fine barges including *Raybel*, *Phoenician* and finally *Olive May*, at 108 tons the largest wooden barge ever built. The *Rand* was deep laden with sand and was sheering violently from side to side in the strong ebb. Her anchor dragged and she swung across *Kathleen's* bow, hitting it with such impact as to cause a split from top to bottom in her stempost. Unfit for a trip to Whitstable, *Kathleen* had to be repaired at Shrubsall's yard at Point Wharf, Greenwich, the work taking until 6th May. *Kathleen* left London on the 8th with more wheat for Ipswich; this time the trip was accomplished without incident.

Kathleen lying astern of *Savoy* in the Pent at Dover in the late thirties.
F. Wraight collection

A return cargo from Dover was not unknown, but the 50 tons of cable strippings carried to London on 3rd July was certainly unusual. Its origin is not recorded.

A cargo of pit props was delivered to Faversham from London in May, 1938, for the Kentish coalfields, but this was virtually the only non-cereal freight in that year. In the following November *Kathleen* took 620 quarters of wheat to Ipswich again. Quickly unloaded, she waited at Shotley, in company with two score others, for a fair wind south. They all came away together with a good breeze from the north-west. Before long, however, the breeze became a gale and a number of barges, including some of Goldsmith's "ironpots", ran before it, ultimately ending up on the Continent. It says a lot for *Kathleen* and her crew that when driven hard under such conditions she could keep up with the "flyers". Of the forty or so barges that left Harwich harbour earlier that day, only *Reminder*, *Edith May* and *Kathleen* rounded the Mouse that tide.

Three freights later it was 1939, the year when Britain had to face up to the tragic reality of Hitler's Germany. It was also the year that "H. K." died and Harry Blaxland, subsequently assisted by Frank Nicholls, son of *Kathleen's* former skipper, took over the reins of the Daniels business.

In July, 1939, *Kathleen* bent on her last complete suit of new sails, made as usual in Goldfinch's loft, a stone's throw from the harbour. The mainsail, topsail and mizzen were to the same dimensions as previously, but the foresail was cut shorter in the luff and leech in order to clear more readily the bitts and forehatch top. The complete suit cost just £118 12s. 3d., the mainsail and topsail £53 8s. 9d. and £24 respectively. Compare these prices with those of ten years previously; £61 4s. and £28 7s., a reduction of around fifteen per cent. This may be accounted for by the change from hand to machine stitching.

By the end of 1939 the formation of the Cereals Import Board to manage the decentralised cereal stores had had a profound effect on *Kathleen's* trading pattern. While destinations remained as previously, the cotchel freights became virtually a thing of the past, with regular full cargoes of wheat dominating her activity.

In 1940 the British Expeditionary Force was forced to retreat from the advancing Nazi hordes until what remained of the army was cornered at Dunkirk. The first day of the evacuation found *Kathleen* arriving at Dover with 650 quarters of wheat, and while she was unloading during the following days her crew watched the trickle of vessels coming into Dover with men from Dunkirk grow to a torrent. In all some 1,200 craft rescued almost 350,000 British and French troops in just over a week, a number of barges taking part in this heroic rescue, but *Kathleen* was not among them; she was ordered back to London on 30th May.

In London, the city office of the firm had been bombed and new accommodation was found as sub-tenants of E. J. & W. Goldsmith's in Fenchurch Street. The Dunkirk evacuation and the bombing of London were significant events in a national sense; no less significant in a way was the installation of a Kelvin 66h.p. auxiliary diesel engine

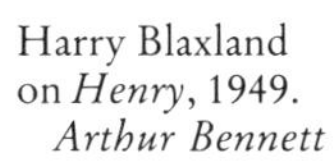

Harry Blaxland
on *Henry*, 1949.
Arthur Bennett

in Daniels' *Vicunia*. Whether this had been planned prior to "H. K.'s" death or whether it was attributable to Harry Blaxland's forward thinking is not clear. What we can be certain of, however, is the dramatic success achieved by the conversion, followed at intervals by similar installations in other barges of Daniels' fleet.

Twenty-seven freights were carried during 1940 and twenty-six in 1941. London to Whitstable, Ramsgate or Dover, nine out of every ten trips deep laden with around 700 quarters of wheat, with the occasional cargo of maize, flour or potatoes. This south-east corner of England was deeply enveloped in Britain's bid for survival. The war at sea, the battle of the skies, all were fiercely fought around *Kathleen's* trading routes, the bombers, the mines, the long-range cross-Channel artillery all attempting to sap the nation's resistance.

By the end of 1941 mines had become one of the sailorman's worst enemies. It was beginning to be realised that some of the magnetic types were even sensitive to the ironwork on a wooden barge. Daniels' *Globe* had been sunk by a mine off Sheerness in February, 1941, and on 10th May the *Duluth* was lost, not blown up herself but foundering after running over the wreck of a steamer mined a short time previously.

Later that year *Kathleen* was lying in the Swatch with a breeze that looked like coming on to blow a gale. Fred Snr asked his son to go on deck to give *Kathleen* a little more chain. Young Fred had only fleeted a few extra fathoms when *Kathleen* reared up in response to an enormous explosion alongside. Columns of water leapt skywards, accompanied by huge lumps of the muddy seabed which soon rained down on deck. A quick inspection revealed that, miraculously, the *Kathleen* was undamaged by what was obviously the explosion of a German mine.

Fred Wraight Jnr. when mate with his father in *Kathleen*.
F. Wraight collection

Not so lucky was Daniels' *H. K. D.* In January, 1942, three barges, all members of the "firm" and crewed by Whitstable men, were brought up overnight upriver of the defence boom which stretched from Shoebury on the north shore to Sheerness on the south (the remains of this construction are still visible today). They were the *Savoy*, of 69 tons, built at Rochester in 1898, skippered by George Fryer with his son Alf, previously with *Kathleen*, as mate; the *H. K. D.*,with Alf's brother Albert as master; and the *Kathleen*. At first light all three barges got under way, a light south-easterly making progress a little slow as the boom was opened to let them through. Remaining in close company, the three barges continued on their way until they arrived at the edge of the Cant. Without warning the sea erupted, and in an instant the *H. K. D.* was no more. The sky filled with debris as barge and cargo disintegrated before the shocked gaze of the other barges' crews. The *H. K. D.'s* 170 tons of bagged wheat drifted down to the sea as *Kathleen* altered course towards the wreckage which covered the area.

It is remarkable that anyone should have survived such a blast, but there in the water were the skipper and mate, very much alive. The *Kathleen* touched her anchor on the ground, lowered her boat and picked up the lucky pair, covered from head to toe in soggy grain; it might well have been the cargo which had cushioned them from the main impact of the blast.

The mate had a painful hip injury, and both Albert Fryer and he were obviously in a state of shock. Alf Fryer, mate of the *Savoy*, which had anchored nearby, joined his brother aboard *Kathleen*. While a hot drink had done much to restore them, the *H. K. D.'s* crew were in need of proper medical attention. It was about the time that the estuary minesweepers could be expected to be homeward bound after their daily sortie to clear the shipping lanes, so *Kathleen's* crew sorted through the international code flags and hoisted a signal to advise the sweepers that they required urgent assistance. A string of minesweepers came into view, but when the first was almost abeam it became apparent that *Kathleen's* signal had not been seen. Fred Junior and Alf Fryer leapt aboard the barge's boat and pulled off on a course to intercept, finally managing to force one to stop by getting almost across her bow. They shouted details of their predicament to the crew of the wallowing vessel, which radioed their message through to Sheerness. In a matter of minutes a fast motor launch was creaming its way to the scene with a doctor aboard. When some distance off, the motor launch stopped in deep water and indicated its unwillingness to venture into an area which only shortly before had claimed the *H. K. D.*, so *Kathleen* raised her anchor and sailed towards the launch to transfer the survivors, before continuing on her way with the *Savoy*.

It is said that the English will survive as long as does the Englishman's humour. Even in these dark days of war there were still amusing incidents which brought a smile to the *Kathleen's* crew. On one occasion in the dead of night, pursuing the bargeman's presumed right to free coal for the cabin stove, Fred Junior was stealthily approaching a handy heap of "black gold" stored in small lighters, having been removed from the bunkers of the many trawlers which were converted for minesweeping at the Albert Dock. With the whole of Britain's capital city darkened by the blackout, Freddie had felt his way to the objective and started to fill his old sack with coal. "I've watched you fill it up, now I'm going to watch you put it all back, mate." The voice from the dark was enough for Fred. Abandoning his ill-gotten gains to the watchman, he retreated at the double to the sanctuary of the barge.

It was the lure of coal that led to another amusing incident; amusing, that is, for some. Off the Long Reach Tavern were Cory's barge roads, a good place for coal with the added bonus of a waterside inn, replete with good beer and some of the most flexible drinking hours on the river. It was a remote spot, and with the paraffin lamps burning behind closed shutters, drinking went on till the early hours of the morning. One night with the wind southerly and high water just passed, *Kathleen's* boat was tied to the tavern causeway, the offshore breeze keeping it well afloat, provided Fred popped down from time to time to move the painter lower as the ebb began to empty the river. Checking the boat around 1 a.m. revealed that although the water was around her, she was on the bottom, fast on the mud. All Fred's efforts failed to move her. She was a heavy thing, large and cumbersome, even fitted with an inboard engine, which rarely worked.

Father was summoned from the bar, but still no luck. What was needed was a stout pull on the painter to slew her head round so she would slide down the mud into deeper water. Fred thought of the six officers in the tavern. The military would help, he was sure. Right enough, the causeway was soon graced by the elegant uniforms of the officers. Fred passed them the painter and positioned himself so as to ease the boat's stern round as they took the strain. To their misfortune, the painter was not man enough for the job. As it broke, the military were catapulted backwards off the causeway and into a confused heap on the muddy foreshore. The boat floated clear. It was all that the Wraights could do to prevent themselves bursting out laughing on the spot, but their helpers were less amused. The story raised more than a chuckle, however, whenever it was recounted to others of the barging fraternity.

Twenty-four round trips were completed in 1942, every one with wheat. By the spring of 1943 a small measure of variety returned to the scene, maize, barley and occasionally timber filling *Kathleen's* hold.

After lying at Whitstable for two weeks cleaning and repairing, *Kathleen* twice collected wheat from London, arriving back at the harbour on the 15th and 23rd September, each time returning empty to the bomb-ravaged docks of the upper reaches. Then followed a sequence of passages unlike any before or after. Until this time virtually all *Kathleen's* trips involved sailing light to London and then leaving loaded for her destination. The exceptions in forty years' trading numbered fewer than a score; scrap metal from Dover being the most prominent return freight. Starting on 6th October, 1943, Kathleen carried 700 quarters of wheat to Whitstable. On the 19th she left for London with 714 quarters of wheat, returning to Whitstable with 41 standards of timber seven days later. Then 716 quarters of wheat were loaded for London on 19th November, and *Kathleen* arrived in London the same day. This was followed by 700 quarters of wheat back to Whitstable within the week. A few days later, another cargo of wheat was delivered to London and more wheat taken on for delivery to Ramsgate, arriving there on 20th December.

Leaving light, by then the exception rather than the rule, the Wraights managed to arrive home on Christmas Eve and spend the fourth Christmas of the war with their family. The first passage of 1944 was from Whitstable to Dartford, recommencing the pattern of wheat in both directions which was to continue, with the exception of 150 tons of manure carried on 5th March, until the 25th of that month, when *Kathleen* sailed from Ramsgate to Whitstable for repairs.

The Dartford freight was almost 160 tons, the largest cargo ever to reach the head of Dartford creek by sailing barge. For a while it appeared as if it might never get there. *Kathleen* locked through into the non-tidal basin and felt her way towards the town. Just below the discharging berth was a lifting bridge which had been raised

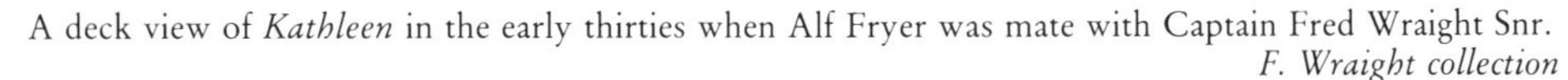

A deck view of *Kathleen* in the early thirties when Alf Fryer was mate with Captain Fred Wraight Snr.
F. Wraight collection

to allow her through. Loaded to her marks, if not even a little more, her draught was just too much for the silted creek and *Kathleen* stuck fast in the middle of the bridge opening. Those waiting to cross wondered how long the barge would remain. No amount of shoving and heaving was of any avail. The Wraights ran out a long wire from the dolly winch to a mooring ring on the quay ahead, but still she would not shift. The weir alongside the entrance lock comprised both fixed and variable sluices to control the level of water upstream; even with the variable sluices closed the water spilled over the fixed sluices into the river beyond, and still *Kathleen* would not budge. The only option then left was to allow more water into the basin from further upriver. This new surge of water swelled around *Kathleen* as it raced towards the weir. Just for a moment the water level was an inch or so above the maximum weir height, and *Kathleen* slipped through.

The apparent shuttle of wheat deliveries was not the result of some bungling bureaucrats at the Cereal Board. The freights from London comprised fresh Canadian wheat imports which had to be distributed to the decentralised cereal stores set up to protect the nation's food supplies from the effects of the blitz. The grain headed the other way was English wheat from Kentish farms for the London flour millers, McDougalls, Hovis and Ranks.

Following the successful engine installation in the *Vicunia*, it was decided that the *Azima* and *Kathleen* should be converted to auxiliary power. With this in mind, *Kathleen* was put in the hands of Anderson, Rigden and Perkins on 26th March, 1944, with instructions that she should be refitted to Lloyd's specification in readiness for her auxiliary engine. This thorough overhaul, by far the most major repair and maintenance work since the 1923 sinking, took almost six months to complete.

Much of *Kathleen's* deck was removed, as well as covering boards and rails. This enabled the shipwrights to fit new inner wales without removing any of the iron knees installed to give extra support to many of the deck beams and carlings. The new wales were fitted in two halves, an incredibly skilled task which necessitated the new timber being accurately shaped before fitting. There could be no offering up of the timber to check dimensions. When the shipwrights were satisfied that the new pieces were ready, they were greased, then worked in from each end, under the main deck beams, with what could only be described as a battering ram applied to the ends. As the new timbers, under great strain, inched their way into position, the long scarfs on each half began to meet. With the last tap of the ram the scarf was perfectly joined amidships and the fastenings then made through to the frames. This was an ingenious and remarkable example of the shipwright's skills.

New covering boards from 13½ inch × 3 inch oak and a lot of new pitchpine deck planks, plus new rails, were fitted. Varnish was not so easy to obtain, so *Kathleen's* sprit was painted for the first time, mast colour brown. Everything else was painted as it had been before, steering gear, carlings and beams maroon, wheel and wooden deck fittings brown, inside coamings pale blue, ironwork green. The

Carrying bagged grain and cereals, *Kathleen* enters Whitstable harbour at the end of one of her voyages from London. The hufflers have already boarded *Kathleen* to assist her into harbour.
F. Wraight collection

quarter boards, once painted brown by the Kelseys, were kept white, as were the hounds, mastcap, and topmast pole. The transom was painted pale green and the hull given two coats of black varnish. The mastcase from Daniels' old *Thomas and Frances* was fitted to replace the previous one which was badly pitted with rust.

All this work was undertaken while *Kathleen* lay in the harbour, paying £3 a week for her berth. During this time the Wraights were paid by the owners around 8s. a day for five days a week, a far cry from the income earned while trading. They managed to fit in a bit of fishing and by selling their catch added to their £2 a week from the firm.

When *Kathleen* re-emerged into trade on 13th September, 1944, she was in the words of her master and mate "As good as new".

The shipwrights' work had cost almost £700 and a lot more would need to be spent when the Kelvin diesel was available for installation. But *Kathleen* had been earning well, and for the next twelve months often continued to enjoy a laden passage, whether bound up for London or down to the ports of Kent and East Anglia.

CHAPTER NINE

Power and Sail

PEACE came to Europe with the surrender of Germany on 8th May, 1945. The war with Japan still endured, and industrial strife had come to London's dockland; here was a hotbed of dockworkers' dissatisfaction. Money, demarcation, manning levels, all the oft-heard ingredients of union disputes manifested themselves among the acres of Thamesside and dockland quays.

A go-slow greeted *Kathleen* when she arrived at the Millwall Docks on 3rd June, 1945. She had orders to load 150 tons of potash from a half-laden Liberty ship, Christophersons of Ipswich being the consigneees. As far as the dockers were concerned, the longer the loading took, the better. It took over a week to fill the forehold, largely on account of the dockers supposedly "working" aboard *Kathleen*. One of them, seated comfortably in a deckchair he had set up in the hold, would in a half-hearted manner attempt to unhook the strop on the huge cargo baskets using a broom handle with a nail at one end. Not that he would get up if he could not reach, the ship's derrick operator being required to improve his accuracy to enable "work" to continue.

After almost three weeks, the owners told Fred Snr, "Whatever you get today, you go". So with somewhat less than her intended 150 tons, *Kathleen* quit strife-torn Millwall and set out for Ipswich on the 22nd.

Kathleen's troubles were by no means over when she arrived at Ipswich. The grab employed to unload the potash made no impression, the cargo having set like concrete. Pneumatic drills were brought aboard to break it up, and this noisy work took nearly a week.

There were complaints that the cause of the problem was a wet hold; but *Kathleen* was always a tight barge in the dry cargo trade, and she had not long returned to work following her overhaul. In reality, potash often has a high moisture content and a few showers during loading would be enough to give it the characteristics of half-cured mortar. The agents were not happy about loading grain, so the Wraights were given orders to sail to Colchester Hythe.

Not even her sinking in 1923 had given rise to more than a few lines of editorial on the inner pages of the Kentish local press. It is therefore perhaps ironic that front page fame for the first and only time in *Kathleen's* career should come at a new port of call, courtesy of the *Essex County Standard*. Under the headline "An Old Industry

Barges, including the *Kathleen*, in Whitstable harbour in the winter of 1948.
Arthur Bennett

Revived" in the issue of 13th July, 1945, was a picture of three barges loading bales of straw, as the "stackies" had done in years gone by. In the foreground was *Kathleen* with the *Gladys* and a genuine stackie, the Maldon-built *Dawn*, beyond. These three were to take the straw for papermaking at Bowaters' new mill at Ridham Dock on the Swale. This was the first consignment of what was to become regular work, though not for *Kathleen.*

Loaded high with over 1,000 bales, weighing a little over 40 tons, *Kathleen* left Colchester on 8th July. With the breeze easterly, she sailed in company with *Gladys*, arriving in Ridham Dock next day. The satisfaction of a good passage was marred by the death of one of the two pet alsatians aboard the *Gladys*. The dogs were tethered by a rope leash to the mizzen rigging whenever the skipper and mate left the barge unattended, and at Ridham they returned after an absence of some hours to discover that one poor dog had either slipped or jumped from the barge's quarter and hung itself.

Kathleen left Ridham Dock on 19th July bound for London. After two months and five more wheat cargoes, the last of which was carried with her mizzen already removed, she arrived at Whitstable to be converted to auxiliary power.

Kathleen's bluff runs made her ideal for an engine installation, only a minimum reduction in carrying capacity resulting. As was the practice almost universally adopted for motorising sailing barges, the engine, shaft, and propeller were installed parallel to the main keelson, to one side or the other; *Kathleen's* 66h.p. Kelvin was

Loading straw at Colchester Hythe on 8th July, 1945—a picture from the *Essex County Standard.*
Essex County Library

fitted to port. The traditional cabin was gutted to accommodate the machinery, and a small skipper's cabin constructed principally from tongued and grooved pine matchboarding. Access was via a newly constructed wheelhouse fitted in place of the mizzen gear; a "spiral staircase" from the cabin to the wheelhouse was situated right aft in the "Yarmouth roads", the old companionway having been displaced by the engine. The new wheelhouse, its back perched on the saddle chock and the front skilfully shaped to the contours of the cabin top, was, like the cabin below, built mainly of tongued and grooved pine. It was glazed with four panes to the front and one in each of the two doors, with railway carriage style leather straps used for the raising or lowering of the glass. There was also a small window beneath the curve of the "whaleback" roof to give visibility astern. In the starboard aft corner was a toilet, an undreamt of luxury for a spritty's crew!

The spindle of the steering gear was shortened to accommodate the wheel within the wheelhouse. The engine controls were routed to the steering position, and the engine exhaust, asbestos lagged, was led aft and vented through the transom.

In addition to the major works related to motorising *Kathleen*, the Wraights organised the usual round of annual maintenance; scraping and oiling the topmast, a lick of paint here and there, and Goldfinch's attention to the barge's rigging and sails.

Prior to her re-entering service *Kathleen's* particulars were to be updated for the Registrar General of Shipping and Seamen. This new registration document was the first amendment to the original, prepared nearly half a century before. Under the section "Particulars of propelling engines etc (if any)" was made the entry covering her Kelvin diesel. Number of engines, one. Number of shafts, one. Description of engine, Internal combustion four stroke single acting. Whether British or Foreign made, British. When made, 1945. Name and address of maker, Bergius Co Ltd, Glasgow. Number and diameters of cylinders, Three 6″. Length of stroke, 9″. Estimated speed of ship, 4/5 knots.

The "Particulars of Tonnage" were revised to take account of the engine room space and other alterations, reducing the registered tonnage from 59.56 to 53.18.

Anderson, Rigden and Perkins' bill for the work, including the cost of the engine, was £2,162 4s. 6d., by far the largest sum ever spent on *Kathleen*, around twice her original building cost.

Kathleen left Whitstable for London with 123 tons of English wheat on 21st April, 1946, her first passage as an auxiliary. During the next three months she managed ten round trips, three more than in the same period of the previous year, despite quite a bit of work to Dover, obviously more time-consuming than the London—Whitstable trade. It appears that, as with the *Vicunia* before her, the benefits of an engine were soon reflected in her rate of work.

It was not unknown for a barge to load and unload wheat without actually moving. This apparently futile phenomenon was not as crazy as it at first appears. Grain driers were not commonly found on Kentish farms in the forties, so the local wheat was often shipped to London with a high moisture content. If on arrival the

Form No. 19. *Signal Letters (if any)*

Transcript of Register for Transmission to Registrar General of Shipping and Seamen

Official Number	Name of Ship	No., Year and Port of Registry
113708	KATHLEEN	5/1946 ROCHESTER

No., Year and Port of previous Registry (if any) FORMERLY 24 IN 1901 REGISTERED ANEW ON INSTALLATION OF MOTOR

Whether British or Foreign Built	Whether a Sailing, Steam or Motor Ship: if Steam or Motor how propelled	Where Built	When Built	Name and Address of Builders
BRITISH	MOTOR SINGLE SCREW	GRAVESEND	1901	LEWIS & GLOVER GRAVESEND

			Feet	Tenths
Number of Decks	ONE	Length from fore part of stem, ~~under the bowsprit~~, to the aft side of the head of the stern post	82	8
Number of Masts	TWO	Length at quarter of depth from top of weather deck at side amidships to bottom of keel		
Rigged	SPRITSAIL	Main breadth to outside of plank	19	7
Stem / Stern	STRAIGHT / SQUARE	Depth in hold from tonnage deck to ceiling at midships	6	03
Build	CARVEL	Depth in hold from upper deck to ceiling at midships, in the case of three decks and upwards		
Galleries		Depth from top of beam amidships to top of keel		
Head		Depth from top of deck at side amidships to bottom of keel		
Framework and description of vessel	WOOD CARVEL	Round of beam		7
Number of Bulkheads	TWO	Length of engine room, if any	9	5
Number of water ballast tanks, and their capacity in tons	NIL			

PARTICULARS OF DISPLACEMENT

Total to quarter the depth from weather deck at side amidships to bottom of keel ..... Tons. Ditto per inch immersion at same depth ..... Tons.

PARTICULARS OF PROPELLING ENGINES, &c. (if any)

No. of sets of Engines	Description of Engines	Whether British or Foreign made	When made	Name and address of makers	Reciprocating Engines: No. and Diameter of Cylinders in each set	Reciprocating Engines: Length of Stroke	Rotary Engines: No. of Cylinders in each set	~~N.H.P.~~ B.H.P. ~~I.H.P.~~ Speed of Ship
ONE	INTERNAL COMBUSTION FOUR STROKE SINGLE ACTING DIESEL	Engines BRITISH	Engines 1945	Engines BERGIUS CO LTD GLASGOW	THREE	9"		66 ESTIMATED
No. of Shafts: ONE	Particulars of Boilers: Description ... Number ... Loaded Pressure ...	Boilers —	Boilers —	Boilers —	6"			4/5 KNOTS

PARTICULARS OF TONNAGE

Gross Tonnage	No. of Tons	Deductions Allowed	No. of Tons
Under Tonnage Deck	71 · 13	On account of space required for propelling power	14 · 82
Space or spaces between Decks		On account of spaces occupied by Seamen or Apprentices, and appropriated to their use, and kept free from Goods or Stores of every kind, not being the personal property of the Crew	8 · 50
Turret or Trunk		These spaces are the following, viz.:— FOREWARD	
Forecastle		(Number of seamen or apprentices for whom accommodation is certified 2)	
Bridge space		Deductions under Section 79 of the Merchant Shipping Act, 1894, and Section 54 of the Merchant Shipping Act, 1906, as follows:—	
Poop or Break			
Side Houses			
Deck Houses			
Chart House			
Spaces for Machinery, and light, and air, under Section 78(2) of the Merchant Shipping Act, 1894	·33		
Excess of Hatchways	9 · 54	Cubic Meters	
Gross Tonnage	81 · 05 / 229 · 37	MASTER'S ACCOMODATION 4·55	4 · 55
Deductions, as per contra	27 · 87 / 78 · 87		
Register Tonnage	53 · 18 / 150 · 50	Total	27 · 87

NOTE.—1. The tonnage of the engine room spaces below the upper deck is 8 · 14 tons, and the tonnage of the total spaces framed in above the upper deck for propelling machinery and for light and air is ·33 tons.

NOTE.—2. The undermentioned spaces above the upper deck are not included in the cubical contents forming the ship's register tonnage: NIL

Name of Master ..... Certificate of Service No. ..... Competency No. .....

Names, Residence, and Description of the Owners, and Number of Sixty-fourth Shares held by each .. viz.,

DANIELS BROTHERS (WHITSTABLE) LIMITED HAVING ITS PRINCIPAL PLACE OF BUSINESS AT 78 HARBOUR STREET WHITSTABLE IN THE COUNTY OF KENT

SHARES - SIXTY-FOUR

Dated FOR CERTIFICATION SEE ATTACHED FORM 6 S R 13A SIGNED ILLEGIBLE Registrar

NOTE.—Registrars in the Colonies are requested to distinguish the Managing Owner by placing the letters "M.O." against his name.

C. 345 N.B.—To be sent in an envelope addressed to the Registrar General of Shipping and Seamen, Llantrisant Road, Cardiff.

Instructions to Registrars of British Ships, para. 37.—Sec. F.66 (Sept. 1968)

A copy of the registration particulars filed on the installation of a Kelvin engine in 1946.

unloading berth at the mill was not available a portable suction elevator would be set up to unload one laden barge into another lying alongside; in this way the damp grain was kept cool and the risk of it germinating, or even catching fire through spontaneous combustion, was avoided. Sometimes the freight would be moved from one barge to the other and back again day after day until eventually it was lifted into the drier at the mill before being ground or stored.

Hardly a greater distance was covered by the two freights done by *Kathleen* at Dover during August. Arriving from London on the 14th, she unloaded 625 quarters of wheat during the following two days. Fred Jnr, who did most of the business ashore, went to see Mr Rylands at Hammonds, Daniels' agents at Dover.

"How many bags of mail will *Kathleen* carry?" inquired Mr Rylands. "I don't know," replied Fred, "two or three thousand, I suppose." Mr Rylands laughed, obviously of the opinion that Fred didn't know what he was talking about. "Well, the way I see it," said Fred, "we can load 700 quarters of wheat which comes in 1,400 bags weighing 2¼ cwt each, and mail bags must be much lighter than that."

There was a Liberty ship lying in the outer harbour with cargo for Dover from Africa. She was carrying mails for England, and the big Dover Harbour Board tugs *Lady Brassey* and *Lady Duncannon* were ferrying the mail bags to the Admiralty

Kathleen's sail plan as an auxiliary from 1946 to 1954. Drawn by the author.

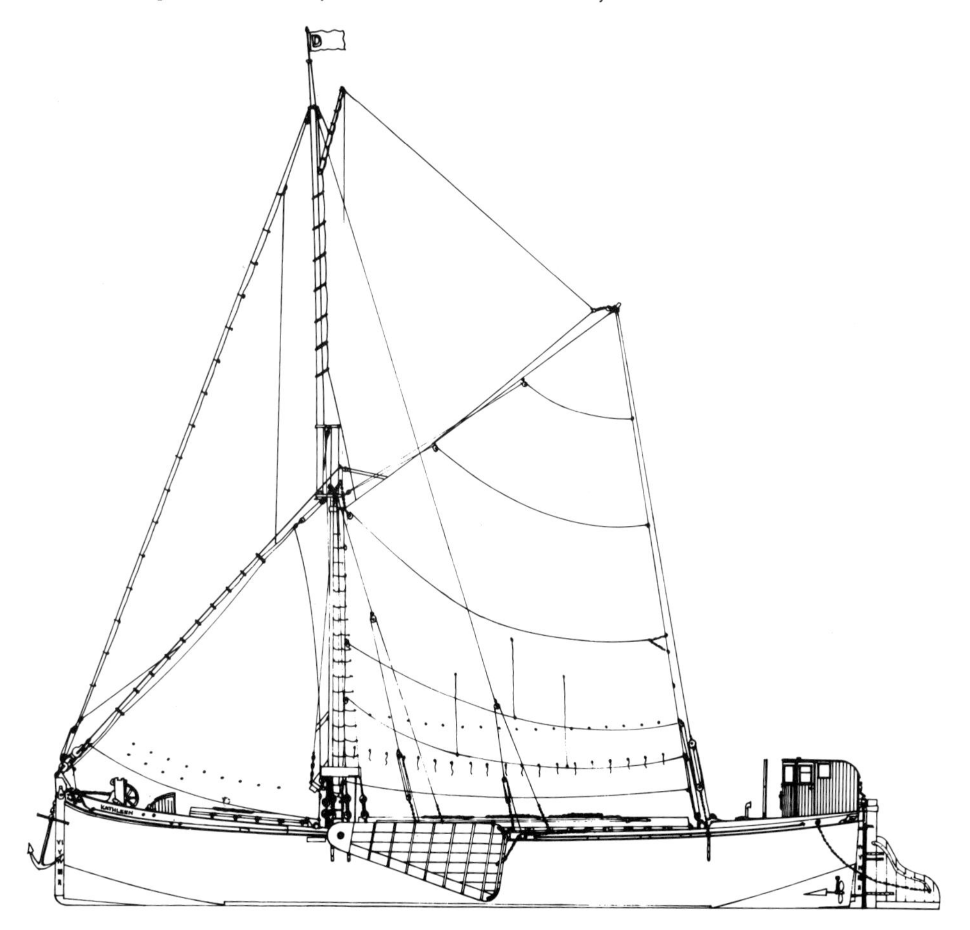

pier, where they were loaded by waiting postmen into trucks bound for the sorting offices at Canterbury and London.

The tugs would come alongside the Liberty ship, whose crew would throw the bags on board; the mail was stacked on and around the lifeboats, by the funnels, in fact anywhere a space could be found, but even so, a full load was never more than a few hundred, and it was an expensive and time-consuming exercise.

Fred Snr went to Hammonds' office and it was agreed that *Kathleen* would help the tugs for £25 a day. The work would continue until the mails were unloaded, and 2s. each per hour was to be paid to the Wraights for stowing the bags in the hold.

Kathleen left the wet dock to go alongside the ship in the outer harbour. One of

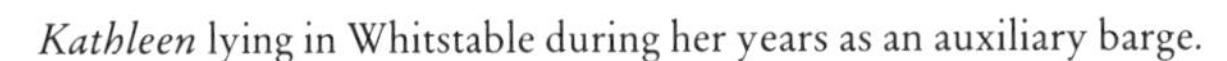

Kathleen lying in Whitstable during her years as an auxiliary barge. *F. Wraight collection*

the Harbour Board tugs had loaded a few hundred bags and set off for the pier. *Kathleen's* hold was cavernous by comparison with the tugs' capacity and she swallowed as many as were thrown down to her before carrying them to the waiting G.P.O. vans. One more trip cleared the remainder and they were soon unloaded by crane in huge nets. Lucrative work, but all over in a day.

More wheat to Whitstable and Dover, timber to the corporation pier at Southend, and a couple of freights of flour, one ex-ship and the other ex-mill, occupied *Kathleen* during September, October and November. Warmly welcomed in October was a new boat from Anderson, Rigden and Perkins for £47 10s. Although its predecessor, the heavy tank boat, had managed to cause amusement that one dark night on the Long Reach causeway, it had for the most part proven far from handy. The flour ex-ship was Canadian or Australian, stropped and swung into *Kathleen's* hold and stowed. The ex-mill flour was always loaded from a shute. The skilled dockers in the barge's hold would catch and turn the sack with a flick of the wrist, a knack which always left the cargo properly stowed without the sack being physically lifted at all.

On 4th December, 1946, *Kathleen* arrived at Felixstowe from London laden with bagged wheat from Australia. The freight was to be unloaded by suction elevator, so full sacks were taken from the centre of the hold and piled on either side to form a trough into which the elevator hose was lowered. The sacks were then slashed with a knife, one after the other, highest row first, their contents spilling into the trough and keeping the elevator supplied until the hold was emptied.

Within a few days a freight of flour, 125 tons, was fixed for London. Leaving Suffolk on 12th December, *Kathleen* arrived in the capital on the 15th and discharged a day or so later. She then loaded 625 quarters of loose wheat for Ramsgate, hosed in from Thomas White's silo. It was not properly trimmed, the forehold being far from full, and with the extra weight of her engine aft *Kathleen* sailed the morning after Boxing Day as light-headed as a Christmas reveller. Arriving off Ramsgate next morning just before high water, she set course for the harbour entrance, only to have her head caught by a gust of wind and the strong east-going tide. In no time at all the barge had swung towards the harbour wall. The anchor was hurriedly let go, but to no avail; within seconds *Kathleen's* bow had struck the unyielding stonework. The Wraights soon regained control of the barge, but the damage was done.

With Fred Jnr pumping continuously they locked into the inner harbour. The Harbour Master gave *Kathleen* every priority. It was not long before a string of lorries organised by Daniels' following Captain Wraight's urgent phone call were being hurriedly filled on the quayside with *Kathleen's* cargo. This work went on apace until eventually the damaged bow rose above the level of the surrounding water, enabling temporary repairs to be effected.

On the last but one day of 1946 *Kathleen* slipped away from Ramsgate light, carrying the flood back to Whitstable. She lay in the harbour for almost two weeks while her damaged planking was replaced with new at a cost of £116 3s. 9d.

KATHLEEN

CHAPTER TEN

Decline

FOR nearly half a century *Kathleen* had been gainfully employed. What of her less fortunate sisters?

After reaching a peak in 1907, the sailing barge population had been in decline for many years. The fleet, which numbered around 1,650 at the end of the First World War, was ravaged further by the slump of the 1930s, leaving only 600 in active work at the beginning of the Second World War. War losses were high, both as a result of enemy action and through the deterioration of those other barges which had lain virtually without maintenance as storage hulks or balloon moorings.

As *Kathleen* completed her first busy year as an auxiliary the number of barges under sail had fallen to fewer than three hundred. Some, well maintained by large companies, and in particular those in specialist work such as the gunpowder fleet, still looked certain to continue trading for many years. Gone, however, were the days when fifty or more barges could be regularly seen working their tides from some Kent or Essex estuary. The competition of the lorry on land and the motor coaster at sea was sounding the death knell of coastwise sail.

Despite this overall deterioration in demand for sailing tonnage, Daniels' barges were in fact busier than ever, with Harry Blaxland chartering extra capacity from the Chatham-based Whiting Brothers' fleet.

Kathleen's appetite for the carriage of wheat continued virtually uninterrupted throughout 1947. The occasional cargo of flour, barley or maize broke the sequence, as did a strike-breaking cargo of baled hemp and jars of gelatine loaded ex-ship at Gravesend towards the end of September and discharged at Black Eagle Wharf, just below the entrance to the St Katharine Docks. Altogether *Kathleen* made thirty-seven laden passages during the year, all but one involving return to London empty, averaging a round trip every ten days.

Her voyaging in 1948 was almost a carbon copy of 1947, with thirty-seven laden passages, thirty-two with wheat, those London-bound often for destinations above the bridges. This work involved lowering the barge's gear and motoring to the unloading berth, sometimes Battersea, sometimes Westminster, before heaving up again to allow access to the hatches. This procedure had, of course, to be repeated for the return journey. When loading a Faversham freight in the first few days of the year *Kathleen* suffered an accident which could have led to tragedy. A team of men was

Kathleen lying off Whitstable, 1948. *Arthur Bennett*

working under the open forehatch loading superphosphate in 2 cwt bags from De Passo's Wharf at Creekmouth, Barking, when, as the quayside crane swung its jib for more cargo, the ball and empty hook caught around *Kathleen's* topmast and broke it, sending large splinters showering into the forehold. Miraculously nobody was hit, though many pieces of the silver spruce spar, originally the topmast from the successful racing barge *Queen*, were large enough to have inflicted serious if not fatal injuries.

On 24th June, 1949, bound for Faversham again, this time with coir yarn, *Kathleen* came upon the tank barge *Cub H* ashore, with her stern in the narrow channel. In attempting to tow her clear *Kathleen's* stern swung round and stuck on the mud. As the tide ebbed the rudder lifted, bending the long arm of the steering gear and distorting the support for the brake and fore-bearing. This damage put *Kathleen's* rudder out of action, so the Wraights dismantled the affected components and Fred Jnr walked to Pollock's shipyard towards the head of the creek, whose personnel obligingly straightened the distorted metalwork. *Kathleen's* rudder post

Kathleen in Whitstable about 1950, with *Major's* wheelhouse visible beyond. *Author's collection*

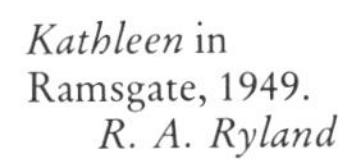

Kathleen in Ramsgate, 1949.
R. A. Ryland

had also split, and this was repaired back at Whitstable along with the remaining ironwork by Anderson, Rigden and Perkins.

Having abandoned the usual practice of spending a couple of midsummer weeks lying at Whitstable for maintenance since she was motorised, it is hardly surprising that *Kathleen's* first "cleaning and repairing", commenced almost four years later on 14th February, 1950, should have taken nearly two months to complete. A bill of something over £300 from the shipwrights, plus lesser charges for chandlery and sail repairs, was a consequence of this long period of virtually continuous activity. A few new products had been carried during the late forties, perhaps when cereal cargoes were scarce or a more lucrative freight was in the offing. There was 150 tons of potash to Ipswich, with 135 yards of sand from Alresford on the River Colne providing a useful return cargo. She also carried bones from London to Faversham, to be ground down for use in fire extinguishers, and thirty standards of timber Ipswich-bound from a London wharf. Overall, however, it was still wheat that dominated the pages of *Kathleen's* cargo books, exactly as it had done for most of her working life.

Her refit was completed on 12th April and was followed by thirty-three freights during the remainder of the year, twenty-nine in wheat, two in barley, one in cattle cake and one laden with logs to a remote wharf opposite Creeksea on the south bank of the River Crouch in Essex.

For two more years *Kathleen* motor-sailed the waters she knew so well, adding Chatham to her regular ports of call and carrying two freights to Sandwich, the old Cinque Port so often passed on the way to Dover but never previously visited. Variety came by way of scrap steel, 98 tons of wallboard, some sulphate of ammonia, 103 tons of potatoes, linseed meal, and a cargo of oats for Faversham. Oats, once a regular freight, had not been carried for over ten years.

The years 1951 and 1952 could certainly be considered among the more mundane and undistinguished in *Kathleen's* life. By contrast 1953 was to bring fame, or perhaps notoriety, to the barge and mixed fortunes to her owners.

Thursday, 1st January, 1953, found *Kathleen* slipping light from Faversham creek bound for London. After loading over Friday and part of Sunday with 40 tons of flour and 100 tons of wheat, her first mixed cargo for nearly a year, she took the evening tide downriver. Having reached Whitstable on the Sunday she started unloading on the Monday and when empty left the harbour for Anderson, Rigden and Perkins' slipway, a few hundred yards to the west. Daniels were unable to afford the high cost of new tonnage, and the ageing fleet of wooden barges, though still serviceable, began to demand more attention from the yard. *Kathleen* was to be fitted with a new main keelson to replace the small section "rail" type incorporated by her builders. The new keelson, an "H" section rolled steel joist, would be fitted in two sections, the forepart running to the stem and the afterpart to her sternpost, joined in the middle by a long steel plate. While arguably weaker at the join, a major strength advantage would result from the inclusion of steel strapping at each end of the keelson bolted to the apron, a timber on the after side of the sterm, and a corresponding fixing at the stern. A major problem as barges grew older was the tendency for the bow and stern to drop, mainly due to the fact that the main keelson often stopped well short of the maximum inside length of the hull, and chine keelsons and inwales rarely went much further than the hold bulkheads. Other work to be undertaken at the same time included replacement of the chine keelsons, plus new lining and ceiling where necessary. The work of taking out the old was commenced.

In Norfolk around the 28th of the month, King's Lynn ambulance driver Bertie Hart, a resident by the Great Ouse for sixty years, first noticed that the ebb was not getting away as it usually did, the young flood finding a lot of water still in the river

In Whitstable with a cargo of 700 quarters of loose wheat about 1952. *Fred Cooper collection*

when the tide had turned. For the next two days he witnessed the same scene, each successive tide finding the river perceptibly fuller. On the afternoon of Saturday, 31st January, the day of the full moon spring tide, Mr Hart stood at a local football match watching the players battle against the increasing north-westerly wind as well as against as the opposing team. A river pilot who had been at work the night before remarked that the motion of the sea had been strange, unlike anything he had previously experienced.

In Essex a policeman, casually observing the River Blackwater that same Saturday afternoon, noticed that the tide appeared not to go out at all, the gale force winds apparently holding the water within the estuary.

In Kent, *Kathleen* lay on the slipway at Whitstable, her hold stripped of chine and main keelsons, a fragile shell awaiting repair.

In the early darkness that January evening the population of England's eastern seaboard went about their business as usual. The gale force winds that rattled window panes, occasionally dislodged slates, and caused branches, even some trees, to fall to the ground, seemed nothing too much out of the ordinary for a mid-winter's night. Yet Britain was only hours away from disaster, one of the greatest in her peacetime history.

As the night wore on mountainous seas broke over and in places breached miles of coastal defences, inundating some 150,000 acres of land, drowning more than three hundred people, wiping out farm livestock by the thousand, and inflicting millions of pounds' worth of damage to property from Lincolnshire to Kent.

At Whitstable, dawn revealed the full extent of the devastation. Much of the

The morning after the floods of 31st January, 1953, *Kathleen* lies against the remains of the shipyard shed. The hoses in the foreground were being used to clear the floodwater from Whitstable town.

R. K. Anderson

A close-up of *Kathleen* embedded in Anderson, Rigden and Perkins' shed. *Kentish Express*

town had been engulfed by the invading seas, even some first-floor accommodation being flooded by the silt-laden water. The foreshore was a shambles, with small craft, and some not so small, smashed to smithereens; and serious damage to those which could be considered to have survived. At the height of the onslaught *Kathleen* had been washed from the slipway and thrown sideways up the beach. For hours she pounded on the shifting shingle and against the yard buildings, coming to rest as the flood tide subsided with her starboard side half buried under the remnants of Anderson, Rigden and Perkins' sheds. Of the slipway there was no sign; it had either been washed away or buried under tons of shingle.

It was sad to see *Kathleen* so mauled by the breakers, yet gratifying to see her quite remarkably intact considering what she had endured. As the Wraights, accompanied by George Richards, foreman shipwright at the yard, and Harry Blaxland from "the Firm", picked their way over the strained hull, the extent of her damage became obvious. The twisting and wringing of the previous night had sprung many planks; the shingle had cut into her bottom doubling and chines like a coarse file scouring balsa wood; her deck seams were cracked open, and many of her stout timbers damaged beyond repair.

Few craft over fifty years old, subjected to such a battering, would be worthy of reconstruction, but *Kathleen*, at fifty-two, was no ordinary vessel. Somehow, as in 1923, she seemed to summon up her will to survive, convincing those connected with her operation that she should be rebuilt for further service. Once the decision was taken, there was really no option but to carry out repairs where she lay, high up on the beach parallel to the water's edge and a long way from the clutches of even the highest normal spring tide.

On 5th July, with the aid of lorry jacks to raise the hull sufficiently for greased planks to be slid under her chines, *Kathleen* was relaunched sideways down the shingle slope to the sea. She had been extensively refurbished, and her main keelson gave the hull great strength.

Many who knew her, however, said that she never looked the same again.

Following her relaunch *Kathleen* lay at Whitstable while her engine was removed and stripped down completely, many new parts being fitted before it was reinstalled.

Left: The day of *Kathleen's* relaunch, 5th July, 1953.
F. Wraight collection

Opposite: *Kathleen* enters the water.
C. Ashby collection

Her repair had proven expensive, £952 for the work originally envisaged and £1,305 attributable to the flood damage, this latter amount probably being met from the Lord Mayor's Flood Relief Fund.

On the morning of Wednesday, 5th August, *Kathleen* went back to work, leaving Whitstable under engine and arriving eleven hours later at London's Victoria Dock, her refurbished hold ready to receive a consignment of wheat for Chatham.

The loss of *Kathleen's* capacity during the first half of the year was only one of the problems that faced Daniels' in 1953. A great question mark hung over the future of Whitstable harbour itself. For years it had continued to decay, the old east quay was falling to pieces and was closed to all vessels over 35 feet; the rail connection had closed down, and only a fierce battle by solicitors representing local interests prevented the railway authority shutting the harbour as well. The flooding had brought home to the local administration that the harbour, unless improved or closed altogether, would continue to be a weak link in the sea defences. What were to develop into long-drawn-out negotiations began with the British Transport Commission with a view to the ultimate purchase of the harbour by the urban district council.

One event in what was otherwise a rather bleak year for the firm did somewhat

compensate for Daniels' misfortunes. The association with Whiting Brothers did not endure, their fleet being sold to the London and Rochester Trading Company, and to replace this capacity Harry Blaxland arranged to work with Cremer's Faversham Freightage Company, their craft taking equal turns with those in the Daniels' fleet. The plain red house flag of the Faversham firm was an appropriate companion to the white and blue of Daniels' barges, for it was the Coronation year of Queen Elizabeth II.

After a gap of fifteen years, the Thames Championship was revived in honour of the royal occasion. There were three classes, champion bowsprit, restricted staysail and auxiliary, this latter class established for the many trading under power and sail. One of the few engineless barges in the Daniels' and Faversham Freightage fleets was Fred Cremer's *Esther*, a little 43 ton vessel built at Faversham by Alfred White Jnr in

Immediately after launching, 5th July, 1953.
C. Ashby collection

1900. The White family was renowned for constructing some of the fastest barges ever built, so she was chosen to represent the two companies in the Grand Coronation Match.

Skippered by Percy (Beefy) Wildish, her master for thirty-eight years, *Esther* was one of five entries in the restricted staysail class. She was very much the outsider of the group, perhaps the most fancied barge being Eastwood's *Westmoreland*, with a history of high placings in the pre-war matches. *Clara*, like *Westmoreland* and *Esther* a product of the White family's genius, had raced once previously in 1896, her year of building, when she took second in the Medway match to the crack *Haughty Belle*. Also from White's yard was the *Dreadnought*, at 70 tons by far the largest barge in the class; she had a second place in the 1927 Medway match to her credit and was destined to join the elite group of barges kept only for racing and to notch up a string of victories in the Thames staysails that was without equal. The fifth entry was *Revival*, ex *Eldred Watkins*, built by W. Orvis at Ipswich in 1901 and known to the working sailorman as a fast passage maker, although not previously raced. *Dreadnought* and *Revival*, both in ICI ownership, sported the company's livery of green rails with the regulation red wales of an explosive carrier, a most distinctive colour scheme.

There was virtually no wind at all as the barges in all three classes made their way to the starting line off Hope Point, having lain at the Denton anchorage overnight. It was Thursday, 21st May, just twelve days before the Coronation. The course was downriver to the North Oaze Buoy, and back upriver to the finish at Gravesend, just a few yards upstream from *Kathleen's* birthplace.

The gun went at 0900, but the light conditions meant a slow start. *Sara*, in the champion bowsprit class, was first away at 0905 followed by *Esther*, the smallest barge in the match, some three and a half minutes later. Then came *Xylonite*, *Revival* and *Edith May* in quick succession, with the rest of the fleet strung out behind. As the light airs continued for some time, the race committee aboard the excursion vessel *Royal Sovereign* decided to shorten the course and the committee boat anchored off Southend to act as the turning mark. In the restricted staysail class *Revival* overhauled *Esther* and just beat her to the mark; *Westmoreland* lay third with *Clara* fourth and *Dreadnought* last. The wind had begun to freshen and eventually settled south-west three, rising four. As the barges turned to windward back up the river *Dreadnought* worked her way back into contention with *Revival* and *Esther*, the three of them battling it out until *Esther* managed to open up a small lead. At the finish it was *Esther* six minutes ahead of *Revival*, with *Dreadnought* third in the class, a further minute and a half behind. After almost eight hours' racing *Esther* had completed the course in only twenty minutes longer than the winner of the champion bowsprits, a truly creditable performance. Silver medals and pewter tankards were awarded to the crew at a ceremony aboard the *Royal Sovereign*, with Harry Blaxland stepping forward to receive the class trophy. The Coronation Match

Kathleen's sail plan, 1954.
Drawn by the author.

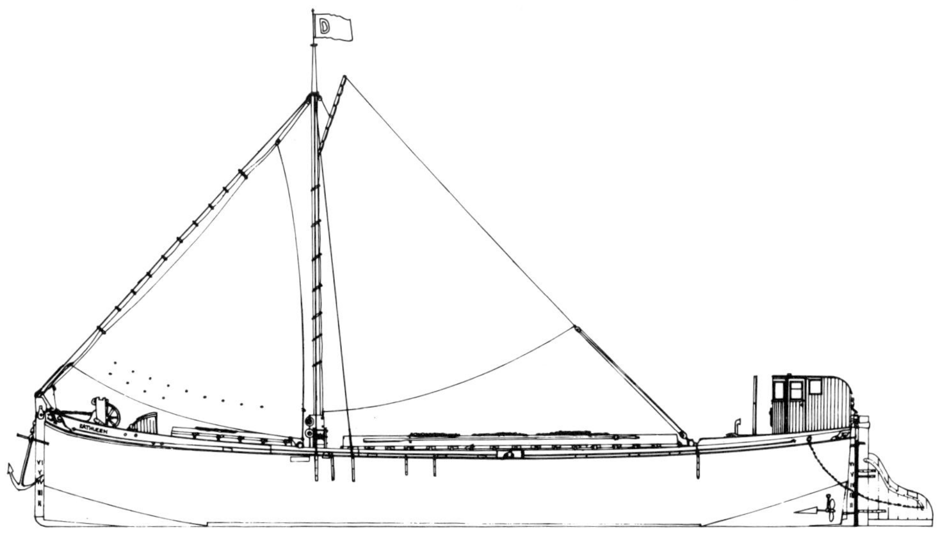

Kathleen arriving at Ramsgate in September, 1954. *Photo by Philip Kershaw, Fred Cooper collection*

was *Esther's* one and only race outing, for although the matches were continued annually for some years, she was stripped of her gear and converted to power before the 1954 race.

Since *Kathleen's* conversion to auxiliary power, she had become increasingly reliant on her engine to ensure regular passages. While few opportunities to gain an extra knot by setting some sail were ever missed, her spars and rigging were really no longer vital to her performance at sea and had become a hindrance at the docks and wharves, where a clear deck meant easier and more efficient cargo handling. On 24th May, 1954, *Kathleen* sailed light from Ramsgate to Whitstable and during the following five days had her mainsail and mainmast removed and her topmast set up in the mainmast case. When she left Whitstable for Millwall Dock on Sunday, 30th May, her sail plan was reduced to foresail and old topsail only, with a small derrick mounted to a gooseneck on the topmast to lift the boat on and off hatches in place of the old burton tackle once rigged to the sprit. The old topsail was soon found to be unsatisfactory when set on the pole mast, so a purpose-made trysail, or "leg of mutton" as they were often called, was ordered from Goldfinch's, to be bent on when *Kathleen* was next in for maintenance or repairs. Unusually, she did not visit her home port for over two months and it was not until 11th September that *Kathleen*, with quite a long list of work to be done, sailed into Whitstable harbour where she lay until 28th October.

During this time the trysail was rigged; her engine decoked and overhauled, needing new pistons and liners; her sterngear and the new propeller, fitted earlier in the year, were checked; and her exhaust system repaired. The time-consuming task was, however, the rebuilding of her port bow, with new uprights and hull planking, covering board and lining. A complicated task, if the bill for the work, £460 15s.11d., is anything to go by.

Her first freight following the repairs was 121 tons of wood pulp from Dover for New Hythe on the River Medway, a destination made much more practical since *Kathleen's* cut-down sailplan made it easier to work above bridges.

A comparison of diesel oil usage before and after *Kathleen's* rig alterations is most revealing. Approximately 2,500 miles were covered in three summer months during 1953, when she still traded with her full auxiliary rig, and over a similar distance and period in 1954 and 1955, after her rig had been reduced, fuel consumption improved by more than ten per cent. This seems to indicate that the windage of the gear aloft was a significant performance inhibitor when under power, and throws into question the whole principle of the economics of the auxiliaries against the ex-sailormen trading under engine alone. It is known, however, that some auxiliaries had been inadequately engined, with insufficient power to work effectively under mechanical propulsion alone.

By 1954 the barge fleets had dwindled astonishingly. In the eight years since *Kathleen* had been motorised, those under sail alone had been reduced from around three hundred to just over thirty. The auxiliaries numbered about forty-five, and those under motor alone about eighty. The creeks and rivers of Kent and East Anglia were becoming littered with hulls as the once-proud sprittles retired, occasionally for further use as a houseboat but more often to lie abandoned, soon to be derelict, and ultimately to rot away.

Kathleen unloading at Whitstable, 1954. *Fred Cooper collection*

KATHLEEN

CHAPTER ELEVEN

The 'Firm' Sells Out

WHITSTABLE saw much less of *Kathleen* from the mid-fifties. Of forty-four cargoes carried during 1955 only ten were to her home port. In previous years the figures would usually have been almost the opposite, with only around twenty or thirty per cent of freights delivered away from "home". Erith, the Isle of Grain and Deal were new destinations that year, and while drums of oil were the only new cargo, there was much more variation in freights from trip to trip.

In 1956 the number of cargoes to Whitstable had fallen to three, but the general level of activity remained very high, with thirty-five laden passages in the year, despite almost seven weeks spent on maintenance in August and September. The emphasis had swung back to wheat, much of it to Ramsgate, perhaps delivered there as a result of the collapse of Daniels' silo at Whitstable during the summer. This spectacular event, the more remarkable in view of the restoration work carried out during 1954, was a major setback to the company's fortunes. Four people were working at the silo when suddenly the walls began to give way, there just being time for them to get clear before the building fell apart, spilling hundreds of tons of grain on to the harbour's north quay.

As if this was not enough misfortune for one year, 1956 also saw the loss of two barges, both large vessels and recent additions to the fleet. *Ardwina*, built in 1909, of 60 registered tons and bought in 1951, was laid up in Whitstable harbour following a collision in the Thames and was subsequently sold for yacht conversion. *Colonia*, a fine 62-tonner built by Feltons at Sandwich and purchased by the firm in 1950, was wrecked in October on Pollards Spit, off the Isle of Sheppey, her crew of two being rescued by the Southend lifeboat.

Daniels' were left with only the *Kathleen, Savoy* and *Azima* on the firm's books, aided by *Edith* and *Esther* from the Faversham Freightage Company. Perhaps as a result of this reduction in capacity, all the vessels were kept fully occupied; despite having given 279 years' service between them, they were still in fit condition to carry dry cargoes such as grain and cement.

Thirty-nine freights were carried by *Kathleen* in 1957, with East Anglian destinations becoming commonplace. In addition to Southend and Ipswich work, there were cargoes of maize for Fingringhoe Mill on the River Colne and Battlesbridge Mill at the head of the River Roach.

Kathleen unloading at Whitstable in 1954. Her sail plan has been reduced to a foresail and leg o' mutton mainsail set on her old topmast.
Fred Cooper collection

After the setbacks of 1956, there seemed to be better auguries for the firm in 1957. A referendum in the town had approved the district council's rescue plan for the harbour and a new era of prosperity for this still predominantly maritime community was expectantly awaited. While the problems of obtaining cost-effective replacement tonnage for the few elderly units in the Daniels' fleet loomed ever larger, trade was still buoyant and the future looked brighter than for many years. But it was not to be, for in June, 1957, Harry Blaxland died. Despite the efforts of his wife and son, assisted by Mabel Carlton, "H. K.'s" niece, to manage the business, it was ultimately decided to sell out to the London and Rochester Trading Company Ltd in June, 1958.

None of these happenings seemed at the time to affect the work of the barges;

Vic Foreman, who replaced Fred Wraight Jnr. as mate of *Kathleen*.
V. Foreman collection

certainly *Kathleen* was kept gainfully employed, another forty-two freights being delivered during 1958. It is noticeable, however, that following the takeover many passages were made with the hold far from full, and some of the lucrative bulk grain work seems to have been taken over by units of the London and Rochester fleet.

Daniels Bros (Whitstable) Ltd retained its own separate identity and for the first time in over forty years was to receive a brand new vessel. Being built in Holland by Gebroeders Coop at Hoogezand, she was designed to load 225 tons and was to be powered by a 120 Deutz diesel.

Around April, 1959, while *Kathleen* was lying at Chatham discharging wheat, a gentleman stepped aboard and introduced himself to Fred Jnr as Mr Clarabut, a director of the London and Rochester Trading Co. He offered Fred the job of mate and engineer in the new vessel, his reputation for a knowledge of engines and mechanical matters seemingly having percolated to the boardroom of his new employer. "What do you think of the idea?" inquired Mr Clarabut. "Not much", replied Fred. "Why don't you give my father and I one of the modern coasters such as the *Silver* or *Gold*, and then when he retires I can take over the ship as master?" Mr Clarabut was not enthusiastic. "You think about the offer I've made you, and if you decide to take it up, let me know."

Fred Snr was anxious that his son should not leave, and young Fred was equally keen to stay; he was happy enough where he was. Lying in his bunk that night he began to wonder about his future. He was in his forties, and with the odds and ends of cargoes they had been carrying, his money had been as little as £4 or £5 a week. He recalled Mr Clarabut's comment that nothing more would be spent on *Kathleen* and decided that leaving her was the only sensible course. Next morning he went to the office and offered his services aboard the new coaster. Fred learnt that she would be delivered around July, and in the meantime he was to carry on with his father.

Named after the first two letters of the christian names of the London and Rochester directors, Maurice Gill and Guy and David Clarabut, the *Maguda* took to the water on 26th June and was handed over at Rochester about a month later. It was almost twenty-four years since Fred Jnr had joined *Kathleen*. It was the twilight of her working career, of that he was in no doubt.

George Green, the P. L. A. grain clerk at the Albert Dock, organised the loading of Fred's last freight aboard *Kathleen*, 600 quarters of wheat for Rochford Mills in the River Roach. On the morning of Friday, 17th July, *Kathleen* left the dock and motored for twelve hours to Shore Ends, just inside the River Crouch, where she anchored to await tide and daylight for the last few twisting miles of her journey. Fred Jnr had news that the *Maguda* was ready, so made his way from Rochford to ship aboard, excitement and perhaps a little sadness keeping him company on his journey. His father took on Vic Foreman, a Whitstable man, as his new mate.

Orders were received to load English wheat from Faversham for London. *Kathleen* sailed light from Rochford on 21st July, arriving at the Kent port the same day. Just 117 tons were loaded, and even less from London for Whitstable on the

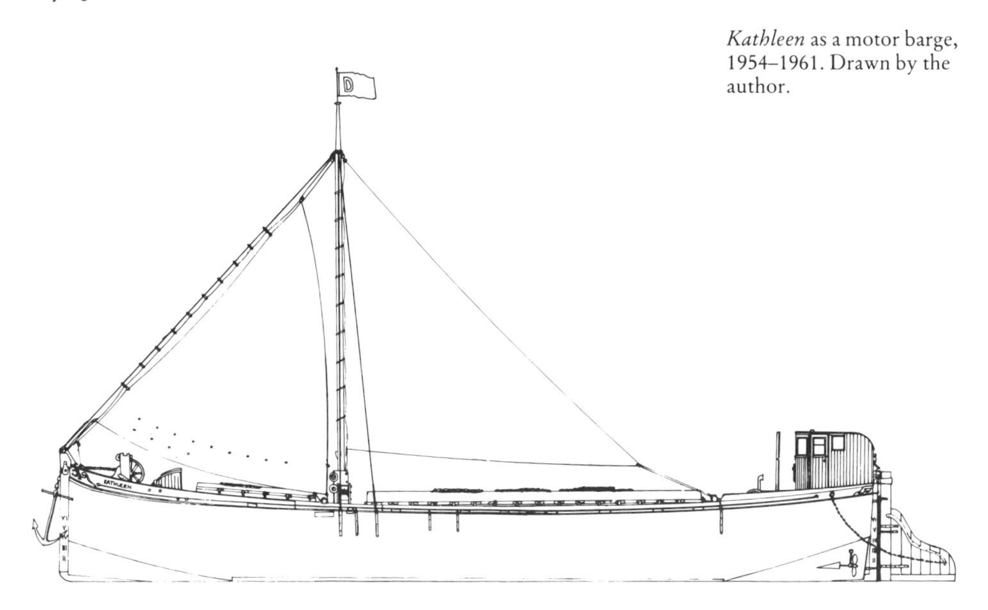

Kathleen as a motor barge, 1954–1961. Drawn by the author.

Left: *Kathleen* in the Albert Dock in the late fifties.
Joe Hines collection

Opposite: *Kathleen* waiting to load in the West India Dock in August, 1961. Also to be seen are the Sittingbourne-built *Maria* and the *Lord Roberts*, the latter being almost hidden by the L. & R.T.C. motor barge *Pepita*. *Tony Ellis*

30th. In the middle of August, 75 tons of pollards were carried to Sittingbourne, and later that same month 12¼ standards of timber, less than half *Kathleen's* capacity, consigned to Creeksea. Then 40 tons of paper bags, 120 tons of barley, 115 tons of bonemeal, all these small cargoes followed during the ensuing weeks, and by year end fewer than a dozen freights in twelve months had filled the barge.

By October Fred Snr decided that he had had enough. With only essential repairs being carried out, and with many of *Kathleen's* contemporaries being withdrawn from service and replaced by modern steel coasters, he felt that the time had come to retire. So after thirty years, during which time he had seen good times and bad, monotony and adventure, and had sailed *Kathleen* the equivalent of eight times round the world, Fred and his barge parted company.

Vic Foreman stayed on to serve under John Herbert, *Kathleen's* new master. All sorts of freights came along during 1960; peas, pulp, wheat, oil, cement, paper bags, hooves, even tinned tomatoes, rock, and two freights of something called Napthalene Cyamite. It was *Kathleen's* last full year in the coasting trade, and despite a fortnight on the London and Rochester yard at Strood for repairs, an impressive forty-five freights were delivered. As to destinations, it is noticeable that she was by this time working only within the limits of the Thames Estuary, her last Ramsgate passage having been made in September, 1957; Dover had last been visited towards the end of 1956.

In the middle of 1960, after just less than a year aboard, Vic Foreman left and a new mate, Melvin Silcox, signed on. The next year started as busily as any in *Kathleen's* long career, and in April, surprisingly, she went on the yard for a refit. Not that money and attention were exactly lavished on her, but a new mast case was fitted and the old topmast replaced by a short pole with a derrick just long enough to swing the barge boat on to the hatches. The trysail and foresail were removed completely, so without canvas for the first time in her life *Kathleen* went back to work, but not for long. Perhaps with a measure of defiance, *Kathleen's* whaleback wheelhouse suddenly sported a white letter D in the Daniels Brothers' style, but this nostalgic gesture could not turn back the clock. How fitting that *Kathleen's* last cargo should be a full load of wheat, the commodity around which her career had been built; and was it mere coincidence that its destination was Whitstable? As she slipped away from the harbour empty on the second Tuesday in October, none of the onlookers who idly watched her departure could have realised that they were witnessing a proud vessel's last farewell to the place which had been her home for over fifty years.

She lay for a few more weeks at Strood without work or crew while her engine and other equipment were taken out, then on 23rd November, 1961, sixty years and seventeen days after her launching, a ledger entry tersely recorded:"*Kathleen*, stores removed, etc. Laid up—Out of Commission."

CHAPTER TWELVE

Dinghy Sailor

RE-RIGGING Thames barges was not, by any stretch of the imagination, a common occurrence in 1965. One barge still traded under sail, the *Cambria*, and there were the auxiliaries *Will Everard* and *Thyra*, while the *May* occasionally took a freight. Possibly there were a few others.

Some former sailing barges still traded with diesel engines, sometimes supplemented by a "leg of mutton" sail or rigged like the *Beatrice Maud* as a pseudo stumpy. The last sailing fleets, comprising Horlock's, Cranfield's and the ICI powder barges, had been disbanded some years previously, the craft passing individually into private hands for conversion to barge yachts.

Motor barges did come on the market from time to time, some as a result of the London and Rochester Trading Company's policy of phasing out wooden craft, and others as skipper/owners retired or small fleets went out of business through their inability to combat modern competition.

How then did I, a Hertfordshire grocer's son, never having sailed anything larger than a small dinghy, come at twenty-three to be the owner of a Thames barge? The answer, strangely enough, concerned my job. Not that there is any connection between the sign and display industry and the sea. As senior buyer of a showcard company, I was reponsible for the purchase of Scandinavian cardboard through board merchants in the City of London. A sales representative from such a firm called one day to discuss business and suggested at lunchtime that we should adjourn to the *White Horse* in Enfield for a beer and a sandwich. During the ensuing chat, the representative mentioned that while waiting in reception he had overheard talk of my dinghy sailing exploits and volunteered to lend me a book which had been gathering dust on his bookshelf for many years. The book was delivered the following day on indefinite loan.

After a quick glance at its dust cover I treated Hervey Benham's *Down Tops'l* to a continuance of its previous fate, albeit on a different bookshelf, for the story of the East Coast sailing barges held no interest for me. Sailing was the exhilaration of counter-balancing the effect of the wind by leaping about in a racing dinghy, and in pursuit of this hobby in the summer of 1964 I was competing in the East Coast area team championships of the Enterprise class. It was during the second race that something happened which was to change my boating habits significantly.

The event was being hosted by the Maylandsea Bay Yacht Club and the course of the race took us out into the Blackwater, tacking to the windward mark just west of St Lawrence Stone. There was a sprightly breeze and it was quite hard work on the fetch to the next mark. One of the unwritten rules of dinghy racing is to concentrate on catching up the boats in front rather than concerning oneself with what goes on behind, and it was because of this that I did not see a barge come round from St Lawrence Bay until she was some hundred yards astern of our racing fleet. Despite being on nearly our fastest point of sailing, here was this lumbering black box of a ship, carrying masses of sail, passing by us with ease. *Marjorie*, Ipswich, I read from her transom, and back at the yacht club I was told that she was one of a number of Maldon-based Thames barges which berthed at the ancient Hythe Quay. I was determined to include a diversion in my journey home to get a closer look. Some hours later, as I feasted on the many hundreds of photographs (now sadly gone) that adorned the walls of the Maldon *Jolly Sailor*, I knew I was well and truly hooked. My bedroom light was hardly off all night as I read through *Down Tops'l*, a superbly detailed account of the East Coast sailing barges.

A few days later I visited Foyle's bookshop and was fortunate to find a copy of Fred Cooper's *Handbook of Sailing Barges*, their last copy, in fact; and also the then recently published *Racing Sailormen*. I must admit that while much smaller in size and content, it was the handbook that interested me most, and from reading its contents I began to accrue some surface knowledge and understanding of the spritsail rig.

For all my new-found enthusiasm, not once had the possibility of owning a barge occured to me. I was content to spend my weekends visiting the many creeks

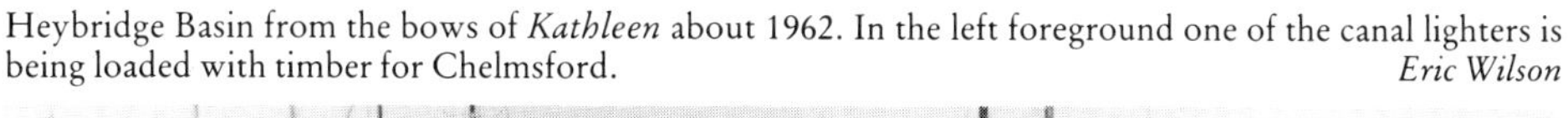
Heybridge Basin from the bows of *Kathleen* about 1962. In the left foreground one of the canal lighters is being loaded with timber for Chelmsford. *Eric Wilson*

and backwaters referred to in *Down Tops'l*, at the same time logging any hulk, regardless of condition.

I remember being thrilled at the sight of the *Will Everard* discharging cargo at Colchester, and it was still possible from the ranks of privately owned craft to see sailing barges passing by along the coast, occasionally loaded with cargo, often just cruising for pleasure, or sometimes with fare-paying passengers on charter work.

Nevertheless, the majority of hulls and hulks spotted were in a sorry state. Barge remains at Whitewall Creek off the Medway and at Murston near Sittingbourne, Kent, reflected the rapid disappearance of these beautiful and efficient craft.

Heybridge Basin about 1963 with the *Edme* in use as a timber lighter in the left foreground. *Kathleen's* stern is visible to the right of the auxiliary *Varuna*, and other timber lighters can also be seen. *S. J. Shipman*

Sometimes, however, the apparent condition of a barge was worse than reality; I well remember a weekend in waders exploring the back channel at Maldon. The hulks *Agnes & Constance, Beaumont Belle* and *Leslie West* lay mouldering close to Sadds' timber yard. They all looked in a pretty poor state, and the *Leslie West*, half full of water aft, had a mass of grass growing from her ceiling under her open forehatch.

Anyone could have won an easy pound from me that day. It appeared inconceivable that she would ever move from that resting place. Yet some months later I saw her being towed down Colliers Reach, apparently bound to sea.

Later that same afternoon, via the towing path of the Chelmer and Blackwater Canal, I arrived at Heybridge Basin. The commercial trade to the Basin was in timber, lightered in former sailing barge hulls from the anchorage off Osea Island, where timber-laden ships, too large to navigate the basin lock, would lie to unload. In the Basin the timber was transferred again to some specially designed, shallow draught steel barges, small enough to navigate the canal up to the timber wharf in Chelmsford.

In the Basin at the time were the sailing barges *Edith May*, a magnificently re-rigged auxiliary built by Cann of Harwich in 1906 and previously worked under the Sully flag, and *Mirosa* (ex *Ready*), a typical Maldon stackie built by Howard as long ago as 1892. These two barges, together with Tate & Lyle's *May*, another Cann barge some fifteen years older than the *Edith May*, were to dominate the four annual barge matches for many years. Also in the Basin were four of the local timber firm's lighters, the barges *Lady Helen*, apparently already sold, *Dawn*, *British Empire* and *Kathleen*. The latter had been their most recent acquisition, invoiced by Daniels Bros on 29th November, 1961, at £500 "m.v. *Kathleen*, for sale as is, towed Maldon", and delivered to Heybridge just before Christmas, 1961.

Dilberry Clark, who was responsible for maintaining the barge hulls, explained that the canal company had lengthened the lock, thereby allowing the Baltic timber ships direct access to the Basin and the steel barges. As a consequence the fleet of ex-sailing barge lighters was being sold.

It was then that the feasibility of re-rigging my own barge really came to the surface. Waterfront pub talk indicated that, not long before, the timber merchants would have accepted £1,000 for their whole fleet, then approximately a dozen barges, but that after they had been on the market for a long time someone had purchased three for next to nothing and sold them for a handsome profit.

Dilberry Clark, after explaining many reasons why I would be crazy to attempt to re-rig a barge (a point rather lost on me in view of the progress being made on the *Mirosa*), went on to say that the *Kathleen*, having been out of active trade the shortest time, was probably the strongest. The *British Empire* would probably be a bit cheaper, and the *Dawn*, built at Cook's yard within view of the Basin, was a stubby little thing with no headroom to speak of. I inquired of Mr Clark for his assurance that the *Kathleen* was in good sound order. "They've all got rot in them, it's just that some of them have got more rot than others; the *Kathleen*, well, she's all right."

Undaunted, I went for another look at her and liked what I saw. I stood at the wheel, hoping nobody was watching, and imagined her under sail. She was steered from right aft, a modification made at the time her whaleback wheelhouse was installed. Her coasting-cum-river barge ancestry was apparent from her large hatches combined with only the smallest of cabin tops in what could easily have been a flush after deck.

It was getting dark by this time, for it was a chilly February Saturday early in 1965. I wandered back to Mr Clark's shed; he told me that if I was interested in her I should phone Mr Auckland at Brown's and discuss the matter with him. He also told me that he thought the asking price was £500.

We were not to know it then, but the sale of Brown and Son's former timber lighters was to have important repercussions on the future of sailing barges, providing a valuable stock of barge hulls. Most of these came to be re-rigged, and without them it is unlikely that barges would still be sailing in any quantity today.

CHAPTER THIRTEEN

Barge Owner

IT WAS on the journey home that evening that it occurred to me; in no way was I in a position to afford such a project. Gradually the reality of the situation filtered through the remnants of my earlier elation.

On Sunday morning I called on my girl friend, Hazel, and told her all about it. She was immediately enthusiastic and suggested that not having enough money was not the sort of obstacle that should influence a decision. We decided that on the Monday morning I would ring Brown's and try to knock the price down, but that even if I failed we would go ahead.

Mr Auckland considered my contention that he was asking too much for the *Kathleen* as a bit of an affront. He informed me that I was rapidly running out of time to buy her at £500 as he was considering increasing all the prices on the remaining barges. He then asked for a £20 deposit in the post, which I promised, and that was almost that.

I only had £16 myself but borrowed the balance from Hazel, who had by this time discovered that her brother, also enthusiastic to help, had got the money we required, but nothing to spend it on. His situation was therefore complementary to ours. We had no money, but something really worth buying. We came to an arrangement and within a few weeks were the proud owners of the *Kathleen*, complete with sixty-four shares as evidenced by a Bill of Sale.

Dilberry Clark found an unlikely ally in my father, who was horrified that I should get involved with such a "heap of rot", as he described it. I believe his considerations were largely financial and on the face of it, my protestations that boats were always a good investment were not really framed with Thames barges in mind. Dilberry's concern was, I am sure, related to ensuring that I fully appreciated the enormity of the task I had taken on in re-rigging such a vessel, which of course, I did not. Neither of these warnings daunted me and I settled down to firing off letters left, right and centre requesting details of barge gear from all the companies mentioned in *Down Tops'l* who had either owned or had close connections with spritsail barges. With hindsight the lack of response does not surprise me, but at that time to have received only two replies to over a dozen letters seemed a bit of a setback.

The London and Rochester Trading Company replied very promptly, advising their regret at having no equipment for sailing barges left in their store and hoping

Girlfriend Hazel's brother Michael stripping off old paint during *Kathleen's* restoration at Heybridge Basin in the summer of 1965. *S. Dyke*

Kathleen shortly after being purchased by the author in 1965, her hull still salt-stained from her last duty as a timber lighter. *S. Dyke*

that I would obtain lots of "amusement" from the *Kathleen*! It seemed a strange response, but if amusement is fun, then fun we had, albeit combined with a lot of hard work.

I had that same week been to Great Wakering to visit the barge historian and skipper Fred Cooper, and a fine welcome was forthcoming. By 25th February, long before the balance of the purchase money had been passed to Brown's, Fred had provided me with a few short historical notes on the *Kathleen* together with spar and sail dimensions taken from Edgar March's drawings. I had decided that these were to be the basis for re-rigging. I knew that she had carried a bowsprit previously but I had no precise details, and in any case many of our decisions on rig would have to be based on what was available. By 1st March Fred had written again giving sizes of a topsail out of the *Millie* which the Thames Barge Sailing Club was prepared to sell. By coincidence the dimensions provided by Harold Eagles of the Club were almost identical to those in Edgar March's drawings. The sail was in an old shed at Eastwood's Lower Halstow brickworks. I told Fred of my interest, and we agreed to inspect it on the first available Saturday.

By early March I had received a favourable response from Mr R. P. Orvis of Paul's Foods Ltd, who was pleased to offer various items of barge's gear which were lying at the old Dock End Shipyard, Ipswich. The prices asked, while really quite reasonable, were certainly more than I wished to pay, and with plenty of other work to do I resolved not to dash off and buy things we did not as yet require and certainly could not afford.

Fred Cooper wrote again within a week enclosing details of all the blocks that we would require, all eighty of them. He had fully detailed the type, size and construction of every one, thereby establishing a checklist against which we could mark off our finds and buys. In the same letter Fred agreed that we should meet on 13th March for the visit to Halstow. This we did, and with a fine day to help us, spread out the topsail in the old brickfield. It seemed all right and we confirmed its suitability sizewise. Digging around, Fred spotted an old foresail in the shed and this we also spread out.

It was not as good as the topsail, but much better than nothing, and it was of appropriate size. We therefore decided to add it to our purchases. It was not possible to be sure of its source but Fred thought it might have been out of Eastwood's *Durham*, whose hulk lay by the lower end of the quay.

Well pleased with the day's work and only £35 worse off, I journeyed happily home, dropping Fred at Great Wakering before pressing on to Hertford. Our first major items had been procured.

By the following Wednesday a further Fred Cooper mail shot had arrived in the post, this time listing all the fibre rope requirements for the *Kathleen*. Without this kind of help it would have been significantly more difficult, if not impossible, to have gone about the re-rigging, and no doubt we would have committed many expensive mistakes on the way.

Later in March Fred wrote again to inform me that the T.B.S.C. was wishing to dispose of the *Asphodel's* mast, which while fairly sound needed a lot of work round the hounds and was a little smaller than the ideal for the *Kathleen* . I turned down the offer and also that of the *Asphodel's* sprit, believing that a letter I had just written to Eastwood's would soon provide the right mast for me. Alas! I shortly received a reply that the spar I had spotted in the grass at Halstow had already been sold, for use on the *Asphodel!* In spite of my pressing on with the acquisition of gear wherever possible, the *Kathleen* was not officially mine until 15th April, when Mr Auckland of Brown's wrote enclosing their receipt and advising that the barge could be moved at

Kathleen as a timber lighter, 1961–65. Drawn by the author.

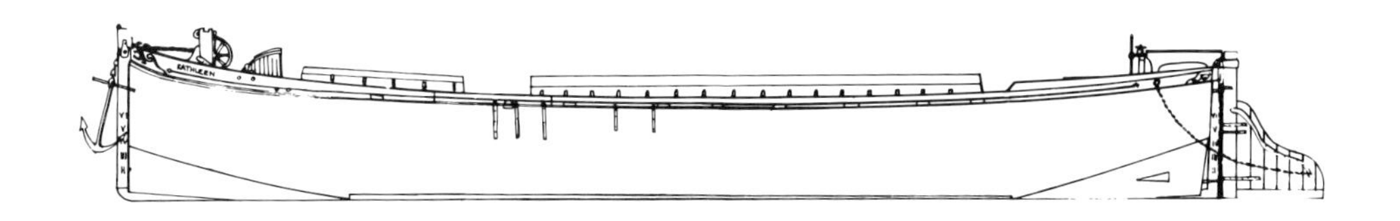

any time unless we intended to stay in the Basin. If this was to be the case, we would be liable to the Canal Company for mooring fees. Shortly after this I received my first fee note for moorings, proudly displaying the canal company's full title, The Company of Proprietors of the Chelmer and Blackwater Navigation Ltd. The detailed charges were written in an almost copperplate hand and the whole effect was reminiscent of an era long since past. The fee itself, however, was sufficient to bring me back to reality.

At the end of April we visited Pin Mill on the Orwell, where we obtained a rather unusual cast-iron mast case from the hulk of the *Charles Hutson* and were able to buy no end of blocks from Reuben Webb, the barge repairer. The rather battered hulk of the *Jess* was lying half way up the hard, her bows cleanly sawn off and shored up with deal boarding in which there was a hole, not unlike a window, about three feet square; this was Reuben's store. He clambered into the barge and began hurling blocks out through the hole in the boarding, shouting in a broad Suffolk accent the purpose for which he deemed each block suitable. In the course of this exercise we were forced to retreat up the hard as the tide came in; the distance, coupled with Reuben's Suffolk accent and our own lack of knowledge about barge blocks, brought a distinct element of comedy into the situation.

It was on this trip to Pin Mill that I met Richard Duke for the first time. Richard, master mariner and arch-enthusiast for Thames barges, was then owner of the barges *Millie* and *Centaur*, and was restoring the *Leslie West* as a house barge. He wrote to me a few days later offering his spare mizzen gear complete for the very reasonable sum of £25, an offer I quickly accepted. The items were duly collected from Cubitt's yacht basin on the Thames at Chiswick.

The mast case had been receiving enthusiastic restoration every weekday evening since its collection and was by then looking like new. All barrels had been restored and the whole thing painted in royal blue. This was to be the first real construction work on board. It heralded the commencement of the re-rigging, which was to continue all through that summer and the following winter, as well as much of the summer of 1966. The die was cast, and our bright blue mast case stood proudly fixed on an otherwise bare deck.

The description bare was no exaggeration. We inherited none of the deck fittings which would have given us a good start. No leeboard winches, no main or fore horse; even some of the chainplates were missing. Those that remained were very wasted and looked unlikely to be adequate to cope with the strains that would be imposed when sailing.

An early priority was to build a permanent roof over the main hatch. Brown's were anxious for return of their hatchcloths, and in any case it was necessary to get some natural light down below as our main hold was to become workshop and store for the next eighteen months.

I drew up a sketch for a special steel tie beam which would allow uninterrupted headroom under the new roof. Bill Hamilton, a pal from dinghy sailing days, kindly made this up and delivered it to Heybridge where we bolted the beam into position. This enabled us to fit four nine-inch by three-inch fore and aft bearers in place of the old hatch beams and use these to support four-by-two-inch softwood joists sprung over the bearers and screwed down on the hatch ledges inside the coamings. On to these were fixed tongued and grooved boards, which were covered in heavy duty roofing felt and then exterior grade eighth-inch hardboard. Finally the joints were covered by battens bedded on to a bitumastic sealing compound. It worked, and with the exception of condensation from the Perspex roof lights and the occasional deck leak, things were getting quite snug down below.

A coal-fired Rayburn room heater was purchased through an advertisement in *Exchange and Mart*. With this installed in the main hold even chilly winter weekends became quite bearable. The roofing programme was to continue for many months, the timber for this work coming by canal from Chelmsford. Any spare time was utilised in the continuing search for barge gear. When picking up the mizzen spars from Cubitt's yacht basin I noticed that there were many barges both inside the basin and lying outside by the river wall. The barge *Wolsey* was fully rigged with big "mulie" mizzen, but for all that she appeared somewhat forlorn. Other barges

Heybridge Basin from *Kathleen* in the summer of 1965. The other barge is *Edith May*. *S. Dyke*

Work proceeding on *Kathleen* in 1965, with the new roof over the main hold providing a useful working space. *S. Dyke*

converted to houseboats sported gay lace curtains and window boxes on their enormous "first floor" additions. The barges outside the basin (the basin is now sadly filled in and developed as a housing estate) were Daniels' *Lord Churchill* and the *Dorothy*, and it was from the latter that a fine pair of leeboard winches was purchased. In addition, the owner of the *Dorothy* was able to find some light irons (supports for sidelight screens) and also a pair of leeboard head iron fittings complete with chains and toggles. Unfortunately a previous owner, when converting her to a houseboat, had decided that her leeboards were an extra he could well do without; failing to understand the simple mechanism retaining them, he opted for the somewhat extensive task of sawing off the fan end and leaving the steel head plates still attached to the barge. In his ignorance he had destroyed a valuable asset. It was becoming clear that, after sails, leeboards would be particularly difficult items to find in suitable sizes. The sailing yacht barges were breaking them every now and again, contributing to their increasing rarity.

Restoration of the winches then became the favourite evening pastime; a few cracked teeth in the winch gearing were soon drilled out and studded. After primer, undercoat, and a final generous covering of our mast case blue, all was set for their installation.

The *Kathleen's* after deck was so cambered as to enable us to fix the leeboard winches without the use of mounting blocks and still get a fair lead for the wire leeboard fall. It was when I removed them from the *Dorothy* that I saw the sense in pushing the fixing bolts up from below; it makes their removal a relatively easy exercise. This can be a very valuable advantage, as I discovered early in 1967. The *Kathleen* was on the starboard tack, thundering down Sea Reach in a stiff breeze bound for a barge match; the port leeboard was held up by a rolling hitch round the pendant, and the winch was in pieces around me while I carried out some pretty urgent repairs! Through following the *Dorothy's* system, by no means universal practice, as evidenced by other barges I have since seen, we managed to put everything back together in time to make our board off Southend.

While on the subject of this *Dorothy*, which should not be confused with the 1885 version, a 44 tonner which scored some racing honours in the thirties, it is worth mentioning the extremes I noticed in her condition. From her leeboard fall sheaves forward she looked superb, decks tight and smartly painted, and down below her floors as square and sound as when she was built in 1898. Astern was a different story: she was all in pieces with holes through her sides, her floors and uprights almost non-existent, and her transom attached by little more than the will of the

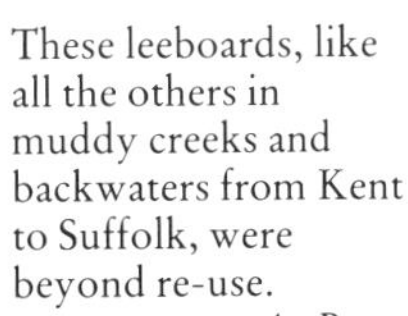

These leeboards, like all the others in muddy creeks and backwaters from Kent to Suffolk, were beyond re-use.
A. Pyner

Almighty. For what it's worth, I'd rather have gone third hand than skipper in her; I reckoned that her foc's'le would float a lot longer than her cabin aft.

In the following weekends on *Kathleen* we gave the deck a long overdue lick of paint, purchased in five-gallon drums from a firm in South London. It went on all right, covered well, and eventually dried, so what more could we expect for just over £3. The penalty for such a doubtful-looking bargain went deeper than the obnoxious smell of the stuff; informed by the salesman that there was an enormous range of alternative greys to choose from, it did not dawn on me that the makers found it impossible to make two cans of the same colour. Each time we bought more and repainted a section of deck a further variation was added to the already extensive range of shades *Kathleen* exhibited! Never mind, protection was what we were after, the cosmetics could come along later.

Bill Hamilton brought down his latest masterpiece one Sunday, a rather complicated steel sculpture intended as our mizzen mast case. Examination of the altered wheel position indicated that the only possible spot to rig a conventional sprits'l mizzen was immediately behind the wheel brake, but this entailed cutting two slots in the top of the steering box to allow the mast case to project sufficiently to accommodate our mast. The structure was some 4 feet 6 inches tall and very spindly but appeared to do the job. Fixings for the shrouds took the form of galvanised eyebolts mounted through the deck. The forestay, which with our peculiar wheel position came down in front of whoever was steering, was fixed to another eyebolt, this time fastened through an angled hole in the cabin skylight frame. I am sure my description sounds precarious, but the system never once gave any problems. A rather strange trait with the mast case came to light the first time the *Kathleen* took the ground after re-rigging; the rudder would ride up, taking the steering gear with it,

Dilberry Clark working on the *Edith May* in Heybridge Basin in 1977.
R. J. Walsh

and somehow tilting the top of the mizzen mast case some three inches forward. As the process reversed when we floated, and no strain was evident, the performance has presumably gone on ever since. I don't think even the most ardent observer would notice that our mizzen gear raked three inches further aft when grounded than when afloat!

By that evening we had our mizzen mast rigged, and though insignificant by comparison with what remained to be done, it gave considerable satisfaction to see it standing there.

We were soon to learn that standing admiring our work was not admired by Dilberry Clark, whose humorous comments as to our work rate would waft across from the shed at regular intervals. A real Essex character, Dilberry had been responsible for maintaining Brown's fleet of barges for many long years, and anything he did not know about barge maintenance and construction was not worth knowing. He possessed many irreplaceable shipwright's tools, including a treenail (pronounced trunnel) plane or mute which he once told me was almost certainly the one used at Cook's Maldon yard to build the *Dawn* in 1897.

I discovered that the port rigging chock was completely rotten, and I remembered having seen one at R. & W. Paul's Dock End Yard at Ipswich. Travelling to Ipswich, I was met by Mr Roy Orvis and agreed to purchase an old chock which had belonged to the big coaster *Lady Jean*; the baulk was 11 feet long and 18 inches high, and could have made at least two chocks for the *Kathleen*. Interesting too were the old chainplate channels, indicating at least a three-foot spacing between each shroud. On the same trip we loaded the wooden fore horse from Cranfield's *Orinoco*, which was to serve as the Kathleen's main horse.

Bill Hamilton, of mizzen mast case fame, brought down his mobile welder and skilfully built up and strengthened the badly worn chainplates. New ones were installed on the rail for the topmast running backstays, and the fixings of the vang (pronounced wang) chainplates were checked and improved to withstand the tremendous strains to which they are subjected, especially when gybing. A generous sprinkling of cleats in strategic places inside the rail completed this aspect of our task.

We took time off on barge match days to watch the *Edith May* achieve the grand slam, winning the Southend, Medway, Blackwater and Orwell matches, a truly remarkable performance. Dilberry Clark was crewing on each occasion, so it is apparent his barge skills extended to the water as well.

It was useful after each match to chat to the other owners. They were always interested to hear of the *Kathleen's* progress, and I was keen to inquire about the whereabouts of any available gear. Not that we very often learnt of anything useful; I began for the first time to wonder if the task would ever be completed. However, it is virtually impossible for even the crew of the last barge home to get despondent on barge match nights, and we invariably got caught up in the revelry, having a wonderful time until the early hours.

CHAPTER FOURTEEN

We Step Up the Search

REALISING that the possibility of having *Kathleen* ready for sailing in 1965 was becoming a pipe dream, I had to rethink our plans. All things considered we had not fared too badly during those first few months, yet there remained some major items such as mainmast, mainsail, leeboards still to be found, and it was becoming obvious that the commercial barge operators and private owners were unlikely to be able to supply these items.

A concerted search of East Coast ports used by the sailing barges appeared to be the only alternative to making everything new. Of course we could have a new mast made, and new sails, but this was quite beyond my already dwindling financial resources.

So early one September morning, on the basis of "start at the top and work down", I set off for Suffolk to commence the search. Around the back of some old sheds on Orford Quay I found two large wooden blocks with patent sheaves undoubtedly suitable for a mainsheet, but that was the only find of the weekend. Not a single trip went by, however, without something coming to hand, either authentic barging gear or some suitable substitute. Often we parked the car some way from the river or foreshore and explored on foot the less frequented creeks which had not already yielded their treasures to previous barge searchers.

On one such walk at Iken Cliff, near Snape on the River Alde, I came across an old man complete with gold earring, speaking Suffolk so broad he was difficult to understand, who turned out to be the huffler (pilot) for the Alde and Ore rivers; for years he had been responsible for navigating laden barges up the tortuous channel to the maltings at Snape. What a character he was! He knew by heart the name of every barge he had brought up the river, and also most of those his father had brought up before him. It would have been difficult to assess his age had it not been for his telling a story of his father, who as skipper of a local barge had been at sea during the great gale of 1888. I concluded that he was unlikely to have been in command at much less than twenty years old, and so his son if born when he was twenty-five would by then have been in his early seventies. Imagine my amazement when he announced that if I came back a week or two later he was sure his father would have shaken off his cold and would tell me the story for himself!

My first important find during the many months of searching was on a visit to

A deck view on *Kathleen* in
Heybridge Basin in July, 1966.
Essex County Newspapers

A much-needed coat of paint is applied to *Kathleen* during restoration. The empty mastcase waits to receive the mainmast, when it can be found. *S. Dyke*

Waldringfield. I had visited Ramsholt, Melton dock, Woodbridge and much of the river wall in between and eventually arrived at this picturesque waterfront village complete with boatyard, pub and a flourishing sailing club. In common with many of the Suffolk rivers the Deben has a number of sandy bays and it was on the "beach" at Waldringfield that I found a main brail winch being used for hauling boats up the sandy foreshore. An inquiry at the *Maybush* revealed that it belonged to the local sailing club, who very generously let me have it for a donation to the club funds and a round of drinks at the bar! An unusual feature of this winch was its complete anonymity; most ironworks embossed their names prominently in the end frame castings, our leeboard winches proudly exhibiting "James Hall & Sons Ltd, Rochester" twice on each, but no maker's name was to be seen on my latest acquisition. Its condition was remarkably good, with very little play in the bearings; every tooth was intact and the pawls hardly worn. There was certainly no cause for the maker to remain anonymous on grounds of conscience regarding its quality. Like the mast case and leeboard winches before it, the brail winch was subjected to the midweek evening treatment, with the result that it was delivered to the *Kathleen* a week later looking like new.

It was a weekend fairly late in September when a man and his wife walked up to the barge and asked to speak to the owner. They had brought along a first edition of Edgar March's book *Spritsail Barges of Thames and Medway*, saying that they had heard the *Kathleen* was re-rigging and wondered if we had a copy. While aware from Fred Cooper that this book included plans and a description of *Kathleen*, I had never before had the opportunity to study the book at all. This generosity is typical of those with an interest in sailing barges. I always felt that the book belonged more to the barge than to me, so when she was sold the book went as well.

Edgar March's dedication always remains in my memory. "To my wife, who has not minded my love for *Kathleen* and her sisters", a simple evocation of the influence of the spritsail barge on the author's life.

The search continued: Felixstowe Ferry, Levington creek, and Ipswich itself, which still yielded the odd bits and pieces like foresail hanks and topmast hoops. There were a few leeboards here too, but they needed a lot of work on them, or so it appeared to me. To my chagrin, I recall that when Hugh Honeywell of the *Remercie* broke a leeboard during a barge race he promptly went up to Ipswich and hung one of these poor-looking specimens upside down as a replacement.

By this time I had covered quite a lot of ground without very much to show for the effort, but there seemed no alternative so I continued to tramp the lonely sea walls and creeks of the Shotley peninsula, taking in places with such picturesque names as Buttermans Bay, where less than thirty years previously barges had loaded grain alongside square-riggers from Australia, and "Johny-All-Alone", a hamlet on the north shore of Constable's River Stour. Steeped in sleepy history they were, steeped in barge gear they were not; so I resolved to take a few weekends off from my East Coast trek and to work at Heybridge on the items we had already assembled.

Back at the Basin Gordon Swift, who had bought the little stackie *Dawn*, was getting on very well and had got things very much sorted out down below, having converted her forehold to provide quite palatial comfort. The lining and coamings had all been sheathed in beautiful ply and sparkled with new varnish. On deck things were also very well advanced. A mast had been found and standing rigging made up by Bill Percy and Dilberry Clark. I was very jealous of the fact that Gordon was obviously going to be under way before us, and his progress spurred me on to greater efforts.

One great advantage of having two barges fitting out together was that a combined search was more likely to succeed than a single-handed one. Invariably I would find something that did not fit *Kathleen* or something we already had, in which case it could be considered for *Dawn*; and Gordon would find things for us. Gordon and Vernon Harvey, owner of the *Edith May*, had the good fortune to buy some of Everards' sail loft remnants, as a result of which Vernon and "Val" Deval, who had re-rigged the *Mirosa*, had their respective barges sporting red-and-white staysails which had been specially made for Everards' queens of barge racing, the

Sara, Veronica and *Dreadnought*. Gordon informed me that the *Dreadnought's* working mizzen, which he thought would be suitable for the *Kathleen*, was available, adding that Alf Naylor, Everards' sailmaker, had assured him it was in good order. I had obtained an estimate from Sadler's at Burnham for a new mizzen, and this came to twice the price wanted for the second-hand sail. I did not need much persuading.

By the next weekend the sail had arrived, and I found that it was like new. There was no sign of chafe in the boltropes and not a patch in the flax anywhere. It had also been recently dressed, so without any hesitation we put it aboard and rigged it on our mizzen spars. It was a perfect fit, as if someone had measured up for the job. Setting a sail, albeit the mizzen and while yet tied up in the Basin, did get the adrenalin going

Victoria, famous for her racing capsize many years before, looking rather forlorn as a houseboat in 1977. *R. J. Walsh*

and I was reminded of my musing the afternoon I had stepped aboard many months previously.

We were soon brought back to reality. "That won't get her finished," shouted Dilberry from the deck of the *Dawn*, so we brailed up and set to work fitting the main brail winch, while other helpers wielded paint brushes to good effect. Renewing my coastal search at Mistley, a sleepy old spa town cum port on the Essex side of the Stour, I was drawn to Horlock's yard, home of the famous Mistleymen. The Horlocks continued to build sailing barges after most other owners had given up, the last of them, *Blue Mermaid*, being laid down in 1930. With the exception of the little *Lady of the Lea*, she was the last Thames spritsail barge built. Unfortunately she was blown to pieces by a magnetic mine during the Second World War. Horlock's were at the time of my visit still motor-barge owners, most of their craft being former Mistley spritties converted to power. I spoke with Peter Horlock and agreed to purchase a pair of davits, but these were hardly the essential items I had been hoping for.

Disappointed, I set off to follow the river eastwards towards Harwich. Just north of the village of Bradfield lies a little-known bay where I discovered the

Victoria, built by White's at Sittingbourne in 1897. She traded under sail until about 1950 and by the time I came across her she was a houseboat. The *Victoria* is remembered from her racing days, not so much for her third and fourth places in the Medway and Thames matches in the year she was built but more for the private match that took place later that year for a £20 wager during which the *Victoria* was caught by a sudden squall and capsized, drowning her owner, Mr Austin, and her skipper Captain Webb. Her condition in 1965 was not as bad as it at first appeared, and her owner took great pride in showing me over her. She had a good main brail winch which could have been bought, but none of the items of which I was short.

The following week started at Beaumont Quay, where the hulk of the *Rose* lay rotting. She, too, had been a former Heybridge timber lighter. Even in her forlorn state the pleasing lines of this Howard stackie were still plain to see. The artistry of her magnificently carved badge boards and transom was a delight to behold. There was nothing of use to the *Kathleen*, however, and, despite calls at Landermere, Kirby and Walton, Hamford Water provided no further reduction to my long list of wants.

Another weekend I found the *Bluebell*, a typical stack barge but this time built at Rochester, hulked on the saltings at St Osyth after ending her working life as a derrick barge at the local boatyard. For much of her life she had been owned by the Wrinches at Erwarton on the Stour, who employed her carrying the produce of their Suffolk farm. All her main standing rigging was strewn about on deck and I thought this might well be of use, so some days later I returned with a van, some more help and some tools and commenced to make piles of all the useful bits of rigging and any other odds and ends. Intent as we were on our work, none of us noticed the tide rising over the saltings until we were surrounded by water. Even when we realised we were cut off no one was too bothered; the highest tide mark we could see was only just to her deck level amidships, so we continued to work away on removing the most obstinate item, a triple sheave stayfall block. Half an hour later we noticed that the water level, apparently ignoring entirely any previous tide lines, was inexorably creeping towards us; to the amusement of one or two watchers from the causeway and from a houseboat nearby, we were all huddled on her windlass and bittheads before the waters receded, allowing us to drag our winnings across the saltings to the van.

Before journeying home I decided that a call on the boatyard would not come amiss. I asked the proprietor what had become of the *Bluebell's* mast and sprit. "I'll show them to you," he said, leading the way to the back of his yard where, neatly stacked, was a pile of timber sawn into six-foot lengths. Seeing my disappointment, he merely said, "If you'd come the week before last you could have seen them in one piece".

Close examination of the rigging when we got it home revealed that it was completely rotten; it was too small for the *Kathleen*, in any case. The only thing we had really gained was a pair of stem blocks, and as events turned out we were never to use them.

A couple of weekends spent exploring Brightlingsea, Wivenhoe, Colchester and Fingringhoe resulted in little more than a couple of deadeyes being added to our haul, and a good deal of effort expended on tracing the owners of the old *Arrow*, which formerly belonged to the Thames Barge Sailing Club, brought no real results. The *Arrow* lay on the foreshore at West Mersea and I was determined to trace her owners, as she still had her mainmast, a major prize. Unfortunately the owners, when I did discover them after many weeks, were unwilling to part with any of her gear unless I took the lot, and at the price asked I just could not afford to be interested. Regretfully I passed that opportunity by.

It was one of Howard's stackies, the *Hyacinth*, which was to yield the next major find. After having driven hundreds of miles during the late summer and autumn, I found her within a twenty-minute drive of Heybridge Basin, hulked in the saltings behind Drake's yard at Tollesbury and apparently stripped of anything worthwhile. The *Hyacinth* was built by Howard at Maldon in 1889 as an identical sister to the *Violet*, both of them being owned by William E. Bentall, the Essex ironfounder who also created the famous yacht *Jullanar*. Bentall sold both barges to George Littlebury of Colchester, the *Violet* "as new" and the *Hyacinth* after five years or so.

When I first saw her the *Hyacinth* was all in pieces, with bits of rotted rigging in the mudflats and nothing to inspire me with hope. Drake's boatyard itself looked almost derelict. The corrugated iron sheds had received no maintenance for many years and the signboard on the premises was peeled and illegible. Down by the slipway was a spar store originally completely closed in but now open in places to the elements. I peered in, and saw a number of old wooden spars on a rack about two feet from the ground. Maybe a topmast among them, I thought, and decided to climb in through a hole in the wall. Despite the gloom, my attention was drawn to a vast spar immediately under the main rack.

Obviously untouched for years, it was a barge's sprit. What a find! Then it occurred to me that it was probably from the *Hyacinth*, a little stackie of 45 tons at the most; the *Kathleen* was nearer 60 tons and, according to Edgar March's plans, needed a sprit 58 feet long.

I paced out the length as best I could. Amazingly it seemed to be even longer than I needed. There was a soft spot about eight feet from the heel, but otherwise it appeared to be perfect. Brushing the dust from near the iron band I was surprised to notice a strange scarf joint about four feet long going a third of the way through the spar. I found another similar scarf about 15 feet towards the heel and concluded that this was a made-up spar rather than the usual one-piece sprit of Oregon pine or pitchpine.

I managed to borrow a tape measure from a man working on an old bawley in the saltings opposite, and he came to help me check my earlier roughly paced measurements. It was 58 feet 9 inches long, and complete with all ironwork. A marvellous find!

The next thing was to trace the owner. The first step in this direction was usually a drink in one of the local pubs, and sure enough over a pint I was soon able to glean that Mr Drake was thought to own the spar, that he was in his late seventies, had suffered a stroke a week or two before and was believed to be still very ill. This made my approach all the more difficult, but I was determined to pursue matters straight away.

I knocked on his front door, which was promptly answered by someone I presumed to be a housekeeper or nurse; she listened sympathetically to my story and promised to impart it to Mr Drake when he was well enough.

There was nothing to do but wait. Within a week I had Mr Drake's reply, written presumably by the lady I had met at his door. The asking price for the sprit was £20, and I was to be responsible if any damage was done to his property while it was being moved. The letter went on to say that it was the sprit from the *Hyacinth* and that it had previously been part of the mast from a J-class yacht which had been de-rigged at Wivenhoe many years ago. The remainder of the original spar had been used to make a sprit for another of his barges.

I replied at once, enclosing the £20, and began assembling a group of strong young men to lift the sprit from its resting place. I guessed that the spar weighed a ton, and because of its length of nearly 60 feet it was necessary to plan a route with no sharp corners. All my heavy gang had to do, however, was launch the spar into the creek, for Gordon Swift had volunteered to tow it out of Tollesbury Fleet and up the Blackwater to Heybridge Basin.

We got it into the water successfully, but it then became obvious that the sprit was intent on enjoying its new lease of life. Regardless of the length of towline or the speed of Gordon's little runabout, the spar yawed about, frequently surged alongside, and even attempted to overtake the towing boat. The sunshine which had blessed the commencement of our voyage began to desert us as we passed the "wrong side" of Osea Island and before long, under a greying sky, the 11-foot boat was thumping into short, steep swells. Looking astern I could often see daylight under the sprit as its centre was lifted clear of the water by wave crests at either end. The entrance to the canal lock at Heybridge was a very welcome sight! With the ebb a couple of hours old we moored the spar outside the Basin to await the next tide. The following day we locked through and brought our trophy alongside.

KATHLEEN

CHAPTER FIFTEEN

The Search Continues

FRED COOPER dropped me a line in January, 1966, offering to carry out the repairs to the topsail and foresail we had collected from Halstow. And then one snowy day in February Fred arrived, complete with spare flax canvas, sailmaker's palm and needles, and lots of patience.

Patching and repairing those sails took the best part of a day; by afternoon I was working alongside Fred, armed with a borrowed palm and stitching "homeward bounders" into the canvas at quite a speed. Fred's bill for the whole day's work, including all the materials he had used, was a paltry six pounds. That sum would hardly buy an hour's labour today from any visiting tradesman.

We were making progress. We had crossed more items off our lists than remained on them. Numerically at least we were past the halfway mark. The major items remaining were mainmast and rigging, and leeboards. A topmast was still needed; and so was a mainsail, for nowhere had we come across anything suitable.

Assuming that there might well be occasions when sail repairing was a necessary skill for the owner of a sailing barge, I left the office at lunchtime on Monday and drove to Thomas Foulkes' emporium under the railway arches in Lansdowne Road, Leytonstone. "Have you a sailmaker's palm?" I asked, noting the worried look on the sales assistant's face and assuming my trip to be in vain. Then I added my punchline, "left handed if you've got one." His eyes lit up. "That's all we have got," he cheerfully volunteered, "thousands of 'em," and promptly disappeared out the back, returning triumphantly a moment or two later with a selection from which I was asked to make a choice. All were marked with the War Department broad arrow symbol and date-stamped 1941. It is a sobering thought that as Britain faced the rigours of the blitz someone, somewhere, was busily contributing to the war effort by turning out thousands of left-handed sailmaker's palms!

I had resolved to compete in a barge match with *Kathleen* during 1966, whatever the odds. Fred Cooper had, very optimistically, included us in the Southend Barge Match programme, but it was inconceivable that we would be ready in time.

I busied myself early in the New Year with hunting for gear and organising some items which I was convinced would have to be made up, one such item being the strap to which the leeboard irons would eventually be shackled. This piece of

The standing rigging laid out on *Kathleen's* main hatch in May, 1966.
C. Atkins

ironwork is bolted to the deck just aft of the mast case, and comprises a piece of steel 2 feet long by 4 inches by 1 inch, with two large eyes for one-inch shackle pins forged in each end. Dilberry Clark had suggested the village smithy at Goldhanger not far from the Basin, so I painstakingly drew a beautiful sketch of what I believed to be required and set off to Goldhanger to have the work put in hand. In no time I was chatting to Mr Emeny, the proprietor, who after letting me explain my drawing and its critical dimensions at length announced that he thought what I wanted looked rather like the strap for securing leeboard irons on a barge.

While at Goldhanger I pottered down to the foreshore past the *Chequers* pub, once run by the late Jack Spitty, who achieved so much racing success with the *Edith May*. There was nothing to be found, only the rotting hulk of another stackie, the *Snowdrop*, built at Frindsbury in 1879 and owned by the Wrinches at Erwarton. Very little of her was left, certainly nothing of use to the *Kathleen*.

If there was to be any chance of sailing in 1966, as I had promised myself, then I had to intensify my efforts to obtain the gear still needed; from late March onwards, with the exception of our ritual pilgrimages to follow the barge matches, weekend after weekend was devoted to the task. Obviously there was not much to be found in Maldon, probably the focal point of the Thames barge revival, and I quickly passed on via Stone and Bradwell to Burnham-on-Crouch.

I was surprised to find Burnham, second only to Cowes as the yachtsmen's Mecca, so steeped in barging history. Besides the barge hulks lying opposite the town on the south of the river there were lots of other indications of a significant involvement with the spritty. The mast heap by the war memorial in the town included at least two barge mainmasts, but both rather rotten and too small for *Kathleen*. There were also a number of leeboards chained to the seawall by Stebbings' yard, but these had long been beyond use.

Reference to Hervey Benham's *Down Tops'l* revealed that large fleets of boomies had once been owned at Burnham by a John Smith, and that in more recent years Prior, the local shipwright, had owned the spritties *George*, the *George and Annie* and the *Jesse*. Reg Prior, the son, owned the *Mayland*, which was trading until 1950, and so it was to his yard I headed first. Until that moment I had thought of Priors only as yacht builders and I can remember admiring the two Buchanan-designed ocean racers *Vashti* and *Jabula*, which achieved great success at the time I was first dinghy sailing as a youngster at Burnham. I explained to Mr Prior that I was interested in any spritsail barge gear he might have around. He thought there was very little but directed me to a large shed where I found, under a long bench running from one end of the building to the other, some encouraging items. First came a couple of bowsprit travellers and then the special "fiddle" blocks used with bowsprit gear. I had not considered *Kathleen* complete with jibs, and therefore put much of this equipment back. I made a heap of things which would be of use to me, mainly blocks of various kinds, a few more foresail hanks, and, the most important discovery, a suitable muzzle for rigging the sprit to the mainmast, and then summoned Mr Prior from his office. I was hoping he might ask less than the ten pounds I was carrying on me, in which case I could have taken everything with me there and then. I was somewhat taken aback when he announced that he would value the items during the following week, and if I cared to call in or phone that coming Friday he would advise the price.

I phoned on the Friday, to be informed that having studied his old catalogues he was asking £50. What catalogues these were I have no idea, but in any case £50 was far more than I expected and I asked him to reconsider. Instead of either refusing to move or offering a reduction, Mr Prior said he would look again at the items during the following week, and if appropriate revalue them. After a further week a price just a couple of pounds lower was offered and accepted, Mr Prior making the point that the muzzle alone would cost that much if made up specially. The bowsprit gear may well still be sitting there to this day.

The remains on the south shore of the Crouch appeared worth a look, so I drove round to the Wallasea Yacht Marina and walked the sea wall to where the old hulks lay ending their days. The Rochester *Argosy*, a former Smeed, Dean barge, was in the best state of preservation and still had a leeboard that warranted a closer appraisal,

Burnham-on-Crouch in the days when sailing barges were owned in the town. *R. Malster collection*

but after waiting for an hour or two of the ebb so I could wade out to it I found that, like the barge to which it belonged, it was far beyond further service.

There remained few places north of the Thames worth investigating, though I did visit Paglesham, where the *Ethel Ada* had been built by Shuttlewood's in 1903. Shuttlewood's shed, which with the *Plough and Sail* pub and a few cottages was all there was to see, still proclaimed in faded lettering "Yacht and Barge Builders"; indeed, Shuttlewood continued building fine miniature yacht barges on traditional lines right up to the mid-fifties.

From there I went to Grays, home of the once-great fleet of spritties owned by E. J. & W. Goldsmith. The old Goldsmith yard lay alongside the right-of-way which had been trodden for years by work-weary or beer-weary bargemen as they walked to or from the *Theobalds Arms*, which even today plays host to seafaring folk, though few vessels lie on the buoys in Northfleet Hope waiting for a freight or perhaps for a better forecast before going down the river to the sea. From the footpath I could see a number of old masts and bits of heavy standing rigging half-buried under earth and rubble. On the foreshore were a few dilapidated leeboards, though nothing that to me looked remotely serviceable.

The disappointment of having drawn a blank for gear was considerably compensated for by a convivial evening in "*The Theobalds*" afterwards. It was in the bar that evening that I heard more barging yarns than ever before, and one in particular concerning the skipper and mate of a motor barge which had brought up for the night just above the old pier at Shotley, where the Stour and Orwell divide inside Harwich harbour. Deciding that the nearest pub, at Shotley, held none of the attractions attributable to *The Angel* in Harwich, the two bargemen set off in the barge's boat on the long scull across the harbour. Tying up in the old Custom House dock, they wandered through the streets to the pub where large quantities of ale were consumed until, and reputedly long after, closing time. During the evening some rather thick banks of fog had been rolling in off the sea. Undeterred, the skipper cast off their boat and the two men, both far gone, set out for their barge.

During the evening a further barge had anchored at Shotley to wait for the tide up to Mistley, and from the deck it was possible to discern the muffled sound of the sculling oar as the almost incapable mate struggled to get his inebriated skipper back on board. Many minutes passed and still their destination eluded them, the sounds of the sculling oar mingling with the drunken curses of the skipper as he harangued the mate for his inability to find their craft.

Now Harwich is an important Trinity House depot, and it is usual for three and sometimes more lightships to be mooored in the harbour. After almost an hour our skipper and the mate were still sculling around aimlessly, apparently completely lost. All of a sudden the cursing and shouting was replaced by a loud "clonk", and then silence. A few seconds later the skipper broke that silence with a shout of rage: "You . . . fool, we've come alongside the South Goodwin, that's fifty miles you've sculled this boat . . ."

CHAPTER SIXTEEN

To *Kathleen's* Home Waters

A FIERCE swell was slapping in against the south wall of the harbour with considerable ferocity, although it was a quiet enough day. I had read of the difficulties of entering Whitstable in an offshore breeze, and now that I stood by the large red grain silo which dominated the area I could well understand the problems faced by a skipper bringing his laden barge into the harbour in such conditions.

The harbour is all entrance, with little room inside. To come alongside the silo a barge had on entering the harbour to get a turn on a bollard on the jetty by the harbour entrance and to turn sharp to starboard to avoid piling up on the other side. It was this sharp turn which contributed to the capsize of Daniels' *Cereal* when arriving deep laden with grain in September, 1929.

Sitting on that all-important bollard, I felt a close affinity with the place. There was something rather satisfying about the little harbour, and I could picture the *Kathleen* and other barges loading and unloading in the days when the towering topmasts of the spritties could be seen from afar.

I had come to *Kathleen's* home port along the A2. Crossing Rochester bridge I had noticed a barge moored among a number of yachts on the west side of the river and had retraced my steps to investigate. She turned out to be the *Russell*, built by Smeed, Dean at Sittingbourne as long ago as 1879 and rebuilt in 1920; at only 44 tons she was much smaller than *Kathleen*, so her gear, which was complete but rather neglected, was unlikely to be of much use to me even if I could have traced her owner.

Whitstable certainly still had atmosphere, I thought as I reflected on the accident which had befallen the *Cereal* all those years before. She had been righted on the next day's tide little the worse for wear; converted to a yacht shortly after the Second World War, she was renamed *Lyford Anna* and eventually became both home and hobby to Frank Lucas and his family, based at Pin Mill during the sixties.

Leaving my seat on the bollard, I wandered along to Anderson, Rigden and Perkins' yard to continue my quest for gear. They had good cause to remember the *Kathleen* and the happenings of 1953, but my inquiries met with no success; the yard was by then better known for racing dinghy hulls than for barges.

Only a few yards further on I spotted a fine pair of leeboards sitting on the beach, one on top of the other. Too good to be true, I thought. And it was! Inquiries revealed that I was too late; they were destined for some other lucky barge. It was then that it occurred to me that I would have to consider making my own leeboards, unless something turned up very soon.

About that time Fred Cooper told me that Sully's auxiliary *Beatrice Maud* was being refitted by Reuben Webb at Pin Mill and that what was left of her sailing gear was to be removed. I wrote immediately; and quite soon I had an appointment to meet Raymond Sully to discuss the purchase of her gear. She was still setting a mainsail and I therefore had high hopes that the lion's share of my outstanding needs would be met. I was informed, however, that her mainmast had been tapered off above the hounds and was not suitable as a mast for a topsail barge. I arranged to meet her skipper, Harold Smy, the next weekend at Pin Mill to collect any gear which might be of use. Harold was somewhat late, but we managed to get the mainsail ashore before the flood had covered the Hard, and additionally I obtained the vangs, rolling vangs, vang fall blocks and also a couple of very old lifebelt corks which Taylor's, the Maldon sailmakers, re-covered and roped for me.

I was also offered the mainsheet block, which I was pleased to accept, but despite much searching it had disappeared. Harold Smy was understandably very annoyed at not being able to find what was, after all, an item unique to the spritsail barge. We had to accept that it was not going to turn up, and as Harold's enthusiasm for the task had given way to anger at this loss of gear, it was obviously time to go. Freddie Webb told me some while afterwards that Harold was convinced that I had removed the mainsheet block before his arrival and had it safely tucked in the boot of my car. I will through these pages protest my innocence!

When I agreed to buy the mainsail, in spite of a large tear in the throat apparently caused by a crane jib, I had presumed that with the *Beatrice Maud's* large mast the sail was certain to suit the *Kathleen's* sail plan. Regretfully that was not the case; when it was laid out and measured I discovered that it was so low peaked it was almost square, and I later confirmed that it was made to suit a mast 35 feet to the crosstrees but only for a 54 foot spreet. Whichever way I looked it seemed impossible to alter; eventually I took it to Mr Taylor who quoted a price for repairs and alterations not much less than the cost of a new sail.

The searching had to start all over again. North Kent was my next objective, with calls at Faversham, where the manager of the shipyard assured me that while they were then building steel lighters they had all the patterns for barge ironwork and would be pleased to quote for casting new leeboard or brail winches, and at Oare Creek, where the old gunpowder wharf was being rebuilt for use by coasters. I found nothing, but did leave my name and address with the new owners of a rather derelict but fully rigged barge on the east bank of the creek.

Later the same afternoon I arrived at Conyer Creek, home of one of White's famous barge yards. The *Persevere*, Fred Cooper's old barge, was right at the head of the creek, looking very smart, as were a number of other barges which were moored against neatly tended gardens. These gardens gave the impression that the barges seldom if ever moved, though a few still had all their spars standing.

White's yard was still owned by the White family, and I was privileged to meet the son of the builder of such famous racers as *Sara* (1902), *Westmoreland* (1900) and *Satanita* (1879). I asked Mr White if he could sell me any old barge gear, having

Barges lying at Pin Mill in the early spring of 1967. Left to right they are: *Cygnet, Venture, Kathleen, Remercie* (in the background), and *Millie.* *R. J. Walsh*

already seen some odd blocks, a couple of sprits and various other pieces of barge paraphernalia in the yard. "What do you want with barge gear?" he asked.

"I'm rigging a barge at Heybridge Basin and I'm still short of many items, and I wondered if you could help," I replied.

"Heybridge in Essex?"

"Yes."

"Sorry, haven't got anything left," said Mr White, turning away and wandering off across the yard.

I was stuck for a response. I had read of the rivalry which was purported to have existed between the Kent and Essex bargemen, though until this moment I had seen nothing of it.

Before I could find my tongue Mr White turned back to me and called over, "Which barge have you got, boy?"

" *Kathleen*," I told him. "Whitstable *Kathleen*."

"And what gear were you after?" he asked me. "Might have some bits and pieces for a Kentishman."

In a short space of time he had found lots of small but useful items which he told me I was to take with his compliments. He also produced a virtually new mainsheet block, a most valuable find, which he sold me for a very reasonable price.

Next morning found me exploring Murston, where the derelict Smeed, Dean works had an almost *Marie Celeste* air about them. The barges lying in the creek were now much decayed, but it was apparent that they had been abandoned with their gear lowered even though the sails had not been unbent; remnants of fabric rotted on the spars and decaying cordage was still rove through rotting blocks. The former blacksmith's shop was still replete with specialist tools hanging around its walls, and the nearby slipway played host to half a dozen old leeboards, all too decayed to be any use.

Further up Milton Creek I came on the old Adelaide Dock, built to serve the Smeed, Dean brickworks. Sailing barges worked up to the dock until 1947, when the *Dunstable*, built in 1891 as the *R. G. H.* at the head of the creek almost within sight of the dock, took away the last freight of bricks under sail.

A few deadeyes was all I had to show for the day's work, but the area was rich in nostalgia and to see where barges had been built and where they had worked in such large numbers filled a niche in the patchwork of knowledge I was absorbing about the Thames barge and her background.

It was barely a month to the year's first barge match; the sands of time were running out. When I arrived at Heybridge the following Saturday to unload some of the acquisitions of the previous weeks I found the *Dawn* virtually finished; she was off to Grays, where Gordon Swift was to put the finishing touches to her before sailing in the Medway match.

Gordon invited me to accompany him on the Bank Holiday Monday race at Southend. I just could not refuse, in spite of the time I knew it would deny me for finishing work on *Kathleen*.

CHAPTER SEVENTEEN

A Mast at Last

ON THE last day of April I travelled south again, this time to Erith with the idea of investigating the saltings. As I set out I had no premonition of my impending good fortune.

The Erith Yacht Club lies among tidal flats a good walk from the river wall, its headquarters being an old lightvessel. I could just discern what looked like the hull of a barge.

On my way to investigate, I was suddenly brought to a halt by a barge's mast lying in the water alongside the track not far from the club. A quickly paced check indicated dimensions closely akin to the *Kathleen's* spar plan, and closer inspection revealed that in addition to the mast, all the main standing rigging was there, together with the crosstrees. I poked around the hounds with a knife and could find no trace of rot. The wire, unusually of the flexible type, also appeared perfectly sound, although some work on the servings would be needed.

I hurried on to the yacht club and was fortunate to find a committee member on board who, an avid barge enthusiast himself, was only too pleased to help. Armed with a tape measure, we returned to the spar and quickly confirmed its suitability. It had been removed from the *Lady Mary*, built in 1900 and formerly one of F. T. Everard's coasters, which the club was using as a spar store and workshop. She traded under sail alone into the mid-fifties and can therefore be numbered among the last handful of cargo-carrying sailormen. There was little other gear on her, although our search revealed a number of stayfall blocks, certainly in better condition than those we had rescued from the *Bluebell* in St Osyth creek the year before.

The club committee agreed to sell me the mast for £25, which seemed a more than fair price, and the money was sent without delay. But how was I to get the mast to Heybridge?

A further chat at the Erith Yacht Club revealed that there was a lighterage company's wharf a little way upriver where it might be possible to arrange for the spar to be lifted ashore. By the following Saturday all was ready, the rigging had been removed and the mast was floated up the Thames, guided by a small dinghy, to the Union Lighterage Company's jetty, where arrangements were finalised for lifting the mast on to a lorry during the following week.

And where was the lorry to come from? When Gordon Swift discovered that the mast he had purchased from the *Asphodel* was beyond repair he had found a replacement at Grays, and this was to be collected by a caravan transporter fitted with special trestles; Gordon put me in touch with the owner, who agreed to collect our mast for £12. On 10th May it was delivered to Heybridge, being unloaded on to the quayside alongside *Kathleen* by a crane from the Blackwater Timber Company.

Looking closer that weekend, I discovered that parts of the heel of the mast were rotten. Had I bought a load of firewood? I voiced my misgivings to Dilberry Clark, who armed himself with a hammer and came to inspect.

"Put your ear to the mast cap," he said. I leaned down and listened. He wandered down to the heel, and as I listened he swung the hammer, giving a light tap in the centre of the heel. The mast rang like a bell. Dilberry pronounced it sound. A few small pieces were glued into the heel to replace the rotten wood, the spar was scraped down and then four coats of clear varnish brought out the lovely grain of the pitchpine; the heel, hounds, and topmast caps were picked out in white.

While I was applying the "cosmetics" to the mast Bill Percy, then foreman rigger at Harland and Wolff in London, busied himself with splicing up a new stanliff to support the heel of the sprit. A yard tackle, temporary head rope and a new stayfall were also prepared, this latter item from two-and-a-quarter-inch flexible wire almost 250 feet long. This was longer than normal, as the stayfall blocks from the *Lady Mary* comprised one three-sheved block and a four-sheved block as distinct from the more usual three-sheave pair of blocks. The advantage in using these was that they provided a greater purchase ratio and reduced the load on the windlass when raising or lowering the barge's spars.

One of the old mainhorse chocks was completely missing from *Kathleen*, and the other, from its condition, ought to have been! Using the existing one as a pattern I proposed to make two new chocks. A suitable piece of seasoned oak had been sawn in half to provide two pieces 18 inches tall, three feet long and six inches thick. Having pencilled on the shape I required the size of the task became apparent.

My inability to cut in a straight line through inch-square deal was a source of concern. How was I to make an eleven-foot cut in six-inch oak? The secret is simple. Firstly, you must not be in any hurry whatsoever; secondly, as Dilberry Clark would say to me, "let the saw do the work"; and thirdly, have someone like Dilberry who could sharpen a saw blindfold to advise and assist. It is certainly true that left to its own devices a sharp saw will cut in a straight line; it is only when the amateur or the clock-watching professional puts pressure on the saw that the problems begin. "If it won't cut on its own, it's not sharp enough," Dilberry would say.

Each chock took about four hours to make, during which time the saw had been sharpened at least three or four times. The finished result was well worth the effort, and the following Saturday, 21st May, our new chocks were bedded down on to the deck, the *Orinoco's* old horse was tailored to suit, and, without forgetting to fit the main horse traveller, the whole arrangement was fastened down. That gave us the chance on Sunday to clear up any non-essential items from the deck in readiness for the mast and sprit to come aboard.

Kathleen was the only barge left at Heybridge Basin on 28th May, as *Mirosa, Dawn* and *Edith May* were all away competing in the Medway Barge Match. We had resisted the temptation to follow the match as there was still so much to be done. The

The *Lady Mary*, Everards' fine coaster, mouldering at Erith. She bequeathed her mast and standing rigging to *Kathleen*. *R. J. Walsh*

quaintly named art of worming, parcelling and serving the stayfall occupied many hours. Firstly we took the heavy coil of wire rope down below and stretched out the first 30 feet or so. This was smeared liberally with waterproof grease and then parcelled by wrapping narrow strips of hessian around it; if the grease was forced through the weave of the sack-like material, enough had been applied; if not, another generous handful was worked into the lay of the wire. To finish off, the wire was served with tarred spunyarn, binding the hessian tightly over the length of stayfall which would be exposed when the barge's gear was hove up. Serving is a two-person task, as without someone to pass the spunyarn ball round the wire the server, armed with his wooden serving mallet, has to stop and wind the ball around to catch up with his work. The purpose of this exercise is to protect the stayfall from salt water corrosion.

We sorted out a set of lower deadeyes and managed to get hold of some four-stranded tarred hemp for the shroud lanyards. All the mainmast standing rigging was laid out on deck and the heavy upper stayfall block bolted to the forestay. The lower block was fixed to the iron eye on the stem band and the stayfall shackled to the upper block, then laboriously threaded round each of the seven sheaves and on to the windlass.

One essential task to be completed was the fitting of the *Lady Jean's* old rigging chock, as the port chainplates were very vulnerable without this support. It was a task that I viewed with a distinct lack of enthusiasm. I was confident that I could assess the shape that was needed to fit the sheer and camber of the deck, but very unsure of my ability to translate the theory into practice as far as the carpentry was concerned. There were plenty of other things to do, so that particular job was left for later. With the prospect of a fine Bank Holiday next day I decided to take up the berth offered aboard the *Dawn* for the Southend-on-Sea Barge Match.

The sailorman's grapevine transmitted the news that Saturday's match had resulted in a win for Tate & Lyle's *May*, with *Mirosa* second and *Anglia* third. This was *Mirosa's* first full season of racing and, as she was a locally rigged and built barge, all talk in the *Jolly Sailor* that evening was of her chances of avenging *May's* victory. Sure enough, Monday's race went to the Maldon favourite, with *May* as runner-up and John Fairbrother bringing *Kitty* into a creditable third place.

At the reception in the evening I took the opportunity of asking around for the gear we were still without. The general consensus of opinion was that leeboards were just not going to be found.

During the following week I decided to check further on the possibility of building my own. I soon discovered that oak planks three to four inches thick by 18 feet long were not readily available, though every hardwood merchant to whom I spoke volunteered the price per cube foot, which when related to my calculated needs put oak completely out of the question. I did not then know that Everard's had once re-equipped their racing barges with elm leeboards experimentally but that these had proved unsuccessful. My own thoughts at the time, contrary to most of the professional opinions that I had sounded out, were that oak was at the time barges were built a most plentiful and relatively cheap hardwood well capable of lasting many years in salt water. I approached George E. Gray, the large hardwood importers, who quickly recommended a timber known as keruing. This has great lateral strength, as evidenced by its use in lorry chassis and coachbuilding. It is also extremely resistant to wet rot, its other main use being for breakwaters. I found that for about £28 it was possible to buy sufficient keruing to make a large barge's leeboard. Ironwork was relatively inexpensive and easy, but the size of timber available, only nine inches by three, necessitated rather more planks than was ideal. The only way I could fasten the whole thing together was with three-eighth bolts, and half nuts to keep the protrusion to a minimum. When shipped the leeboard gave perfectly good service and never gave cause for complaint in operation, though its bristling nuts and bolts caused a lot of comment from other barge owners, who always dashed to provide additional fenders if the *Kathleen* was coming alongside.

The first weekend in June found me at Dixon Kerly's yard in Maldon. I had been told of some long poles there suitable for a topmast, and armed with a tape measure I checked each piece for length. Only one of the eight or nine was long enough for *Kathleen*; but only one was needed, so after agreeing the price the baulk was towed round by water the short distance to Heybridge, lifted over the sea wall and put behind the garages which flank the Basin until I had time to shape it up.

Only the rigging chock was preventing us putting up the mast and sprit, so on the Sunday morning I began to alter the *Lady Jean's* chock to suit; but this was easier said than done. The first task was to reduce the height from 18 inches to nine, and having despaired of successfully sawing the total length with the grain I decided to make a series of vertical saw cuts through the side I was cutting to waste, and then split off the surplus wood with a cold chisel. I struggled all that morning with the iron-hard oak; my attemps with the chisel were totally ineffective. A rule for this kind of circumstance was to stop, swallow one's pride and beg explanation from Dilberry Clark! On this occasion it was time for a pint at the *Jolly Sailor* and a pasty for lunch. Calling at Dilberry's shed on the way I told him of my problem, which he did not seem totally unaware of.

"Adze, that's what you need," he said. "Draw a line where you want it cut and I'll have a look at it after lunch." I went back to the rigging chock, and with the broad edge of a carpenter's pencil I marked the cutting line all round the eleven-foot baulk, and then hurried off to the pub. Some while later I was back at the shed inquiring if Dilberry was ready to have a try. "Been and had a look, but couldn't make a start," he said.

"Why not?" I queried.

"Pencil line's so thick, didn't know which side of it to work to."

I laughed; he didn't, he was quite serious. I told him that if he was able to be that accurate, then the top of the line would suit me best. He was soon astride the timber with the adze swinging between his legs and the oak chips flying. Other than the occasional pause to check on the pencil line, he worked continuously back and forth along the chock until the job was done. The resulting cut surface was as smooth as anything a plane could achieve, and I stared in wonderment. The skills of a lifetime practising a trade are hard earned and well deserved.

With the chock in position on deck I bored with a Scotch auger some holes right through into the tops of the upright frames and spiked it home with 20-inch steel rods of one inch diameter. I was pretty sure that the chock was there for the remainder of *Kathleen's* sailing days.

There was just time that evening with the aid of some stout rope, a couple of tackles and a liberal sprinkling of brain and brawn to heave the huge sprit on board. The fine weather soon dried out the timber and by midweek I had scarfed in a piece of pine where a little rot had got hold.

It was now possible to see the method of construction of the sprit. There was an eight-inch square timber in the middle which ran the total length of the spar; on either flat face were D-shaped additions joined at about 15-foot centres along its length. I presumed that a sprit made up in this way would be at least as strong as, and possibly stronger than, a conventional type. The years of storage had effectively removed all the old paint and I spent just an hour or so with some glasspaper before the primer was applied. Grey undercoat followed and, departing from tradition, black gloss completed the restoration.

The next job was to get the mainmast aboard. When it was unloaded from the lorry this had been left with its heel nearest the lock, but the barge was stern on to the lock and either mast or barge had to be turned; *Kathleen* proved the more willing. With much grunting and not a little swearing we rolled the mast up planks laid from the quayside to the hatch top, and quite soon the heel, well greased, was nestling in the mast case. The top of the mast was supported just aft of the main horse on a specially shaped prop, and a couple of tackles were rigged to the rails to keep the whole thing stable.

With Fred Cooper's *Handbook* laid open alongside, we placed the standing rigging in position, stanliff first, port pair of shrouds next, then the starboard shrouds, port aft shroud and main runner, starboard aft shroud and runner, and finally the

The author in working rig aboard *Kathleen* at Pin Mill in 1966. *East Anglian Daily Times*

forestay resting on a bracket halfway up the doubling. The lower deadeyes were fixed to the chainplates and the shroud lanyards rove through. Then the sprit was attached both to the mainmast muzzle and to the stanliff, the yard tackle was rigged and the vangs fitted to the sprit end. Once the vang fall tackles were shackled to the lower end of the vangs I decided that the big moment had arrived.

While helpers covered the serving on the standing rigging—and themselves—with stockholm tar I wandered to Brown's shed to announce to Dilberry that we were ready to heave up. Dilberry came aboard, inspected our workmanship, made a few small adjustments and announced that he was satisfied; together we manned the windlass.

"Remember to take it nice and steady," he said; "there's no rush to get it up; she's been without for nearly twenty years now, so an extra ten minutes isn't going to matter a lot!"

The pawls of the powerful windlass clanked on the iron ruffles, slowly the slack in the stayfall was taken up and the forestay was stretched taut. "Take a blow," said Dilberry. We stopped winding and he wandered aft to reassure himself that all was well. After winding again for a few moments the mast prop came loose, the total weight of the mast was now on the forestay. The shallow angle of pull imposed a tremendous strain, but everything appeared to be in order. We wound on a little further until Dilberry called another halt. He inspected the standing rigging to see that it was not likely to foul anything such as a batten hook on the hatch coamings, explaining that once caught an axe was sometimes the only way out of the problem. I saw his point; with a load of many tons on the windlass it would be very dangerous to release the pawls and unwind the stayfall.

We carried on winding and suddenly the load felt noticeably heavier. A glance revealed that we now also had the weight of the sprit, which was clear of the transom saddle chock on which it had rested a few moments earlier.

Soon the effort needed to crank the windlass began to diminish as the angle of the mast approached the perpendicular. The whole exercise was completed without a hitch. It was a tremendous thrill to be able to look up at the lofty spars towering above the surrounding buildings. A red letter day indeed for the *Kathleen*.

That same afternoon Jed Green, owner of the Paglesham-built *Ethel Ada*, came to the Basin and we got chatting about his efforts to refit her. I still had the *Beatrice Maud* mainsail; I agreed to sell it to him at the price I had paid to Sully's and at the same time arranged to borrow the *Ethel Ada's* port leeboard if I had not had the chance to make a second one myself.

Early that same evening I set to work on the topmast. Having prepared a plywood template of the topmast caps through which the spar would have to be raised, I planed away until darkness came. By dusk I had made significant headway; the pole was completely formed and the D-shaped heel almost down to size.

I felt that only the lack of a mainsail was likely to prevent us sailing in the Pin Mill match, just nine weeks away.

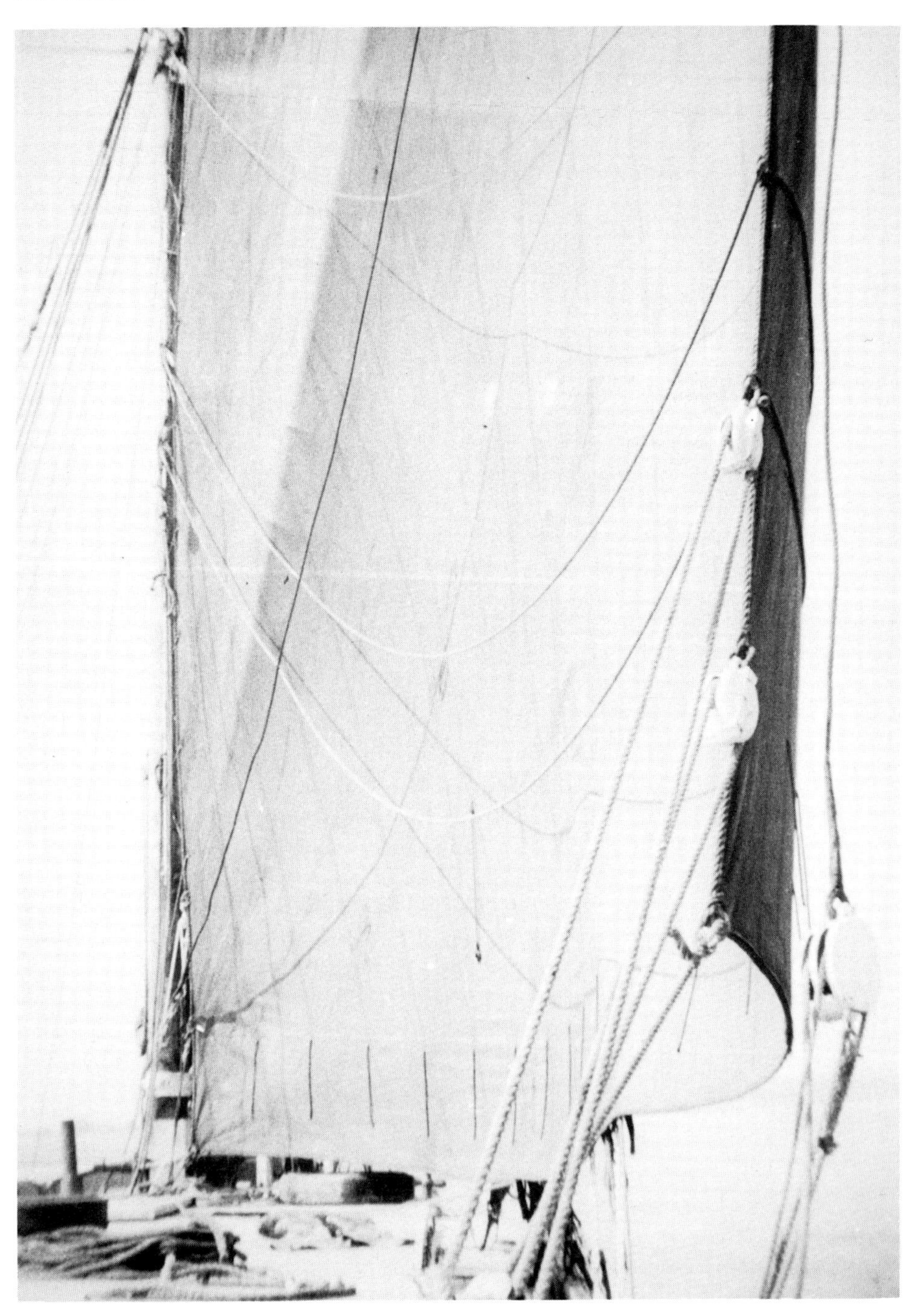

CHAPTER EIGHTEEN

The Mainsail

SHAVINGS lay ankle deep around me. I was back to the job of shaping the topmast, but already it was 18th June and the Pin Mill match was that much nearer.

Initially that spar had seemed only just large enough, yet after all my work the templates still showed it to be oversize. Eventually, however, I was satisfied that the spar would indeed pass unimpeded through the topmast caps, and so I proceeded to fit the various bits of ironwork.

The lower six feet was then varnished, but the remainder of the topmast was oiled so that the topmast hoops when attached to the topsail would slide freely up and down. The pole was painted white and the truck drilled to take the spindle for the flag, or "bob" as it is known to sailormen.

I had asked Bill Percy to quote me a price for the topmast rigging, but my requirement coincided with Vernon Harvey deciding to replace that from the *Edith May*. This was quite new, but had been spliced up too short due to a measuring error. For a couple of seasons the *Edith May* had rigged short strops to extend the running and standing backstays, but this had not proved entirely satisfactory. If we dispensed with the extension pieces, or shortened them, the rigging could be ideal for *Kathleen*. Vernon agreed to sell, and Sunday was spent making the necessary alterations, splicing a wire heel rope used to raise and lower the topmast, and reeving the topmast stay and running backstay tackles.

By mid-afternoon the inevitable Sunday gallery of visitors to the Basin were gathered around, firing their questions at us if we dared to appear on deck. Which way does it go? What is it made of? Bet it cost a lot of money? Those were typical of the rather uninformed questions with which the summer crowds bombarded us. I hope I was never rude or too blatantly anti-social but, anxious as we were to complete our work, we found it more than a little frustrating being unable to achieve more than ten minutes' uninterrupted attention to any on-deck task. Among the bystanders was a Dutchman who came aboard and introduced himself in very good English as the mate on the *Clothilda M*, a Dutch coaster which was discharging timber in the Basin for Brown's at Chelmsford. He expressed great interest in learning more about the Thames barge and its ancestry. Before long we adjourned to his ship to continue our natter.

Until only a few years ago the little-known Chelmer and Blackwater Canal was

Venta's mainsail fitted perfectly, clearing the main hatch roof by about nine inches. *Author's collection*

restricted to commercial traffic, when even such mighty waterways as the Manchester Ship Canal had long permitted the passage of increasing numbers of pleasure boats. Only in the 1970s, on cessation of the timber trade to Chelmsford, was the canal opened up for leisure activities. To my Dutch friend, canals were still the logical means of inland transportation of bulk loads, and he expressed surprise at the lack of waterway utilisation in the United Kingdom.

The *Clothilda M* was a smart little ship which busied herself in the timber trade, making remarkable fourteen-day round trips from the Baltic timber ports to Heybridge Basin and back via the Kiel Canal, loading salt there for shipment to the East Europeans. Such was the speed of these passages that even towards high summer the centre of some bundles of softwood were found to be frozen on arrival at Heybridge.

I learnt much of the ways of the coastal trade that evening. There was a certain irony in our discussion, for it was small motor coasters, many of them Dutch owned, that had done most, after the motor lorry, to speed the decline of coastwise sail in Britain. Many hours and a not inconsiderable quantity of schnapps later I emerged into the late evening and, after closing hatches on the *Kathleen*, wended my way home.

The following Saturday, the first after midsummer day, found us transporting our new leeboard to Heybridge; we had built it much nearer home, mainly in the evenings. It was a relatively easy task to stand the leeboard on edge, rig a tackle from the main shrouds and hoist it into position so that a mushroom toggle could be located on the leeboard iron. The fan of the leeboard was lashed to the rail until the leeboard pendant could be shipped.

Instead of the usual system of chain pendants we decided to follow the example of the *Edith May*, *Mirosa* and *Dawn* and to use semi-flexible wire pendants made from a type of cable designed for towing paravanes in minesweeping operations. This was relatively resistant to corrosion but we found it lethal to work with; unless loose ends are kept whipped the strands will fly apart due to strand tension and as much as 20 feet of the wire could be unlaid in an instant. This made the job of splicing in the thimbles a nightmare, and Dilberry Clarke and Bill Percy spent most of Sunday getting that job done, alternately coaxing and cursing.

By the afternoon we were able to shackle the first pendant to the eye of our new leeboard; the other end was passed through a rail-mounted sheave and shackled to a block through which was rove a flexible wire fall, one end of this being made fast to the main horse and the other end being passed around the barrel of the leeboard winch.

The same operation was repeated on the starboard side, except that we had no leeboard to shackle on; almost certainly we would have to use the one offered from the *Ethel Ada*.

All that week I was on the telephone, trying to locate a mainsail, but there was nothing available. I was too poor to have a new one made, but all the effort we had expended so far was going to be worthless if we could not find a sail. It was already the first weekend in July, the Blackwater match was on the ninth and then it was just five short weeks to the Orwell match at Pin Mill, the last race of the season.

I spent Saturday morning at Taylor's sail loft in Maldon buying a strip of bunting to make up into our own houseflag and organising rope for the lower, middle and peak brails, used with the wire main brails to furl the mainsail. When I got to Heybridge Bill Percy had finished the wire brails and the single leg which connects them to the main brail winch to port of the mastcase. I sorted out the various brail blocks and gave them a lick of paint, laying them out to dry in the sun.

I had chosen a blue flag so as to imitate the Daniels' "bob" under which *Kathleen* had traded for fifty years. Without the patience to sew on an intricate motif, I decided on a white diamond design which when applied in paint conveniently soaked through the bunting, providing an identical image on the other side.

Richard Atkins, a regular and enthusiastic helper, had turned up some beechwood handgrips to replace those long since lost from our "chaffcutter" wheel. It was a relatively simple task to fit these, holding them in place with wedges similar to those used to retain the head on a hammer.

Another task accomplished that weekend was the fitting of our fore horse, which had been made up from heavy wire instead of the more usual timber. This had been specially spliced by the Talurit system, as a conventional splice at both ends would have obstructed the free travel of the foresail sheet.

Much had been done, but still we had no sail. Then, late that Sunday afternoon, Paddy O'Shea visited us. Paddy was owner of the *Nellie Parker*, a product of Shrubsall's prolific Ipswich shipyard in 1899, and was collecting gear in the hope of re-rigging her, but he had a long way to go.

"I understand you need a mainsail," he said inquiringly. "I've one you could borrow if it'll fit."

This was astonishing, incredible news. Where was this sail? On board the *Nellie Parker*, moored outside the Basin in Colliers Reach, no more than a stone's throw away, said Paddy.

Out it came, and out came the tape measure. Our luck was in! It was near enough just what we required. The sail was folded into a long sausage-shaped parcel and lifted by a gang of helpers over the lock gates and on board *Kathleen*. Paddy was happy to lend us the sail, and all he wanted in return was a chance to sail with us in the Pin Mill match. A most generous gesture.

CHAPTER NINETEEN

Sail Dressing

DURING the week that followed I busied myself with some of the much-neglected "admin" required of the barge owner. I wrote to the insurance brokers advising them that we would shortly be under way and asking that the cover be altered accordingly, confirmed to the Pin Mill Sailing Club our entry for the Orwell match, and dealt with a long unanswered letter from the Ministry of Defence asking for confirmation that I was owner of the dumb barge *Kathleen*.

To that letter I replied that I considered their description most unfair to the lady concerned; while she was certainly without an engine she would very soon be capable of making passages under sail. Some months later a similar letter to the first was received, again describing *Kathleen* as a dumb barge, so her re-rigging was obviously not significant to the resources of the Ministry of Defence small craft register.

Such was my conviction that the completion of *Kathleen's* re-rigging was no more than a matter of "hoisting the sails", so to speak, that I arranged with Tom Bottomly that we should follow the Blackwater match from the deck of his sturdy motor fishing vessel *Tomanko*, which was acting as one of the committee boats. She was in communication by radio with the *Maureen Brush*, one of Alan Brush's ballastmen, and also the other committee boat, so it was almost like following the event on the television; not only were we able to follow what we could see of the race but were kept up to date by radio of what was happening elsewhere in the fleet.

After the prizegiving the crews adjourned to the *Jolly Sailor* to relive the excitement of the match. I had during the day heard confirmation that men who had skippered barges in trade had to be carried as masters in the barge matches, and in any case although I had sailed since I was nine I was by no means confident that I could safely handle the *Kathleen* without advice and tuition. While discussing "the form" for the forthcoming Pin Mill match with Gordon Swift I asked whether he knew of a skipper who would sail the *Kathleen* up to the Orwell and in the race. Gordon said that his skipper, Syd Milbourn, had a brother who was also an ex-bargeman living in Grays.

Next morning started somewhat later than usual, accompanied by more than the merest hint of hangover. Nevertheless, I was keen to lower down in order to rig our fine new topmast and make ready to receive the sails once they had been dressed. Dilberry Clark came aboard to show us how to lower the gear without placing unnecessary strain on the windlass and bittheads. The stayfall had not been stowed below, as would be the case when fully rigged, so we soon had three turns around the windlass barrel and from there the stayfall was led to the top of the port bitthead and made fast. I removed the hemp stopper, a rope bound around the stayfall between the two giant stem blocks to prevent any movement in the wire. Once this was unhitched Dilberry smoothly lowered away without a pause while I ran aft to guide the sprit on to the starboard side of the saddle chock and position the mast prop. I rigged tackles from the masthead to the main horse chocks to ensure nothing could move and then we manhandled the topmast, over 40 feet long but relatively light, into position on board without too much difficulty. The heel was lashed to the mainmast while the heelrope was rigged. Without forgetting to fit the requisite number of topmast hoops to suit our topsail , the topmast rigging was fitted over the hounds and the spindle which carried the house flag was hammered into the topmast pole. Finally I removed the temporary headrope which had been supporting the upper end of the sprit; all was ready for the sails.

Naturally I was anxious to get the sails bent on, but I wanted to dress the foresail and topsail before bending them; I intended to make an early start, but the morning of 16th July was one of those damp summer mornings so familiar to the East Coast sailor and an intermittent drizzle put paid to my plans. By late afternoon things were brightening up, so we started with the smallest first and soon had the mizzen bent on to its spars. When the sail was set the boom sagged a bit, so we shortened the stanliff,

Lowering the mast to bend on the mainsail. Captain Les Milbourn is by the windlass and the author can be seen near the mastcase. *Author's collection*

which peaked up the sail and cured the problem. The mizzen is sheeted to a chain from the rudder blade by a tackle on the boom, the sheet fall being led to a cleat on the mast by the goose neck. This system ensures that when the barge tacks the movement of the rudder sets the mizzen sail to windward, thereby assisting the turn by effectively luffing the barge into the wind. I was aware from a study of many

Lowering down; the foresail has already been seized on to the forestay. *Author's collection*

books that barges will turn to windward in narrow and shoal waters like no other vessel of their size; the books are certainly right.

Sunday morning was just the opposite to Saturday; a clear blue sky and gentle breeze foretold a settled and warm day, in fact a sail dressing day. The exact nature of that foul-smelling concoction, a barge's sail dressing, is usually the closely guarded secret of the sailmaker or bargeman that prepares it. General consensus exists over the basic ingredients: red and yellow ochre, which provides the colour and body, liquified with water and by the addition of linseed oil and cod oil. A barge's sails are permanently exposed to all weathers, and this rather weird mixture maintains the flax sailcloth in a supple and waterproof condition. I have heard it said that when you stop getting covered in sail dressing it is time to dress the sails again; the stuff gets on your hands, your face and your clothes. If the sails are allowed to dry out they become susceptible to chafe, and if kept brailed up too long without use they can deteriorate quite quickly.

As soon as the dew had gone from behind Dilberry Clark's shed we turned our attention to the foresail, spreading it out on the grass and brushing generous quantities of Dilberry's rust-coloured mixture over one side of the sail with a stiff broom. Judging by the smell, I would say that mixture was based on the original recipe, with certain undisclosed additives. I was certainly well pleased to be using the same dressing as had been used for both *Edith May's* and *Mirosa's* sails; fast mixture indeed!

Applying the mixture does not take long, but the sail has then to be allowed to dry in the sun before it is turned over and the operation repeated on the other side. While it was drying I took the opportunity to carry out a further messy but vital task, brushing stockholm tar on to the foresail boltropes to protect them against rot. By contrast with the evil odour of the sail dressing, stockholm tar has a delightful aroma. By the time I had done that job the foresail was dry, so we turned it over and dressed the other side.

The same exercise was then carried out on the topsail; it was only possible to finish one side before the sail was in shadow, and there was no chance of getting it dry. Both sails were left where they lay and it was not until we returned to Heybridge the following Saturday that the topsail was finished off and the foresail lifted back aboard. It was a relatively simple if somewhat time-consuming exercise to seize the foresail to the hanks already on the forestay. Unlike the topsail, the foresail is more easily bent on with the gear lowered down, leaving the forestay horizontal some few feet above deck level.

The foresail halliard was shackled to the head of the sail and the downhaul attached at the head. A chain sheet was passed around our wire forehorse and made fast to the two cringles in the clew of the sail. With the addition of the bowline (a rope used to hold the foresail aback when tacking) the whole arrangement was complete. By mid-afternoon we were able to start bending on the mainsail. To prevent any undue strain on the sail, I rigged a loose wire throat lashing and purposely fitted no jackstay shackles to the luff of the sail where it adjoins the mainmast. The main brails were rove, followed by the lower, middle and peak brails, the lowers and middles leading to the mast case, the peaks to the cleats on the main shrouds, and the main brail leg to the winch to port of the mast case.

Sunday morning started bright and we made an early start, though there was more wind than I would have liked for the job in hand. Les Milbourn came aboard and introduced himself; he was obviously enthusiastic about sailing but he might have been somewhat daunted by the fact that all our gear was far from new and totally untried since the re-rigging. He set to work with us, at the same time checking that all the running rigging had been properly rove; in general our work received his approval.

Les and I took to the windlass handles; the rhythmic clank of the pawls began to ring across the Basin. *Kathleen* was about to become a sailing ship again, sporting a full suit of sails for the first time since the end of the Second World War.

Ever mindful of Dilberry Clark's advice, Les and I checked frequently to ensure that nothing was fouled. The number of turns of the stayfall on the windlass barrel increased slowly; the weight of the sails made a noticeable difference to the load, but we kept going until the mast was nearly vertical and the weight on the windlass was much reduced. I went to the mast case to judge when we had wound far enough; the bolt was slipped into the after side of the case and then the hemp stopper was wound tightly around the parts of the stayfall, and as a safety measure two U-clamps were also fitted. We unwound the rest of the stayfall from the windlass and fed it through the small deck fitting to starboard of the bittheads and down into the foc's'le cupboard, where it was coiled neatly away.

Our blue-and-white flag atop the topmast stood as flat as a board in the strong breeze. I had hoped to set and check the mainsail later in the day, but unless the wind went down with the sun it would not be possible.

We busied ourselves with the topmast next, connecting the heel rope to the mast case winch and slacking off our temporary lashing. Inch by inch the 40-foot mast was wound skywards until at last the spar was fully raised. By climbing the mainmast shrouds I was able to insert the fid, an iron bar which passes through a hole in the topmast heel to rest on the lower cap and hold the spar in position. We slacked away the heel rope and then set up the topmast stays. Our flag flew proudly some 80 feet above deck. After belaying the various halliards in their appointed places we adjourned to admire our handywork from the quay. There remained only the topsail to be bent on aloft, a job for the following Sunday.

We rigged her many times over at the bar of the *Jolly Sailor* that night. At closing time we walked to the barge and I stood listening to the wind in the rigging and spars. Even with her sails brailed up the windage aloft was considerable. Her five-inch mooring warps were bar taut, as if *Kathleen* and the wind had a pact to try and be free of the quay.

"Not long to wait, old girl," I thought affectionately.

CHAPTER TWENTY

Sailing Again

THE stockholm tar on the boltropes combined with the sail dressing to make our already tatty working clothes into a real mess. Our faces, too, began to look as though we were in Indian warpaint.

Saturday, 30th July had dawned bright and cheery and we were astir early, seizing the topsail to its headstick and making up the sail so that it could be hoisited aloft. The week had dragged by at the office and I had been eager to return to Heybridge—and here I was, getting grubbier by the moment.

Undeterred by the deterioration in our appearance, we pulled the sail up on the staysail halliard until it was lcvel with thc mainmast head. Then I climbed aloft and sat on the mainmast cap, my tools strung from my belt, to shackle the topsail halliard to the headstick; then the topsail tack, clewline and sheet were shackled on, and as Les Milbourn, standing on deck 40 feet below, hoisted the topsail I lashed the topmast hoops to the sail. The gasket, a rope for stowing the topsail, was fixed in position.

After a break for lunch we turned our attention to the mainsail, running the heavy mainsheet block aft and hooking it to the main horse traveller. The peak brails were let go from their cleats on the aft main shrouds, the lower and middle brails released from the mast case, and the main brails slacked off on the brail winch. The sail was sheeted home, and immediately a major problem was apparent; the mainsheet block fouled the after headledge on the main hatch. Whether the new horse was lower than her original, the hatch had been "rose upon" since the *Kathleen* became a motor barge, or our mainsail was shorter in the foot, was irrelevant. The fact was that with less than a fortnight to the Pin Mill match, we could not set our mainsail without major surgery to our new hatch top.

We called upon Dilberry, who advised that the only thing to do was to slope down the rear of the hatch to a height of nine inches from about six feet forward of the main horse. With the cure agreed, all that remained was to administer the treatment. Easier said than done. The headledge was oak and riddled with thick iron spikes fastening through the deck planks into the main beams beneath. I was anxious to be ready for the tug at two o'clock next day, so I started dismantling the new hatch top straight away. By early evening all the new timber work, so patiently completed the previous autumn, had been removed, exposing the original timber coamings and headledge. I located a chainsaw, which I felt would make light work of the task. Within half an hour I was one third of the way through the timber and two-thirds through the stock of spare chains, and had completely exhausted the patience of local residents, who besides being subjected to the high-pitched stutter of the two-stroke saw had also suffered TV interference from its unsuppressed motor which had blotted out all local viewing of England beating West Germany to win the World Cup. It was obviously time to stop.

Next morning I succeeded in reducing the hatch top sufficiently to sheet down the mainsail clear of any obstruction. Temporary hardboard panels formed a rather ineffective new roof, which I covered with a tarpaulin in the hope that it would resist all but the most torrential downpour.

It was an exciting day for *Kathleen* and her helpers. Letting go the mooring warps, we turned her bow towards the lock gate and the open river beyond. Stebbings' motor-boat had arrived in Colliers Reach, so we manoeuvred *Kathleen* into the lock, and with the Blackwater only a couple of feet below the level of water in the Basin it was not long before the dock chamber had emptied sufficiently to allow the huge single lock gate to be slid open. With a towline made fast to her bittheads, *Kathleen* was eased out into the river, her ancient timbers floating in saltwater for the first time in over two years. Thoughts of that first occasion when I had stood at *Kathleen's* wheel some eighteen months previously came flooding back. This time it was real. A turn of her chaffcutter wheel sent us obediently in the wake of our towboat. Looking over the transom I could see the foaming bubbles of our wake seething round the rudder post and gently spreading astern.

Before long the well-known panorama of Maldon waterfront came into sight; it was not long before, with a friendly hail and a wave, we were cast off and came alongside the other spritties lying at the Hythe. Critical eyes roved over our spars and rigging; apart from the occasional frown at our non-standard leeboard, our efforts received the approval of the local experts.

With little of the afternoon left, we abandoned work for the day and yarned to the other barge folk until opening time. Our memorable first "voyage" was sufficient excuse for consuming large quantities of ale during the early evening. It was suggested that before departing for home we propose a toast to *Kathleen* from a bottle of scotch purchased for the purpose.

"Do you take any water?" asked the barman. "Not as far as I know," I replied, "but I'll look before I go."

I had not realised the misunderstanding until his amazed face disappeared into the other bar, leaving behind howls of laughter from my friends. Obviously my thoughts were with the barge.

At least an hour later than intended, we slipped out from the crowded pub and went back aboard. *Kathleen* had taken the ground as the river reduced to a small trickle with the last of the ebb. All was well aboard; not forgetting the incident in the bar an hour or so previously, I checked for signs of water in the bilges. The dust which had not been disturbed since we bought her was still not even damp, indeed a tribute to the skills of her builders.

During the week I arranged with Les that he would arrive at Maldon under his own steam around 10.30 on Saturday. As soon as we floated the job of transferring

Kathleen leaves Maldon Hythe for her first sail after being re-rigged. A towline has just been passed to Sadd's old yacht, which is plucking the barge off a lee shore. *A. Pyner*

the *Ethel Ada's* leeboard could take place, and subject to a favourable wind we could punch the last of the flood for an hour and use the whole of the ebb to Harwich, giving us a favourable tide up to Pin Mill in early evening. Even the best-laid plans go awry; the transfer of the leeboard was a traumatic task which consumed the whole Saturday morning. By the time everything was sorted out the tide was ebbing and we were lucky to be still afloat.

Up went the topsail, this time very much in earnest; then we set the foresail and mainsail. Les took station at the wheel, our lines were let go and we were off. The long-awaited moment had arrived.

Under sail alone for the first time in twenty years, *Kathleen* had joined the small handful of pure sailing barges which keep alive the traditions of their three thousand predecessors. The hours of toil and effort of the previous eighteen months were repaid tenfold by the thrill of that moment.

Such romantic thoughts evaporated when our skipper voiced his doubt about us weathering a trot of moored boats. As we slowly slipped to leeward of them I visualised us drifting on to the saltings on a falling tide. Just when it appeared that nothing could stop us going ashore, Sadd's beautiful old yacht, at no small risk to vessel and crew, motored under our lee and passed us a line. Slowly *Kathleen's* head came round and within a few minutes the breeze from below Maldon church found

Captain Les Milbourn, *Kathleen's* racing skipper in 1966 and 1967.
L. Milbourn collection

our topsail. We gathered steerage way; with profuse gestures of appreciation we cast off the towline and were soon into Colliers Reach, passing by Heybridge Basin. Northey Island slipped astern and as we came abreast of Osea Pier a slight swell began to move the barge and the deck canted to the increasing wind. Les handed over the wheel to me and placed an order for his first cup of tea, a ritual which became a regular feature of Captain Milbourn's barging. Two cups later we were off Bradwell power station, an ugly scar on the estuary skyline but a welcome guide to the coastal navigator.

I eased the mainsheet and weather vang as we bore away north-easterly along the low-lying Essex shore. The breeze had begun to ease a little and by the time we could see the holiday resort of Clacton abeam to port the sun was beginning to dip towards the horizon.

I had already discovered that on many points of sailing *Kathleen* was content to steer herself, little if any attention to the wheel being needed. I wandered forward to the mast case to consult with Les about our estimated time of arrival. With Walton's pier still some way off our port bow, we agreed that our passage would not be over until well after dark. Les took over the helm and I went below to search out our navigation lamps. Lights I found, but oil we had none! A powerful torch was all that could be mustered to warn off any approaching ship we might encounter.

By about eight o'clock the light buoy marking the Medusa Channel was flashing about a mile ahead through the gathering dusk. By the time we reached the channel, called Medusa after Nelson's ship of that name, total darkness had replaced the twilight.

We gybed just short of the buoy, having dropped the head of the topsail to reduce the strain on the topmast and rigging. Everything held, and we enthusiastically reset the topsail as we sped into Harwich with the breeze beginning to get up again. Navigation lights were seen fast approaching from astern; a Sealink ferry, Les announced, as we luffed up close to the Harwich shore in the hope that the lights of the town would silhouette our shape to the on-rushing ship. Her siren boomed out, and before long she swept across our bow on her way to Parkeston quay.

As we entered the Orwell we were confronted by a port light faintly gleaming in the dark some distance off. Les sent someone forward to keep watch. Our lookout yelled aft that the vessel ahead was now showing green, and accordingly we bore away to the north shore to pass on the proper side. "She's dead ahead," he called; then a moment later "Red showing now." Les sighed with relief. "Much further and we'd have been on the putty," he said. A few moments later a cry from forward indicated that both navigation lights were now showing again. In the pitch blackness it was impossible to see what was going on.

"To hell with this!" Les yelled above the breeze, "if he holds his course he'll be ashore and we'll be with him inside a minute." Hauling on the mainsheet and swinging the wheel almost in the same movement, we rushed up to windward to pass the offending craft on the wrong side. The gap between us rapidly narrowed. "Bloody yachtsmen!" shouted Les as we swept by a small yacht swinging to her anchor in the fairway and burning her navigation lights brightly.

As if that was not sufficient, a couple of cables further on there came a thump from forward and another small yacht, anchored in mid stream but without any riding light, bumped down our side and disappeared astern.

"Enough of this", said Les, "get ready to let go the anchor." We heaved the lead line and crept up to the windward shore without really knowing our true position. We brailed up the mainsail and mizzen and let go in about five fathoms. The foresail was lowered and the tops'l stowed with a hurriedly arranged gasket.

We all fell in below, lit the tilley lamp and brewed the last of the tea before a hearty fry-up rounded off our day. Up on deck again, I rigged a riding light on the stays'l halliard and Les, with the benefit of previous experience, wound on the rudder brake and fixed the preventer chain to the quarter, then dropped a fender between each leeboard and *Kathleen's* side. "Now we'll get a quiet night's sleep," he announced as he went below to turn in.

Sleep! some chance! I thought; my mind was busy reliving the events of the previous hours and contemplating the days ahead. Eventually the realisation that I was very tired persuaded me to leave the magic of the deck and climb into a sleeping bag below. Les may have made things relatively quiet, but there were still many creaks and rattles that were foreign to me. Nevertheless, the gentle swell which was causing the *Kathleen's* curtsying movement eventually rocked us all to sleep.

I woke early and was soon on deck to ascertain where we were. No more than twenty feet astern lay a massive mooring buoy, with another one a hundred yards beyond and two more large buoys not far ahead of us, and four smaller ones well inshore. Reference to the chart soon identified our whereabouts as Buttermans Bay. Les, who had the kettle on and was shaking the last remnants of dust from the

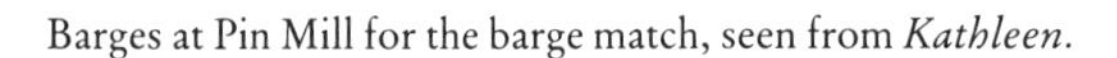

Barges at Pin Mill for the barge match, seen from *Kathleen*. *L. Milbourn*

Just before the start of the 1966 Pin Mill barge match: left to right are *Kathleen, Mirosa* and *May*.
A. Brown

Ty-Phoo packet for his first of the day, told me that he was none too happy with our situation; he was concerned that our anchor might foul the ground tackle of the buoys. As soon as breakfast was out of the way we set tops'l and foresail and hove the anchor short. Les's fears were well justified; despite the power of the barge's windlass nothing would shift our anchor. We stowed the sails and pondered the problem. Les was anxious to get a train home, so we took the dinghy ashore at Clamp House and walked to Pin Mill. Most of those asked were of the opinion that little could be done to regain the anchor, but John Fairbrother, skipper-owner of the *Kitty*, another former timber lighter from Heybridge Basin, offered to come to our assistance in the hope that extra windlass capacity might enable us to lift the offending chain sufficiently to release our anchor. After some hours' effort it was decided that nothing more could be done. We had to face the fact that the only course was to cut our cable at low water, to save as much chain as possible, having run a mooring wire to one of the nearby buoys.

That evening we walked to Pin Mill to arrange for a tow on to the hard on the Monday morning. Inquiries in the bar of the picturesque *Butt and Oyster* revealed that we should contact Frank Lucas aboard his yacht barge *Lyford Anna*; he owned a workboat which fished, towed or undertook any task from which a living could be made. He was pleased to help, and by midday Monday we were secure alongside Richard Duke's *Millie*.

During the following few days we had our first opportunity to scrub round and

A Pin Mill barge match from the air. The fleet, including *Kathleen*, is running down the Orwell in the early morning sunshine before a light wind. *Terry Watson*

freshly tar the hull and undertake the hundred and one other tasks, some cosmetic, some essential, that remained to be completed. We were still short of a staysail, but Richard Duke managed to find us a rather old sail aboard *Millie* which would be better than nothing. For some reason its colour was akin to khaki, but a photographer from the local paper assured us that in black-and-white we would not look too bad!

A whisper was going about that the Board of Trade was to forbid barges to sail beyond the Thames Estuary and rivers, defined as "all navigable tidal waters west of a line from the Naze to the North Foreland." The normal barge match course would have gone outside these limits, but as most of the competitors were running the gauntlet from the Naze to Harwich when coming to the event, it all seemed a bit strange. The Pin Mill Sailing Club wisely set an inshore course, using the River Stour as well as the Orwell and Harwich harbour. Geoffrey Collard, who was responsible for the *May*, kindly loaned us additional lifejackets and a liferaft, and we bought more flares from the local chandlery.

I believe it was Bob Wells, skipper of the *May*, who said that any law which made every barge owner provide two lifejackets for each of his crew and passengers but did nothing to legislate against twenty people getting in a ten-foot pram dinghy to row to America, wasn't worth a light. "If your barge starts to sink," he would say, "it's an idiot that jumps over the side with a lifejacket on. Climb the rigging and tie yourself to the mast, there's few places round our coast where an 80-foot mast won't enable you to keep dry until help comes!"

While we did not really expect to win any trophies, I must admit we were a little disappointed with our last but one position in the match. Our borrowed staysail had blown to pieces very early on and we had not gone on the blocks to clean up underneath our hull. Despite these problems, the day had provided a fitting climax to the summer's labours. The evening social was an opportunity to yarn with other skippers and owners on an equal footing, despite our experience being limited to one trip from Maldon.

The following Saturday we decided to sail to Harwich and up the Stour to Mistley. I was hopeful that we might be able to get another anchor to replace the lightweight kedge we had somewhat half-heartedly rigged to our cable. Les had no time for the kedge, announcing that it was totally inadequate for anything other than slack water on a windless day. There was little wind for the trip and Saturday evening found us anchored at Wrabness half a dozen barge lengths ahead of *Mirosa* and Peter Horlock's tug, which was alongside. I sculled our boat over and climbed aboard. Sounds of revelry and merrymaking abounded, it was Val's birthday; the corks were popping and a really great atmosphere pervaded the barge's hold. I think Val and Peter found our circumstances rather sobering; if we were desperate for an anchor, what were we hanging on now? They were hardly reassured by my description of our kedge and Peter promised delivery of a replacement anchor early the following morning.

I returned to the deck to untie our boat and commence the hard slog over the flood tide back to *Kathleen*. No such problem, the kedge had dragged and I could almost jump the gap between us! This was hardly a satisfactory situation, and Peter kindly towed us to better holding ground for the rest of the night.

Peter Horlock's interests on Mistley River, as the Stour is sometimes known, were far-ranging. I once heard it said that he had a different uniform for each day of the week, one for harbour master, one for pilot, one for commodore of his own fleet and so on. When asked why his ballast dredger had not worked on a wonderful gravel deposit just above Wrabness he is reputed to have replied, "I know it's the best ballast in the river, but if I move it there'll be no need for the pilot, so I'll leave it where it is!"

By mid-morning our new anchor was aboard. We thanked Peter for his help and then ran to Harwich with the last of the ebb, turning to windward with the flood back to Pin Mill.

The season was drawing to a close, and within a few weekends we were lowering our gear and laying up for the winter, close under the windows of the *Butt & Oyster*. A staysail, mainsail and leeboard still needed to be found by the following summer. Les agreed to skipper in '67, so we opted to enter all the matches in our first full season.

KATHLEEN

CHAPTER TWENTY-ONE

Southend and Medway, 1967

THE BEGINNING of May saw all the Pin Mill based barges, including *Kathleen*, rigged out with freshly varnished spars, newly oiled topmasts and brand-new "bobs" fluttering in the breeze.

We had entered for both the Southend match and the Medway match, but the arrival of the entry forms in March had proved a reminder that we still had no mainsail for the season, Paddy O'Shea being reticent about lending his again as he did not want it worn out before he could rig the *Nellie Parker*. Rumours that the *Edith May* was to have a new mainsail raised hopes, but these were dashed when Vernon Harvey told me he was keeping his old sail for another season.

Salvation came in the form of another loan, this time from Jocelyn Lukens, owner of the much-travelled *Venta*, which had just sailed back from Scandinavia and was moored off Dolphin Court on the Embankment, seemingly as a house barge. *Venta's* mainsail really was a perfect fit on *Kathleen's* spars. And John Bassett, owner of *Venture*, which had been one of Cranfield Brothers' last sailormen in the grain trade, arranged to sell me one of two almost-new staysails he had just bought; it was a little short in the luff but significantly better than nothing.

It appeared unlikely that Jed Green would require his leeboard for the *Ethel Ada* that year, so with plenty of other jobs to occupy our time we put off building our second leeboard.

Early May also found the social season getting under way, and on the 6th there were Saturday night parties aboard both *Venture* and Richard Duke's *Millie*. A week or two earlier I had had what turned out to be a final bust-up with girl friend Hazel, so when I found myself aboard the *Venture* I was not very much in the party mood. Bill Simpson, who looked after the *Venture*, kindly sculled me to the *Millie* so I could sample the other party! As a "gatecrasher" I kept a low profile to start with, chatting briefly to a very attractive blonde standing, albeit complete with boyfriend, by the main horse. It was the best party I ever went to; not that the choice in refreshment, beer or water, was anything to write home about; not that I found the blaring gramophone much to my liking; the fact is I ended up marrying the blonde! Not that evening, of course, but early in 1969.

Two weekends after the party we sailed for Grays on the lower reaches of London River with the intention of dropping down to Southend just before the barge match on 27th May. We left Pin Mill with a fickle breeze around midday on the Saturday and as darkness fell we were wallowing off Jaywick with hardly a breath of

Kathleen seen from the pierhead when taking part in the 1967 Southend match. *Tony Ellis*

air to give us steerage way. With the night came the merest hint of wind from the North, and slowly we picked up speed towards the Wallet Spitway. A ballastman bound for the Colne throbbed passed us without lights as we entered the narrow channel. The wind by this time was blowing about force three–four and we were scudding along in fine style.

A carelessly dropped winch handle broke our compass, but navigation was easy with visibility of at least three or four miles. Then from nowhere a blanket of fog rolled in from the sea, accompanied by ever-increasing winds. By sounding the channel we sailed onwards, Les having calculated that we should come across the N.E. Maplin buoy after twenty-five minutes. If it was there, we didn't see it. The swirling fog was thicker than ever and the wind increased in strength until, despite reducing sail, *Kathleen's* hull was creaking and groaning under the strain. Les announced that we would have to anchor; even in such shallow water he thought forty fathoms of chain would be needed. I went forward to the windlass, brailing the last of the mainsail on the way, and started to pull up the anchor chain from the locker down below. After twenty fathoms had been heaped on deck it was apparent that the chain had not been used for many years; the links were rusted to the extent that I really doubted that they would stand the tremendous snatching which they could expect in such conditions. Terry Smith, a friend from sailing club days who with his wife Linda had come along as our crew, rallied round to help, taking the wheel while Les came forward to inspect the chain. "Just give her twenty fathoms," he said.

The barge headed into the wind and I let go the anchor. As it hit the water an explosion of phosphorus leapt in the air, adding a magic unreality to our isolated world. We quickly swung to the anchor; a hand rested on the bar-taut cable as we bucked and reared in the rising seas was sufficient to convince us that we were certainly dragging. We agreed to chance another five fathoms of chain, and this eased our motion so that we rode much more comfortably among the ghostly fog and rushing wave crests.

We believed that we were now not dragging appreciably, so watches were set for the night and those not involved on deck turned in below. After a fitful sleep Les woke me up for my watch. We checked the bilges for leaks; good old *Kathleen*, not a drop of water. On deck I found the wind much moderated and the fog thinning appreciably. Dawn was only an hour or so away and I was sure I could hear the monotonous clang of a bell buoy some distance off.

By daybreak the fog had dispersed, leaving an overcast day with sea and sky merging as one. My bell buoy was easily visible not more than a mile away, and other than our own vessel was the only object in the bleak seascape. The wind had subsided further and the worst of our ordeal seemed behind us.

A decent fry-up for breakfast, followed by gallons of steaming hot tea, soon had us well recovered and eager to be under way. With topsail, foresail, main and mizzen all set we ran to our bell buoy to identify our position. It was the Maplin Spit. We had obviously come much further up the Thames Estuary than we had thought.

We knew where we were all right while we were in sight of the buoy, but without a compass the moment we headed away from the buoy we were hopelessly lost. It was with a lot of luck and just a little skill that we found ourselves off Shoebury a couple of hours later, and with the breeze freshening again we were on the buoy at Grays in time for a couple of lunchtime pints at the *Theobalds Arms*. Grays was crowded with laden motor barges whose skippers presumed we had come up from Holehaven, a few miles downriver, on the morning flood. They were disbelieving when we told them we were up from Ipswich; they were apparently waiting at Grays for the weather to improve before setting out!

Our hectic experience had resulted in some damage to our port leeboard winch, so I dismantled it in order to stud a couple of broken teeth before going home to face another week of work ashore.

Les was already aboard when I arrived at Grays on Thursday morning for the trip to Southend to find the *Cambria* the only other craft sharing the buoy with *Kathleen*. Her boat was at the end of the right-of-way leading from the foreshore past Goldsmith's old yard to the *Theobalds Arms*, and just as I was about to hail Les, Bob Roberts, skipper-owner of *Cambria*, the last pure sailing cargo vessel trading in Northern Europe, offered me a lift to *Kathleen* and saved Les the trip.

Bob was in a pretty foul mood, not surprisingly, as he had sailed from Pin Mill the night before with the promise of freight to Ipswich from the Surrey Docks, only to find on phoning from the pub to advise his arrival that the cargo had gone to a motor coaster. Without a cargo Bob and his mate "Ginger" Latham were without pay, so to lose a freight was a considerable hardship.

Les was well organised aboard, the topsail sheet was out, the brails let go and one of our two mooring wires already slipped. Inevitably a "cuppa" was also brewing. We were anxious to be on our way, so Les, confident that we could weather Tilbury without tacking, suggested that the leeboard winch could be re-assembled on our way. Bob Roberts was not so sure, and looking at the *Cambria's* flag streaming out in the stiffish breeze, he gave us a fifty-fifty chance of making our heading without a board to the windward shore.

We cast off, wishing Bob and "Ginger" better luck with their search for work, and felt well satisfied when we just pinched past the point and bore away down Gravesend Reach. The winch was re-assembled in time for us to wear round into Leigh Ray Gut, where we brought up for the night.

Next day our race crew came aboard and we scrubbed round on the Marsh End Sands at low water before sailing down to Southend, anchoring just west of the mile-and-a-quarter long pier. Saturday was fine but with little or no wind. Simon Lainé, owner of the *Saltcote Belle*, had lent us a magnificent staysail much larger than anything else we had; nothing could have suited the conditions better, so we awaited the 10.30 start cautiously optimistic that we would improve on our first match result at Pin Mill the previous year.

The starting gun saw us poorly placed among the tail-enders as we tacked with

Millie follows in *Kathleen's* wake during the Southend match in May, 1967. *A. Pyner*

the new flood to the West Leigh Middle buoy. Last but two around, we reached down the Estuary for the South Shoebury buoy some eight miles distant and, much to our surprise, soon began to leave the last two barges further astern and began to overhaul first *Kitty* and then Gordon Swift's *Dawn*. By the time we were off Shoeburyness, the wind had almost died away and the flood tide was at its strongest. Two of the leading barges had kept the last of the breeze to the buoy and were being carried upriver in fine style, but other competitors had not fared so well, having been swept to the west by the strong tide before rounding the mark; they were now behind us as we held on well beyond the buoy before tacking. To minimise the effect of the adverse tide we crept over the Maplin Sands in water barely deeper than our draft; the bottom was so clear that we could see the scurrying flatfish as our approach disturbed their sunbathing.

After much discussion we decided to lay the mark, and all appeared well; we were holding our course and were now lying in third place. Just when it seemed we were about to round, Les bore away past the black conical buoy and headed up into the wind. Contrary to my own thoughts, Les was right in assuming that the mark was to be rounded to port, certainly an impossibility from the north shore under the prevailing conditions. We were quickly swept upstream and our chances of a place disappeared.

A little later the committee boat hailed us and the other barges advising us to retire as there was no chance of completing the course in time for the evening's festivities. Regretfully we complied, as did most of the opposition; only *Mirosa*, *May*, and *Venture*, coming from the Medway shore, successfully completed the course to take first, second and third places respectively.

We consoled ourselves with the dubious honour of being "best loser" and anchored back at the pier ready for the trip across the estuary next day for the Medway race on Bank Holiday Monday.

The Medway approaches are dominated by the vast bulk of the Sheerness fortifications which loom straight out of the river on the port hand. We had little more wind than on Saturday and narrowly avoided getting caught up in the fierce eddies and tide rip off Garrison Point. Once through the entrance, however, we were greeted by much smoother, broadening waters and by a freshening breeze from the South.

Disaster struck as we tacked up Kethole Reach, the topsail tearing along the boltrope and then about eight or ten feet up the cloths, the tear getting worse as I scampered forward to let go the halliard and sheet, heaving on the clewline as the sail ran down the topmast. Unfortunately our misfortune had occurred on the wrong tack; half the sail was on one side of the mast cap and the rest, including the headstick, still flogging about on the other side. With very little room to manoeuvre the barge in those confined waters there was little we could do to prevent the topsail continuing to tear itself apart; it was some time before I could go aloft and pass the gasket round the tattered remnants.

All was gloom when I returned to the deck. It was already late afternoon, and with the race starting early the following morning there seemed little chance of our taking part.

We anchored off Gillingham pier among many other barges, most of which had arrived an hour or so before us. Repairing the sail seemed our only chance, as a suitable replacement could obviously not be found, so once the inevitable cup of tea had been taken care of, the topsail was unbent and lowered to the deck for inspection. While our worst fears were not confirmed, the damage was severe. We decided to cut up an old hatch cloth for the repairs, the sail was spread out on the main hatch and the arduous work began. An additional sailmaker's palm was borrowed from the *Millie* so that two could work at the same time round the ten-foot-long patch.

One by one the crews from the other barges set off for an evening's merrymaking ashore, made all the more enjoyable by the good-natured rivalry over who was going to do best on race day. Frequent shouted invitations to join the party were regretfully turned down, and our predicament explained to those that sculled by us. Soon the barges all around us were deserted, with riding lights rigged and lit for the impending night. Aboard *Kathleen* we toiled on, stitching "homeward-bounders" into the stiff canvas to the accompaniment of our own curses as thumbs and forefingers blistered from our urgent labours.

As darkness fell we still had much left to do, so we rigged Tilley lanterns to work by. The last stitch was done as somewhere in Gillingham a clock struck midnight. With no chance of bending on the sail in the dark, we turned in below, fed up with having missed the barside chatter and ale but consoled by the thought that we would after all be competing in the morning.

An early start to the day saw our topsail rigged before breakfast; we were under way in good time, anxious to test the results of our sailmaking skills before the breeze became too strong. The extent of our stitching was there for all to see, the bright green of the tarpaulin patches contrasting vividly with the deep rust colour of the sail dressing.

Despite quite a good start we were soon overhauled by most of the faster barges as we ran with the wind from the South-west towards the turning mark off the beach at Sheerness. There was not much strength to the breeze and the outward leg took a

long time to complete, especially the last mile against the first of the flood. Once round the mark our progress improved, and with the wind increasing and veering more southerly very long tacks were possible toward the north bank. On some reaches we fetched through without putting in a tack at all. With the fleet so spread out there was little competitive element left in the race for us tail-enders, but excitement briefly reappeared as we entered the closing minutes of the race. We had hardly noticed how we had been creeping up on the *Millie* until we passed Folly Fort, some few cables from the finish. She was well to leeward and would almost

Opposite: Riding lights are rigged on *Kathleen* and other barges lying in the Medway after the 1967 Medway match. *A. Cordell*

Right: A fine bow view of *Kathleen* taken during the 1967 Medway race. *A. Brown*

certainly have to tack just before the line, whereas a windshift in our favour looked likely to carry us straight across. No such luck; the wind veered again as we approached, forcing us to bear away quite violently and allowing *Millie* to finish a minute ahead.

If nothing else, we were well pleased with the way the tops'l repair had held together and were confident that the passage to the Blackwater could safely be attempted, weather permitting, the next weekend. Les, myself and a couple of friends assembled on the Friday evening at Gillingham pier and put off aboard. We were the only barge from the previous weekend's match still anchored off the pier. All was well aboard and we agreed that with tides the way they were and the forecast announcing south-westerly, force one to two, there was little point in getting under way much before 09.30 next morning.

At 5.30, however, we were rudely awakened by a boat's hooter followed by distorted shouts of "*Kathleen* ahoy" through a loud hailer. Tumbling on to deck in our pyjamas, Les and I found ourselves facing the Royal Navy. A crisp-looking sub-lieutenant commanding an immaculate pinnace ordered us to move immediately; we were apparently obstructing the entrance to Chatham Dockyard, and a newly re-commissioned submarine was waiting to leave. Just as I was about to reply that we would do our best to get out of the way, Les cupped his hands to his face and shouted "We're not planning to move till half past nine, we've no engine, there's no wind, and the tide's against us till then," adding as an afterthought, "If you can't wait, it'll have to go underneath us!"

Our sub-lieutenant, noticeably ruffled, consulted with two of his crew. I can only suppose that they had a certain respect for the stubbornness of the average barge skipper as, with the muffled roar of powerful engines, they sped off whence they had come without another word.

With so little wind we hardly had steerage way as we carried our tide out into the estuary. We narrowly missed being set on to the s.s *Richard Montgomery*, that infamous American ammunition ship wreck which stands guard at the Medway approaches. As we wallowed in the slight swell the otherwise mirror-like sea bore a rubbish-filled tea chest abeam of us. By some quirk of tides, first the tea chest overtook us, then we the tea chest, and so on for an hour or so. Eventually a slant of breeze was "bought" by Les, who in true sailorman tradition had been pitching his small change over the side in order to purchase a little wind.

Most of the day was behind us by the time the Shoebury shore was reached. We anchored to wait for the ebb, which then took us down the Essex coast during the early hours of Sunday morning, enabling us to anchor in time for a drink and lunch in the *Jolly Sailor* at Heybridge.

The familiar faces of friends in the bar made this a bit of a homecoming. It was, after all, some ten months since *Kathleen* had left the Basin, and many people were keen to hear of our wanderings.

CHAPTER TWENTY-TWO

Fourth Home!

KATHLEEN slipped quietly over the finishing line at Maldon to the applause of the crowd on the Promenade, who presumably believed that we had achieved a memorable class win and a creditable fourth place overall.

Alas, we felt more than a little guilty at receiving that applause, for we had hauled down our code flag some time earlier to signify our having retired from the race. I mused that it was unlikely we would ever deserve such an ovation.

We had never been in with a chance. By the time I had arrived at Heybridge that morning Les was organising a lift to the *Kathleen* aboard the Swedish galeas *Borneo*, which was leaving the Basin to follow the day's racing. Les was as usual wearing his immaculate white cheesecutter cap and was travelling light, his kit comprising only the race instructions, his lunch box and, of course, a packet of Ty-Phoo.

There was as little wind for the Blackwater match as there had been for any of the other 1967 matches. Many of the barges coming down from Maldon Hythe were being towed towards the start line, and Les and I were concerned that we would not make it in time unless we too were able to arrange a tow. We were mightily relieved when John Kemp hailed us from the East Coast Sail Trust's barge *Thalatta* inviting us to throw him a line.

Only the crack auxiliary barges took the trouble of removing their propellers to reduce drag; thus the *Thalatta* was able to use her auxiliary to take her down to the start way downriver at Osea Island. We stowed all the sails we had just set, with the exception of the topsail, and followed *Thalatta* towards the start line. We would make it!

We would have done, too, except for a shouted comment being misunderstood aboard the *Thalatta*. Our towrope was let go! Thus we found ourselves crossing the line many minutes after the starting gun and already at the back of the fleet, behind even the faster barges which had started half an hour after the rest. Our own class were just specks on the horizon.

The slight breeze which came up as we started had fallen away again by the time we were off the Colne. Laid-up merchant ships of the Union-Castle and Blue Star lines anchored in the estuary of the Blackwater provided marks by which we could judge our dismal progress, and we eventually rounded the outer mark just ahead of *Spinaway C*, which was rounding it for the second time. She was leading the class for the faster barges and had rounded the mark for the first time an hour or so before. Not long afterwards the *May* and then *Mirosa* overhauled us, and by the time we reached the inner mark for the first time the leading barges were ploughing on to the finish, and even the slower barges in our class were well on their way back to the outer mark, the nearest of them at least a mile ahead of us.

Les was concerned that we would have to sail against the tide to the outer mark and then have to fight the ebb back to the Maldon. It did not need a mathematician to do the necessary calculation; the formula was *closing time minus sailing time equals drinking time*, and in our case this produced a minus answer. This was obviously unacceptable to the entire crew, and the decision was made to press on straight up to Maldon.

Thus it was that we received the undeserved applause of the spectators on Maldon Promenade and came alongside the Hythe Quay on one of the innermost berths, the fourth barge "home". We moored up and then stepped aboard *Spinaway C* to congragulate the crew on their victory before settling down to watch the other barges wending their way up the tortuous channel to the finish.

After the presentation of prizes on the steps of the Maldon Yacht Club we all walked over to the *Jolly Sailor* to while away the time until the organised social events of the evening got under way. The sole topic of conversation at the barge match supper was, as ever, the racing of a few hours before.

The discussion was continued on Sunday morning when, up late, we wandered ashore at opening time to wash away the effects of an indulgent evening with a little more of the same recipe. Sober decisions had to be made, however, and it was decided to sail for Pin Mill the following weekend. Les would not be available, so I decided to take the barge myself and asked a chap from the Thames Barge Sailing Club to come as mate, plus Terry Smith, our crew on the trip from Pin Mill to Grays, as third hand.

We floated just after two on the Saturday morning. Casting off the heavy coir moorings we extricated ourselves from the other barges at the crowded quay. Under topsail and foresail only and with a fair wind over our quarter we slid silently away, down past the Maldon smacks hard by the Promenade and on past the old ballast crane at the top end of Colliers Reach, hardening our mainsheet to sail closer to the wind to weather Northey Island. Narrowly missing a string of unlit timber lighters off the Blackwater Sailing Club, we eased our sheets as we bore away into the ever-broadening Blackwater. With the moon appearing intermittently, a fine wind, and the bright lights of Bradwell power station to navigate by, there could have been no more pleasant job than sailing a barge that warm summer's night.

Dawn began to beckon us from out to sea as we left the estuary behind. Jaywick and Clacton came abeam as the first drops of rain pattered on the deck and hatches. Terry noticed that the dawn had been overpowered by the rainclouds and that it was getting darker again, and we donned our oilskins as the wind began to whip up white horses on the wavecrests. Walton pier and the coastline disappeared from view in the thickening downpour.

The barge was running dart before the wind on a compass course for the Medusa buoy and was becoming difficult to manage. The ebb was still with us, but in the

The *Spinaway C*, formerly owned by Ipswich millers Cranfield Brothers. *R. Malster*

conditions prevailing it was such hard work steering for more than ten minutes at a time that Terry and I took regular turns at the wheel. Despite the rough going, *Kathleen* appeared to be enjoying the weather.

We brailed a few cloths of the mainsail, but we should really have rucked the topsail to make sure we didn't carry away the topmast. Our third hand magicked a flask of brandy from an innermost pocket with the remark that it was "part of his survival kit."

I have no idea what speed we were making, but in a situation where we could not see much further than a couple of barge lengths into the murk I began to get concerned about getting out of the Wallet channel into shoal waters. Our bow wave was still climbing high but the rain had eased and the sky was beginning to lighten from the west, and soon it was possible to discern Walton pier some way behind us, so we knew that the Medusa could not be far. Sure enough, as the clearing sky overtook us and hurried on eastwards the buoy appeared almost dead ahead, half a mile away.

Although our gear had manfully survived quite a battering over the previous few hours, I was very uneasy about subjecting it to a heavy gybe when rounding the Naze. With the wind moderating a little we got ready to tack round. As we came into the wind the mousing of the mainsheet block came adrift, allowing the hook to disengage from the mainhorse traveller. The terrifying effect of this was to allow the mainsheet and block, aided by 1500 square feet of flogging mainsail, to flail around like a demented blacksmith. The thrashing block gouged great lumps out of the hatch top and rail as its violent gyrations continued unabated. It would have been suicidal to have tried to grab at it, so I bore away until the mainsail calmed down against the topmast runner. Terry could then reach the brail winch in safety and retrieve the sail sufficiently to enable us to reunite the block and traveller, this time with a secure lashing.

Once the panic was over we realised that we were already heading into Harwich, still with the wind abaft the beam. To sail east, then north-east, then almost west, all in the space of a few hours, with a fair wind all the time must be an extraordinary piece of luck. We had made such a good passage that there was little water in the Orwell as we took the young flood up to Pin Mill. Despite the fair wind, the trip had been physically exhausting, and I decided to anchor on the north side of the river and to take our dinghy ashore to arrange a tow through the crowded moorings to the barge hard. In the *Butt and Oyster* I found Mick Lungley, one of Paul's barge skippers, who offered to save me the cost of a tug by sailing the *Kathleen* to her berth. He pronounced *Kathleen* much handier than he had expected, and proved it by taking her for a spin up the river, weaving in and out of the Woolverstone yacht moorings as if aboard a racing dinghy. We had taken under eight hours for the passage from Maldon to Pin Mill, not at all bad for one of the slow barges!

Barges lying in the Orwell off Pin Mill under a threatening sky. *R. Malster*

CHAPTER TWENTY-THREE

Charter Work

FOR the first time I was able to see underneath *Kathleen's* hull. She lay on the blocks on Pin Mill hard, having taken the place of Bob Roberts' big mulie *Cambria*, which had been having a lick of paint and a coat of anti-fouling in preparation for a hard winter's trading.

With her towering grey sides making her look every bit of her 79 registered tons, the *Cambria* looked magnificent sitting there on the hard. *Kathleen* did not look too bad, either. The bare pitchpine planks and flat elm keel were virtually clean, and I was spared the task of scraping off weed which would have grown if we had spent long periods afloat without taking the ground. We scrubbed round and repainted her from chine to deck level with shiny black bitumastic.

With a couple of weekends left before the Pin Mill barge match I arranged to sail to Wrabness the next Saturday and for a charter party the weekend after. Both trips held a few surprises for us.

The first outing started very sedately with *Kathleen* drifting off the hard at high water. With a little wind from the North-west we slipped down towards Buttermans Bay between the numerous moorings and the shore, but we experienced some difficulty in staying to windward and, with Pin Mill less than five hundred yards away, we ground to a halt on the sandy beach. We pushed and we shoved, but there we stayed; and we were quickly high and dry. And we stayed there for the rest of the day and for Sunday morning as well; at least we were able to walk back to the *Butt and Oyster* for a drink on the Saturday evening.

At high water at lunchtime on the Sunday we floated off, and under topsail and foresail sailed back towards the hard. With a number of barges gathered for the forthcoming match, the moorings on the hard were very crowded. As we approached it was apparent that our speed was somewhat higher than desirable, so we dropped the foresail and subsequently the topsail to slow *Kathleen* down, but we were still carrying our way a lot further than I expected. It seemed to us and to the people on the moored barges that a collision with one or other of the barges was unavoidable. I dropped the anchor under our stem, and when that did not seem to check our way lowered the leeboards so that they would touch the muddy bottom. With uncanny precision we stopped just eighteen inches short of the *Venture*, much to the relief of those on board both barges. I have to admit that I tried to create the impression that our arrival had been under control from start to finish; whether anyone believed me I have no idea!

The Stansted Abbotts Young Farmers' Club charter was perhaps the least cost-effective business venture *Kathleen* ever undertook in her long trading career.

Not that there is anything incompatible in barges and farmers; for over two hundred years they co-existed very much for mutual benefit. East Coast farms provided feedstuffs for the London horses which drew all the traffic, and the barges which delivered hay brought away manure or "London Mixture" as it was known for spreading on the fields; a totally compatible and inter-dependent trade carried on by spritties which were in many cases owned by the farmers whose cargoes they carried. Sad to say, *Kathleen's* 1968 venture had no such fundamental purpose; my interest in the Young Farmers was their preparedness to part with a very modest £12, and their benefit was to have been a pleasurable weekend's sailing in exchange.

I was on my own for the weekend and would have to rely on the charterers to help with the running of the barge, my intention being to sail with the morning tide on the Saturday and to return at midday on Sunday. The *Butt and Oyster* was crowded on Friday evening; locals like Ephraim Sharman and Bill Simpson, as much a part of Pin Mill as the pub itself, sat in their regular places as they had done most evenings as long as anyone could remember. Then there were the yachting fraternity,

A misty morning on the Orwell. The windward leeboard is partially lowered and is being held out from *Kathleen's* side by the leeway she is making. *R. J. Walsh*

some from the Royal Harwich Yacht Club and others, of course, from the Pin Mill Sailing Club. There, too, were the visiting yachtsmen, those who had popped round from the Walton and Frinton Club just south of Harwich, and others from as far afield as Holland, Belgium and France. The common denominator, other than the alcoholic one, was an interest in the river and the craft that sailed it.

At about eight o'clock the first of the charter party arrived at the "*Butt*". With beers all round as each successive charterer arrived, by the time the whole party was assembled those who had been there at the start were fairly well departed from sobriety. In such circumstances, I was soon persuaded by my agricultural accomplices that we should leave on the high water some half an hour later. Borrowing the *Venture's* boat, ours being totally inadequate for such numbers, I ferried our party aboard. The north-westerly breeze was damp and light, the night pitch black without a star in sight.

My plan was to slip seawards twixt moorings and shore, luffing into the channel just above Buttermans Bay. On such a dark night it would be difficult to judge distance and speed, so I asked one of the young farmers to go forward with a powerful torch. The idea was to illuminate the moored boats to port and to spot the wreck marker laid where a charter yacht had sunk during the previous week. Shedding our mooring lines, I turned our bows eastwards into the gloom.

As we slid through the shallow water my lookout on the bow swept his torch aimlessly from side to side, mainly pointed skyward, and in a manner totally useless as an aid to navigation. The fact that the wreck marker rushed past our side without so much as a murmur from those on watch should have served as a warning of impending problems. Even in the blackness of night, as my eyes began to adjust to the environment I was able to discern the occasional white hull moored to port and the tree-shrouded shoreline opposite, but this awareness was instantly removed by the lookout, who swung his torch aft, totally dazzling me, and at the same time announced that he could see some yachts moored ahead. "How far?" I asked. "A long way off yet," came the answer, "but I'll let you know if we need to alter course."

I calculated that we would soon be below the moorings and free to swing out into the fairway and so on down to Shotley, where we would anchor for the night.

"Yachts dead ahead!" came a shout from the bow. "How far away?"

"Difficult to say in the dark."

"Should I alter course?"

"No," followed by a pause and then, "I'm sure we shall hit them anyway."

I left the wheel and sped forward. There, just in front of us, in a neat line across our path, lay a string of dinghies. Our only hope was to attempt to pass between two of the dinghies, despite the gaps between them appearing somewhat less than our beam. We wound up the leeward leeboard as, back at the wheel, I swung the barge's bow towards one of the narrow gaps. Amazingly, it was beginning to look as if we might get through, despite now realising that we were passing over a line which stretched from one boat to another. When almost clear, the mooring rope was caught between our sternpost and rudder, and almost at once the dinghies on either side veered together and began to follow us. I poked about with a boat hook, hoping I could free the rope, but to no avail. As our way carried us onwards, despite brailing the mainsail and dropping fore and topsail, two further dinghies fell in astern like soldiers, then another two, then two more, and ultimately, with only a hint of resistance, the launching pontoon from the shore joined in astern.

The lights of Clamp House Sailing School were coming on one by one, though what had made them aware of the disappearance of their fleet I could not guess. The throbb of an engine signalled more activity, and from out of the darkness a flashlight scoured the river. We had anchored by this time, swinging to our cable dangerously near the motor barge *Redoubtable* displaying the warning flag and red wale of an explosives carrier. With the ebb running strongly, the Wayfarer dinghies strung out astern were knocking hell out of each other as the sailing school motor boat came alongside. A quick count of the hulls somehow created the impression that we had lost some of our original flock; it occurred to me that any so lost would by then have been dashing out through Harwich on the tide, and with the same thought the motor boat sped off into the night, leaving us to sort out the remainder, which took until dawn. The motor boat returned empty handed; a re-count revealed that no boats were missing anyway. What a relief!

The rest of the weekend slipped by uneventfully, and at lunchtime on Sunday young farmers and *Kathleen* parted company after a short but memorable voyage! The cost of repairs to the dinghies was many times the charter fee.

CHAPTER TWENTY-FOUR

Collision!

THERE was more breeze than we had come to expect on race days for *Kathleen's* second Orwell match, that of 1967. There was a crowd aboard *Kathleen* that day; our usual race crew, plus quite a few passengers, including a reporter and a photographer from the American *Time* magazine; expensive photographic equipment was festooned everywhere, and the cameras consumed film at great speed.

We arrived at the line in company with *Dawn*, *Millie*, *Centaur*, *Remercie*, *Saltcote Belle* and a few more. The five-minute gun had been fired and we sailed about in close company, jockeying for advantage by getting on starboard tack up to windward to ensure a more advantageous first leg. The little cannons belonging to Pin Mill Sailing Club made a very impressive report as they sent the barges on their journey down to Harwich harbour and the first turning mark. As they had done previously, the race organisers set a river course; first down the Orwell to the Cliff Foot buoy off Harwich and then a leg up the equally picturesque Stour to Harkstead Point, back to the Cliff Foot buoy, just seaward of Felixstowe Dock, and then back to Pin Mill. With a split fleet, the faster barges having a later start, and the multiplicity of short legs on the course, the barges sailed backward and forward in all directions.

Despite a respectable start, we had been overhauled by most of the fleet by the time we were approaching the Cliff Foot buoy for the second time. Les decided to put in a long tack to the Felixstowe shore in the hope that the ebb would carry us down a long way towards the outer mark. The *Saltcote Belle*, just astern of us as we came into the confluence of the two rivers, tacked towards Harwich town before standing out for the buoy on a long starboard tack across the harbour. As we winded by the Felixstowe container terminal, the *Saltcote Belle* appeared to have gained from her manoeuvre, and although half a mile away, looked to me as if she would reach the turn just ahead of us.

A few minutes later a slight wind shift headed the opposition and gave us back some of the ground we had just lost. It would be a close thing at the mark, and I asked Les if we should turn to avoid having to tack into the *Saltcote Belle's* lee. He thought that with any luck we would be across her bow with room to spare, an opinion I had my doubts about. There was still plenty of sea room between us and there was no immediate necessity to come to a decision.

After a few more minutes our converging courses still looked likely to require us

An unusual view of the foredeck showing the massive anchor windlass. The foresail is about to have the downhaul wound around it to secure the sail ready for stowing. *Author's collection* to give way to the *Saltcote Belle* as she continued on starboard tack, and therefore with right-of-way. I mentioned to Les that I thought we should tack, but he steadfastly held his course towards the buoy in spite of the rapidly closing gap between the two barges. It was now becoming apparent to the other crew members, and possibly some of our passengers, that unless we acted soon there was a real possibility of a collision. Les was unmoved. He argued that, despite being on port tack, we had right-of-way as we were in the act of rounding the mark.

"She'll bear away under our stern in a moment," he said, concentrating his gaze on the buoy, still some way off.

Somebody on the *Saltcote Belle* was standing in the bow waving his arms at us and yelling over the wind.

Both vessels stood on until only a couple of barge lengths separated us. It was strange how people reacted to the impending collision, which was by this time inevitable. Most stood absolutely silent and still, as if transfixed to the deck. A few people retreated from where they imagined the point of impact would be; our intrepid photographer friend did the opposite and leapt over the hatches towards the *Saltcote Belle's* fast-approaching bow, his camera working overtime as he snapped and wound on.

I just grabbed one of the rubber tyres we used for fenders in the hope that at least some of the force of the blow could be absorbed if I could get it over the side in time. Les also reacted, rapidly spinning the wheel, but he acted far too late to prevent the sickening sound of splintering timber as the *Saltcote Belle's* stempost and port bow crashed into us, just aft of the rigging chock. Both barges reared up from the impact, stopped dead in their tracks, and then quickly drifted apart as the sails were taken aback and then filled on a new tack.

We must be taking on water at an alarming rate! With Les organising a reduction in sail, I dashed down the companion way to assess the damage. Everything looked normal down below, except for a few broken mugs that had fallen on to the steel keelson. A hurried glance at the bilges showed that *Kathleen* remained as tight as she always had been.

Much relieved, I returned on deck. The *Saltcote Belle* had anchored and was presumably assessing her damage. She had also raised a protest flag to her crosstrees, indicating where her skipper thought blame for the incident should lie. Les was unrepentant, and had organised full sail again with the intention of completing the course.

Why had Les not tacked earlier to avoid the collision, I wanted to know. It seemed that his brother Syd had left the *Dawn* and shipped aboard the *Saltcote Belle*

Kitty takes *Kathleen's* wind when racing on the Orwell in 1967.
Fred Cooper collection

KATHLEEN

as skipper; bargemen can be a stubborn breed, and when two brothers are competing in the same barge match anything can happen. And it had!

We completed the course, with at least one or two barges behind us. Over a pint at the bar in the Pin Mill Sailing Club the owner of the *Saltcote Belle* and I talked the matter over; he agreed that his protest would really serve no useful purpose and sportingly withdrew it. He told me that the damage to his barge seemed surprisingly slight and that he felt the whole incident was best forgotten.

* * * *

When Mary, whom I had met earlier in the year aboard the *Millie*, and I decided to get married we needed the deposit for a house. The barge was our only realisable asset, and after considerable heartsearching we eventually advertised *Kathleen* for sale. The response was staggering. We had more than forty inquiries, some from people wanting to transform the barge into something she was not; TV companies wishing to convert her to a Roman galley for film work; a club owner requiring her for a floating restaurant; even a group of Welsh miners wanting to take her pearl diving in the Pacific!

From this array of contacts emerged Pat Murphy, who was interested in keeping her sailing. A price was agreed and from then on *Kathleen's* new owner carefully undertook the work that I wished I had the time and money to do myself. Two Kelvin 44 h.p. diesels were installed, a radio telephone was fitted, and a host of other equipment was put in to provide every facility within the practical family accommodation Pat had organised below.

A fine pair of leeboards were discovered on the *Wolsey*, which by this time was moored as a houseboat on the Thames at Isleworth. After a somewhat hazardous morning removing them, using oil drums as buoyancy, we managed by late afternoon to float them ashore at nearby Lion Wharf. By then it was dark, and our efforts at loading the leeboards on to our lorry were interrupted by the constabulary; it took some time to convince them that ours was an honest though unusual labour. By the time we had done so we were too late to drive straight up to Pin Mill, so it was a four o'clock start in order that the lorry could be returned to Enfield by nine.

Pat Murphy also bought much-needed new sails and had Reuben and Freddy Webb do some long-overdue jobs on the hull. Some new inwale, covering board and rail was fitted, and repairs were done to the ceiling and lining prior to partitioning in softwood for the toilet and bathroom forward and a new cabin aft. The beam under the main hatch forward headledge had a new end skilfully scarfed in, and the cabin top aft was modified to accommodate the engine controls. The whole main hatch top was completed with a glass-fibre sheathing and a proper companionway with sliding hatch installed. By the time these extensive works were all completed, *Kathleen* had lain with topsides exposed to the sun for many months and on her first sail after refitting, in the spring of 1969, dried-out timbers and open seams resulted in some quite serious leaks; the worst of these were cured when a new apron was fitted, and the remainder more or less took care of themselves.

CHAPTER TWENTY-FIVE

To Holland

KATHLEEN heaved and rolled uncomfortably as she set course for the N.E. Gunfleet, whence she would steer direct for Holland.

She had come downriver from Pin Mill under her two diesels, but to steady her it was decided to set the topsail, no easy task when the masthead was describing wild arcs in the sky as *Kathleen* pitched and wallowed in an uneasy sea. Eventually, however, the gasket securing the sail was let go and after coming up into the wind to ease the load on the halliard, the topsail was set.

Pat Murphy had chosen an inauspicious month of 1971 for the trip to Holland. Already *Kathleen* had lain at Pin Mill for the best part of a week waiting for a strong north-easterly wind to moderate, and on the morning she set out under power the 1.55 a.m. weather forecast, a tape of which Pat played over before making his decision to leave, spoke of winds north-easterly 5 gusting 6, with the possibility of some fog. But with the two engines as well as her sails the prospects for the trip did not seem too daunting.

The topsail was soon setting well, but troubles were in store for *Kathleen*. Before she reaches the N.E. Gunfleet the starboard leeboard touched bottom; it was progressively raised as the *Kathleen* stood on, while a couple of yachts which had earlier been nearby bore away to the South. The leeboard continued to kick, and eventually it was wound right up, then the rudder jumped as it touched the bottom in a trough of the rather confused swell. This was almost certainly the Cork Sand, which is avoided by deep-draughted vessels but over which a barge like the *Kathleen* with her shallow draught might safely sail when conditions were right.

She was soon over and into deeper water, but it then became apparent that she was making rather more water than could be ignored. The water was probably coming through seams around her wales and covering board which had opened up; the heavy swell was sluicing around the hull and sometimes spilling on deck. An unfortunate effect of this situation was that fragments of soft timber from the top of her uprights, undisturbed for years, were washed down between the outer hull planking and the lining into the bilges, soon clogging the automatic pumps.

A semi-rotary hand pump was cleared, and this made it possible to keep pace with the incoming water, though to keep the flywheel of the starboard engine clear of the bilgewater it was necessary to pump continuously.

As the day wore on the strong winds and lumpy sea showed no signs of abating. The crew were getting tired and the continuing necessity to keep the pumps going was causing concern. The conspicuous light tower at the entrance to the Schelde was clearly visible in the distance; the Dutch coast was not far off.

There was, though, the prospect of arriving at a foreign port among busy shipping lanes at night. In the circumstances that prospect was not a cheerful one, and the decision was taken to turn back. By lunchtime the following morning *Kathleen* was back at Pin Mill.

She spent three more seasons on the Orwell, and then in 1975 Pat Murphy again planned to sail her to Holland, this time with a view to selling her there. Remembering what had happened in 1971, Pat planned to arrive at the Hook of Holland in daylight.

Thus it was that *Kathleen* slipped away from Pin Mill on the evening of 3rd July, 1975, with her owner on board, together with a few of his family and friends, including a couple of local people from Pin Mill and a prospective purchaser along for the trip.

Once clear of Harwich harbour *Kathleen* romped along, helped by a brisk

The jagged end of the sprit and broken stump of the topmast bear witness to *Kathleen's* ordeal in the North Sea.
F. Everitt collection

breeze from the North-north-east, about force 5. After agreeing watches for the night most of the crew turned in for some sleep, but not before someone had remarked on the water which was beginning to lay to leeward by the starboard chine keelson. The amount was nothing to worry about, no more than was to be expected in a vessel which no longer kept her side planking tight by regular work deep laden; a barge, being flat bottomed and having vertical sides, will soon show bilgewater in the hold if she heels.

As dawn approached the watch was changed. One of the crew occupying the top bunk in the old crew accommodation aft climbed down, waking his compatriot sleeping in the bunk below. Exchanging a few words with his relief, the helmsman handed over the wheel and went below to get some well-earned sleep in the bunk just vacated by his relief. The second disturbance was just too much for the occupant of the lower bunk, who was by then wide awake and decided to "sniff the dawn".

Climbing the companion way, he was greeted by a breeze which had gained a little in strength since the evening before. An offer of bacon and eggs was gratefully accepted by the man at the wheel, so the other crewman went to the companion way in the starboard side of the main hatch abaft the mastcase. Descending the steps, he found bilgewater some two feet deep.

He raced back on deck to raise the alarm. The first concern was to get to the owner's cabin, as this could become cut off if the water rose further, and Fred Everitt left the wheel, dashed forward and descended the foc's'le stairs, from which he waded through the deepening water to wake Pat Murphy.

With the others on board alerted to the danger, there was time to take stock of the situation. None of the pumps was effective and nothing could be done to reduce the steady increase in the depth of water in the hold. For the time being there seemed to be no difficulty in handling *Kathleen*, provided she remained on the port tack, so it was decided to continue. Not many hours went by before the level of water put the starboard engine out of use, for the massive flywheel was scooping up the water and scattering it around the engineroom. The other Kelvin was to windward and so was clear of the water; in any case, its bearers were significantly higher than those of the starboard engine.

As the day wore on the water level rose and *Kathleen's* movements became increasingly sluggish and unpredictable. The mass of water within the hull rushed first one way and then another, often exaggerating the angle of heel when the surge of water to leeward coincided with one of the many squalls which reflected a general worsening in the weather. The coast of Holland was no more than twenty miles away, and *Kathleen* would be in safety in just a few hours.

Suddenly, with a crack like a rifle shot, the topmast snapped a few feet above the mainmast cap and disappeared into the sea to leeward, leaving a tangled mass of rigging and cordage on deck. The topsail, still attached to the barge, thrashed around in the sea, half filling with wind one minute, half submerged the next and acting like an enormous sea anchor. Obviously the sail must either be retrieved or it must be cut adrift. In order to get the sail close alongside, the barge was put head to wind while four of the crew struggled with the unwieldy mass like fishermen hauling an overloaded net.

The deepening water down below caused the barge to wallow and pitch violently, imposing further strain on the gear aloft. The mainsheet block charged from one end of the horse to the other, the peak of the sprit swinging equally violently fifty feet up.

With a splintering of timber the sprit broke just above the yard tackle iron band, the upper part falling vertically to the deck and embedding itself like an arrow in the main hatch cover no more than a foot from the men still struggling to secure the topsail. The lower 30 feet of sprit, with no vangs to control it, swung wildly from side to side and seemed likely also to crash down at any moment.

By good fortune a rope had become entangled in the splintered end of the sprit above the yard tackle attachment, and this line was taken forward and used to secure the broken sprit. The wind had reached force 8, gale force, and the barge, under foresail and mizzen only, had become very difficult to handle, her bows constantly falling off to leeward and the surging water below giving her a mind of her own. The port engine was still operating but it proved of little use in such circumstances, pushing the barge's head further from the wind.

There was no hope of making the Hook of Holland under such a handicap, so *Kathleen* bore away under one engine and what was left of her canvas in hopes of making the Wester Schelde. Progress was being made, and with the Dutch coast close at hand there appeared to be a good chance of *Kathleen* getting through unaided.

It was not to be. At around seven in the evening, with the prospect of darkness seeming very daunting, the mizzen sheet parted and the sail had to be brailed up, leaving *Kathleen* with just the foresail and one engine. A little later, as if to hasten the inevitable, the half-submerged port engine screamed in protest as the bearings, turning in water rather than oil, began to seize.

Just before eight o'clock a distress rocket was set off. *Kathleen* lay near buoy no. 9 in the Oostgat, with just her foresail left and the water down below about waist height. Radio Vlissingen reported the sighting of a rocket to the South Holland Lifeboat Service and by 8.25 p.m. the lifeboat *Javazee*, with Coxswain Cornelius Erasmus in command, was on her way to the casualty; the motor vessel *Stuyvesant* was standing by the *Kathleen* and was reporting her position to the *Javazee*. When the revolving lights of the lifeboat were sighted from the *Kathleen* two more rockets were fired to aid the *Javazee* in locating her, and at 9.45 p.m. the lifeboat came alongside the barge to put a line aboard for the tow into Breskens. It was a slow trip, the two vessels arriving at 11.25 p.m.

A large pump was bought aboard straight away, and by about 2.30 a.m. it was possible to examine the chaos down below. While the pumping was under way Pat Murphy and his crew were taken to the home of Ramon Quekelberghe, the lifeboat's engineer, for much-needed cups of coffee and baths.

By running the pumps every three hours or so it proved possible to keep pace with the leak, and with the help of Coxswain Erasmus arrangements were made for *Kathleen* to be slipped on a yard where the local fishing boats were maintained. The sprung chine seam which had caused near-disaster was soon successfully re-spiked.

Not long after this eventful voyage *Kathleen* was sold to Mr J. J. Schijf, of Bevervijk, who kept her in a small dock on the north side of the North Sea Canal a short distance inland from Ijmuiden. With a new topmast and sprit and with her sails, miraculously almost undamaged during that eventful North Sea crossing, and with a

Sorting out the muddle after *Kathleen* had been towed into Breskens by the lifeboat.
F. Everitt collection

new six-cylinder diesel fitted, she was soon to be seen motor-sailing on the Dutch waterways.

But *Kathleen's* Indian summer was drawing to a close and little if anything was spent on her upkeep. In 1979 she was sold to Adrian Brood, who with two friends intended to refit her yet again. Daunted by the task, however, Adrian's partners dropped out, leaving him with no option but to abandon his plans. She lay almost derelict, for sale at £2,000 or near offer. Some of her sails lay rotting down below under leaking hatch covers; the rest were missing; her engines stood rusting, partly dismantled and totally uncared for; her hold was littered with rotting cordage, corroded ironwork and a variety of neglected domestic items.

Epilogue

IT WAS in the summer of 1981 that I rediscovered *Kathleen* while I was on a business trip to Holland. Her mainmast caught my eye as I crossed the North Sea Canal by ferry; I could see that it was the mast of a Thames barge, but it was only when I went over to where she lay that I discovered that it was *Kathleen*.

I suppose it was inevitable that, as I looked at her languishing forlornly beside that Dutch waterway, I should ponder on the possibility of rescuing her for a second time. On my return I looked into the cost of towage and insurance, and searched for a berth where she could lie while restoration was undertaken. Then I went back to Holland with Mary and the children so we could all see what was involved and so I could make a more thorough examination of *Kathleen's* condition. We were all disappointed when we realised that money and time beyond our resources would have been needed to carry out *Kathleen's* restoration; no insurer would cover the towage risks without a small fortune being spent on her before she even left for England.

All the same, I could not bear to see all those spars and fittings going to waste; I had spent so much time and effort searching for them and fitting them fifteen years before. I resolved to acquire *Kathleen* so that I could remove her winches, ironwork, mast, sprit, leeboards and other items; they could be used to extend the life of some other sailing barge.

In due course I became owner of *Kathleen* for a second time and set to work to strip her bare of so much that I had painstakingly fitted; just four days and two large lorry loads later the task was complete. I had a last nostalgic look around in the dank hold and came across a number of barge match plaques from the sixties and seventies, badly stained and with their varnish peeling. I gathered them up as precious mementoes of *Kathleen's* sailing days and went off to meet Jan Witterman, who had expressed an interest in the barge when he stood watching me remove her gear.

Much to my surprise he was keen to buy her, primarily for her shafts and propellers and for one engine which he thought could be repaired to serve in a large

Plaques commemorating the Pin Mill match of 1966 and the 1967 Medway match still adorning the hold in 1981.

R. J. Walsh

ketch yacht he was building in Amsterdam. A deal was struck and I sold *Kathleen* for the second time, with some grounds for optimism that she might yet have a useful life ahead of her.

She lay in Ijmuiden for two more years without much attention being paid to her, but in the summer of 1983 she was towed to Spaarndam to be refurbished as a houseboat. With luck she may reach her century before the day inevitably comes when she is moved to some remote graveyard, there to lie abandoned and decaying until all trace of her disappears; a fate which has befallen so many of her sisters.

Much of the ironwork and the rigging and many of the spars removed from *Kathleen* live on in the sailing barge *Wyvenhoe*. Built in 1898 by Forrestt at Wivenhoe for Augustus George Hughes, of Providence Wharf, East Greenwich, the *Wyvenhoe* was described by the *Essex County Standard* as "a racing barge . . .

Kathleen lying at Ijmuiden after the author had removed her spars and many of her fittings for use in another barge.
R. J. Walsh

The *Wyvenhoe* taking part in the 1986 Pin Mill match.
R. Malster

designed for use upon the Thames". There is, however, no evidence that she ever competed in any sailing barge matches before being fully converted to power in 1923. Her original owner sold her in 1906 to the Tilbury Contracting and Dredging Company, and in 1916 she passed to the London and Rochester Barge Company, who traded with her until she was sold to Kennedy Marine Freights in 1970. She changed hands again in 1981 when Paynes Marine Transport put her to work supplying B.P. with stores and equipment for oil tankers at their Isle of Grain refinery, and in January, 1983, she was acquired by her present owners, who have carefully restored her to sailing condition. The last barge to be re-rigged directly out of trade, the *Wyvenhoe* returned to sail in 1984 for the first time in sixty years, and she has since enjoyed considerable success in the annual barge matches.

Glossary of Barge Terms

Backstay On a barge the topmast shrouds are sometimes known as "standing backstays" and the topmast backstays as "topmast running backstays".

Bilge The space between the bottom hull planking and the ceiling of the hold.

Bitt heads The tops of the two massive timbers, the windlass bitts, supporting the windlass.

Block A wooden or metal case containing sheaves over which a rope is rove.

Bob The houseflag or owner's flag, which is mounted on a spindle at the head of the topmast; short for bobfly. It is made up both of the flag itself and a wooden frame.

Boltropes Ropes sewn to the perimeter of a sail, usually in the case of barge sails made from tarred hemp.

Boomie A barge rigged with gaff and boom to both main and mizzen sails. While a sprittie brails up her sails, a boomie would lower hers. This is a more suitable rig than the spritsail rig for deep-sea work.

Brail Ropes or wires used to furl the spritsail by drawing it up to the mast in a manner similar to that used in opening a traditional theatre curtain.

Ceiling The inside planking forming the floor of a barge's hold; at the sides the **lining** is carried up to just beneath the inwale.

Chaffcutter A barge's wheel of cast iron which in appearance resembles the style of cast-iron wheel used on agricultural implements, including chaffcutters, hence the name.

Chainplate An iron strap with an eye at one end for the attachment of a deadeye, the other end being fastened to the barge's side.

Chine The angle where the barge's bottom planks meet the side planking; the edge at which the chine side plank and under chine plank meet.

Deadeye A circular turned block of hardwood which is grooved around its circumference and pierced with three holes, used in pairs to secure the shrouds to the chainplates. A lanyard is rove through the holes in the deadeyes to create a purchase by which the shroud is set up taut. Originally "dead men's eyes".

Floor A transverse structural timber to which the bottom planking is fastened. The ends of the floor timbers are joined to the bottom of the frames. The keelson is fastened on top of the floors, and the hold ceiling is fastened to the top of the floors.

Fore horse A transverse wooden or iron beam or wire fitted forward of the mainmast around which the foresail sheet is fastened, allowing the sheet to traverse freely.

Huffler A man employed to assist the barge's crew to take their craft up tortuous channels to remote wharves or through bridges, as in London, Rochester, etc.

Homeward bounder A deep-sea expression for large herringbone stitches used in repairing sails.

Keelson A baulk of timber or a steel girder fitted on top of the floors to form the backbone of the barge; it is through-bolted to the keel, with the ends scarphed to the deadwood at stem and stern. Chine keelsons of more modest dimensions are fitted inside the frames at the junction of floors and frames.

Leeboard A large fan-shaped wooden board fitted at each side of a barge and pivoted at its forward end. When the board on the lee side is lowered it increases the effective draught of the barge and serves to reduce the amount of leeway when sailing close-hauled. It operates in much the same way as the centreplate of a dinghy.

Leeboard irons Iron bars running from a strap by the mainmast case to the head of each leeboard, by which means the leeboards are supported.

Leeboard pendant A wire or chain connecting the leeboard to a single whip purchase, the fall of which is led to a winch on the barge's quarter. The end of the pendant is shackled about half way down the fan of the leeboard.

Light irons Iron bars mounted in sockets by the main shrouds which support the light boxes or screens in which are hung the navigation lamps, port and starboard.

Luff The forward edge of a fore-and-aft sail.
The process of pointing a sailing vessel closer to the wind.

Main horse A transverse beam of timber fitted on chocks abaft the main hatch and shaped so that when the sail is sheeted home amidships it will travel to either side without attention. The mainsheet block is hooked to an iron ring or traveller which is free to move from side to side along the horse.

Mizzen The small mast stepped at or near the stern of a barge, and the sail set on the mizzen mast. This sail, like the barge's mainsail, is usually rigged with a sprit.

Mulie A barge with a sprit-rigged mainsail and a large gaff-rigged mizzen. The mizzen mast is set forward of the wheel and the sail sheeted to the saddle chock.

Pawls Iron "fingers" fitted on the windlass and winches, engaging in the teeth of the barrel to ensure that the windlass or winch cannot reverse under load.

Saddle chock A transverse beam fitted on deck at the stern, directly over the transom and usually supporting fairleads for mooring warps.

Sheet A rope used to trim a sail to the wind. In the case of a barge this is usually of three-inch manilla, hitched to the clew of the sail and passing through a double block hooked to the traveller on the main horse and two single blocks on the leech of the sail.

Sprit A large spar used to extend the peak of the spritsail. It extends between the peak of the sail and the foot of the mast, to which it is held by the muzzle and band; the downward thrust of the sprit is taken by the stanliff. Pronounced "spreet".

Spritsail A sail extended by a sprit.

Stackie A barge designed to carry hay or straw piled up high above her hatches. Stackie barges were generally built with little sheer and a feature was the wide deck between rail and hatch coaming designed to accommodate a standard bale.

Stanliff A heavy wire cable fitted to the mainmast at the hounds to carry the weight of the sprit at the heel. The stanliff is adjusted by taking up, or adding to, the chain links at the lower end.

Stayfall A flexible wire cable rove through a pair of large blocks, the lower one fitted to the barge's stemhead and the upper one attached to the end of the forestay, forming a tackle by which the mainmast is raised and lowered.

Staysail A light undressed sail of flax canvas or cotton set between stem and topmast head.

Stumpy A barge, usually small, which has no topmast and sets no topsail.

Tack The lower forward corner of a fore-and-aft sail.
To tack is to sail into the wind by proceeding at an angle to the wind; tacking is the act of turning at the end of each leg so sailed.
Description of the point of sailing of a vessel relative to the wind direction; a vessel on port tack has the wind on the port side.

Tackle A pair of blocks through which is rove a rope to provide an advantageous purchase for lifting, moving or securing heavy loads, as in raising sails or trimming sails to the wind.

Topmast pole That part of the spar between the hounds and the truck.

Truck A circular wooden cap at the top of a barge's topmast.

Vang Pronounced "wang". A wire cable for the purpose of controlling the sprit; it leads from the head of the sprit to tackles whose lower blocks are mounted near each end of the main horse.

Warp A heavy mooring rope.

Windlass A powerful hand-operated winch mounted in the bow of a barge; used primarily for raising the anchor and also for raising and lowering the mainmast.

Index

Illustrations in bold type

Index of Vessels

Barges unless otherwise stated

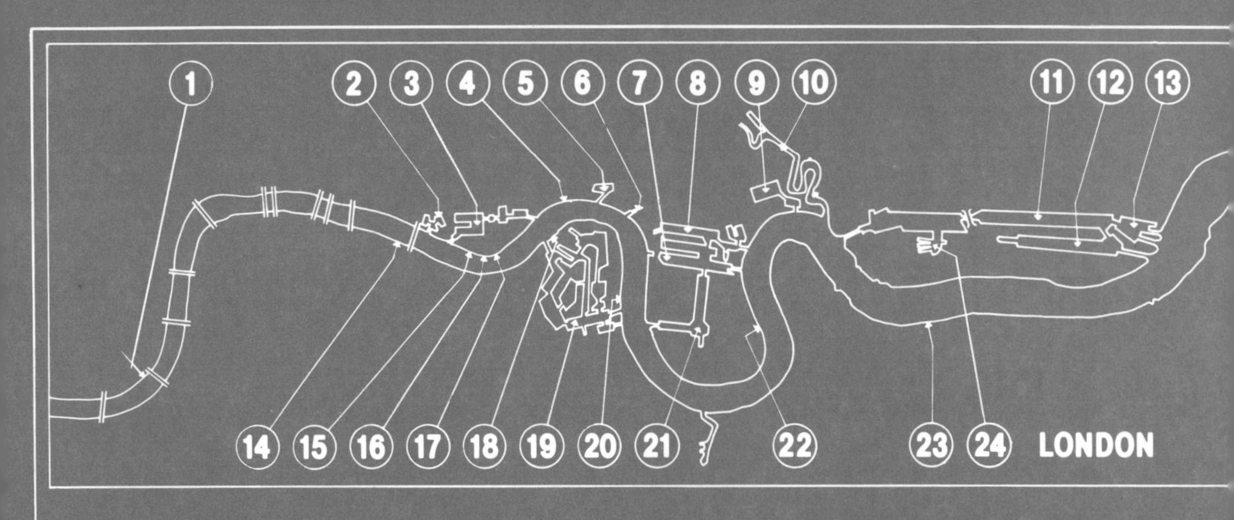

HARBOURS, DOCKS & WHARVES

SERVED BY THE SAILING BARGE

KATHLEEN

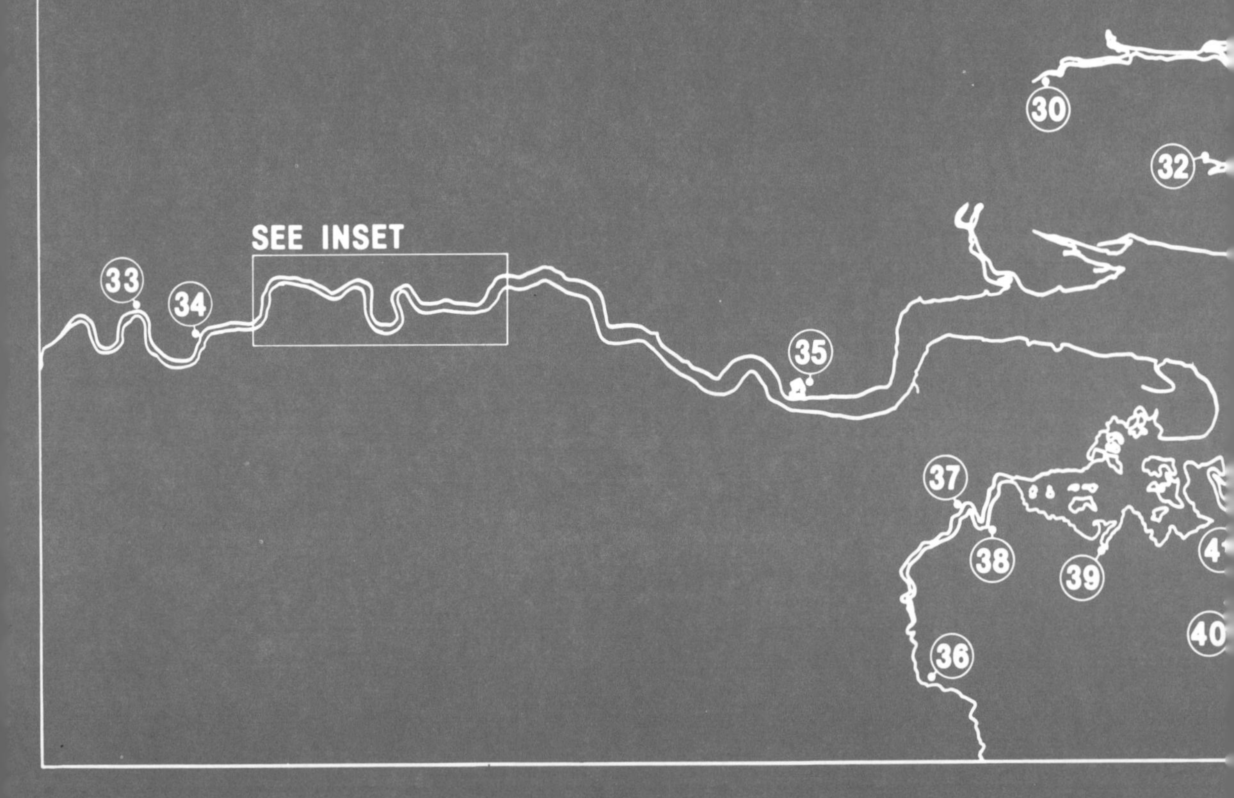